Gender and the American Presidency

LEXINGTON STUDIES IN POLITICAL COMMUNICATION

Series Editor: Robert E. Denton, Jr.

Virginia Polytechnic Institute and State University

This series encourages focused work examining the role and function of communication in the realm of politics including campaigns and elections, media, and political institutions.

RECENT TITLES IN THE SERIES:

Gender and the American Presidency

Nine Presidential Women and the Barriers They Faced

Theodore F. Sheckels,
Nichola D. Gutgold, and
Diana B. Carlin

LEXINGTON BOOKS
Lanham • Boulder • New York • Toronto • Plymouth, UK

Published by Lexington Books
A wholly owned subsidiary of The Rowman & Littlefield Publishing Group, Inc.
4501 Forbes Boulevard, Suite 200, Lanham, Maryland 20706
www.rowman.com

Estover Road, Plymouth PL6 7PY, United Kingdom

British Library Cataloguing in Publication Information Available

Library of Congress Cataloging-in-Publication Data
Sheckels, Theodore F.
  Gender and the American presidency : nine presidential women and the barriers
they faced / Theodore F. Sheckels, Nichola D. Gutgold, and Diana Bartelli Carlin.
     p. cm.
  Includes bibliographical references and index.
  ISBN 978-0-7391-6678-9 (cloth : alk. paper) — ISBN 978-0-7391-6679-6 (pbk. :
alk. paper) — ISBN 978-0-7391-6680-2
  1. Women presidential candidates—United States. 2. Sex role—Political
aspects—United States. I. Gutgold, Nichola D. II. Carlin, Diana B., 1950- III. Title.
  HQ1391.U5S47 2012
  324.9730082—dc23

                                                                      2011050536

Printed in the United States of America

Contents

Preface

In four-year cycles, Americans—led by the media—ask the question, who among the many possibilities is made of presidential timber. The question is asked as candidates surface and as they proceed through a campaign's primary phase. As the surfacing period lengthens, the question is asked earlier and perhaps more often. Some would even suggest that, as soon as a president is inaugurated, the question begins being asked about prospective challengers with the election four years off in view.

This book begins in a conversation about this national mania, a conversation that gives rise to a fundamental question: why are so many men assessed and, then, either acclaimed or rejected, while so few women are? The comparative numbers in politics perhaps once explained this gender gap, but now, there are many women governors and many women in the U.S. Senate, the two likeliest places—history tells us—to find Americans of presidential timber. One would think the number of women vetted by the media and populace would have increased more than it has.

But, even if the numbed vetted has increased just a bit, the number who are found qualified remains low. Hillary Clinton in 2008 got as close as any woman has thus far, but even she, in the Democratic Party's final analysis, was found lacking. In 2012, Sarah Palin has finally declined to be considered, but, if she had chosen otherwise, she probably would have struck several barriers on her path. And Michelle Bachmann, who was a candidate, has indeed struck several. People asked if she is sufficiently qualified; people balked at her sometimes-aggressive tone; people questioned whether her husband's views are a political liability.

It is not for the authors of this study to decide if Palin and Bachmann are truly of presidential timber, but we will argue, for the sake of this study, that there have been many women in the past several decades who have been just as if not more qualified than men who have survived the vetting process almost if not to the end. There were evidently barriers in these women's paths, and it is the purpose of this study to ascertain what those barriers might be. Why have so many political women with public service careers comparable to the men who have been dubbed frontrunners been judged not ready for the White House?

We could have searched the extant literature on gender and politics and developed several hypotheses and, then, tested them against the stories of prominent political women. We chose instead to work in the inductive manner familiar to both rhetoricians and critics. We chose to examine the women and, then, extract from their stories what the hypotheses might be. We imagined that the hypotheses arrived at in this manner might well largely match-up with those that might have characterized a deductive approach. We chose to proceed as we did based on a hunch that the stories, if told without the lens of current theories about gender and politics firmly in place, might point to some new or some differently-cast hypotheses. Put simply, we thought that the stories might lead to a more nuanced "take" on gender and politics than extant research.

Current theories, of course, cannot be ignored, and, as the chapters discussing nine presidential-caliber women reveal, they are not. We use those theories not to generate *the* questions we ask about each woman's experience and rhetoric but to pose some of the question we ask. We let our instincts as critics determine to which issues we turn—media coverage, double-binds, communication style or communication ability, practical matters such as one's political views and how they match (or don't match) the party's. Our goal for each woman studied was to tease out of the account of her experience and rhetoric a plausible answer to the overarching question of "Why not Madam President?" Those answers, put together—we thought—might take us to a richer picture of the barriers in the road to the presidency than if we had proceeded deductively from extant research and posed a set of hypotheses.

The goal was, then, to arrive at a richer set of hypotheses that we—or other critics—might then test. That is, if the hypotheses rang true—that is, fit the nine stories we tell and fit other stories that come into the readers' minds. We think, when the reader reaches the conclusion of this book, she or he will find that our eventual hypotheses do run true and explain the stories of many, many political women.

For this inductive process to work, we had to choose our case studies carefully. An *n* of nine is, of course, not high so we needed a range of prospective candidates that one reading this book would think to be representative—different ages, different regions, both parties, senators and governors. Admittedly, we sometimes chose women we were, for one reason or another, drawn to. (It is, perhaps, no accident that two of the women are Kansans, as is, by birth, one author, and two are Marylanders, as is another author based on having grown up there.) Nonetheless, variety is clearly characteristic of this group of nine. Other names were considered, but we kept returning to these nine. Nine was a doable number for the book, but, more important, these nine seemed to cover the bases we wanted our analyses to cover.

In the chapters that follow, after an introduction that points to extant work on the topic that does indeed inform our analyses, we consider, in order of birth date, nine very interesting women. Each chapter reviews the relevant details of their political lives, attempts to describe what we might term their rhetorical style, and tries to explain why the path to the presidency was blocked for them. Different authors among us wrote the different chapters, and, although we did our best to standardize the approach we were taking, a reader can probably discern which three chapters each author wrote. So be it. That our styles diverge somewhat from each other should not detract from the fact that we are focused on the same three concerns: these women's careers, their rhetoric, and the barriers or forces or circumstances that made them, arguably, presidential timber but not successful aspirants to a presidential nod.

The concluding chapter steps away from the nine case studies and attempts to extract certain general maxims that a woman seeking the presidency must be aware of. These maxims, we suggest, might serve as hypotheses for further work—work that validates or invalidates our conclusions by considering other women; work that evaluates present or future women candidates' chances. We think other past cases will indeed validate our work, and, unfortunately, we think present and future cases will also. We say "unfortunately" because we do hope that, some day, some of the barriers we describe might fall, but, for at least the near future, we think women will be facing much the same barriers as in earlier decades. The next Nancy Kassebaums and Dianne Feinsteins will still run amok if too centrist; the next Barbara Mikulskis and Nancy Pelosis will still run amok if too aggressively outspoken. The barriers we identified that affected the careers of these four women as well as those of Elizabeth Dole, Christine Gregoire, Olympia Snowe, Kathleen Sebelius, and Linda Lingle will prove to be barriers at least in the near political future.

The good news is that there is some suggestion that the barriers facing women are increasingly looking like the barriers facing anyone. A centrist male candidate, for example, would experience the same difficulties in the surfacing and primary seasons as a centrist woman; a male candidate without significant financial support would experience the same problems as an undersupported woman. In the present 2012 season, consider Mitt Romney's situation—too centrist on some issues for the Republicans actively engaged in that party's early deliberations. Consider Tim Pawlenty's—gone because the money wasn't there after the Iowa straw poll. Still, many barriers do seem higher for women than for men, and the ways appearance plays out seem strikingly different. New Jersey Governor Chris Christie was thought qualified by those pushing him to declare his candidacy, but women with more public service have been viewed skeptically as insufficiently credentialed. And the media does not seem to be commenting on the color of Texas Governor Rick Perry's suits or how much silver is in Mitt Romney's hair. Only when the appearance is at an extreme—Indiana Governor Jeff Daniels's height or Chris Christie's weight—is that appearance noted.

Our belief is that political communication research matters, and our hope is that the articulation of the barriers in the nine stories to come and, explicitly, in the conclusion will cause some to ask if these barriers should exist and/or if these barriers should be higher, wider, or more barbed for women than for men.

No study, of course, is just the work of its authors. So, the three authors of this book would like to thank the many political communication scholars—those who work empirically and those who work rhetorically—whose work on the question of gender and the presidency foreground this exploration. There is quite clearly a community of scholars who see this question as both intriguing and important. We are proud to be part of that community.

Professor Sheckels would like to thank the staff of the University of Maryland's McKeldin Library for assisting him in locating materials that fleshed out Baltimore's political atmosphere in earlier decades. He would also like to thank staff members in the Capitol Hill offices of Senators Feinstein and Mikulski and Representative Pelosi for clarifying matters not clear on Congressional websites. Professor Gutgold would like to thank Governors Gregoire and Lingle for granting her telephone interviews and Elizabeth Dole for two gracious in-person interviews. She also thanks her co-authors—Sheckels for imagining this book, Carlin for lending her considerable talents to it. And she wishes to express her immense gratitude to her cherished family, Geoff, Ian, and Emi, for their interest in her work and their love and support. Professor Carlin wishes to thank Abby Pierron for her research assistance on the Kassebaum chapter and for locating photographs; Joe Pierron for his editing and encouragement; Nancy Kassebaum Baker and Kathleen Sebelius for taking time for interviews; and her co-authors for having and developing the idea behind the book and for their patience.

All three authors would like to thank Rebecca McCary at Lexington Books, who initially encouraged this study into existence and Lenore Lautigar at Lexington, who took over for Rebecca and pushed it along through the various photographic and textual hoops.

1

Gender and the American Presidency: Nine Presidential Women and the Barriers They Faced—An Introduction

> "I'm not going to pretend that running for president as a woman is not daunting . . . and it is . . . probably a path that doesn't appeal to a lot of women even in elective office because it is so difficult."[1]
>
> —Hillary Rodham Clinton

Scott Brown had not even been sworn in as U.S. senator from Massachusetts, yet the rights to the domain names scottbrown2012.com and scott-brown2016.com were snatched up the day the charismatic, pick-up driving Republican claimed an upset victory. His win over the Democratic candidate, Martha Coakley, which claimed the senate seat held by Ted Kennedy for forty-seven years, stunned the political world. This enthusiastic reaction to Scott Brown—that he could be the next president—came on the heels of what was an unprecedented year for women in American politics.

In 2008 Hillary Clinton became the first female frontrunner presidential candidate and she *almost won* the Democratic nomination. Hillary Clinton was seen as the best hope for those wishing to see a woman win the White House. She had many of the markers that indicate political success: fame, a well-oiled political machine, and loads of money. Furthermore, her credibility as a candidate was high: most Americans believed that she could do the job of president.[2] As secretary of state, Hillary Clinton's popularity ratings continue to exceed those of the president.[3] In *Big Girls Don't Cry*, Rebecca Traister describes the cultural shifts that made many of the groundbreaking aspects of the 2008 election possible. In an optimistic voice she notes, "Political breakthroughs begat cultural breakthroughs begat comedy breakthroughs begat political breakthroughs."[4] Less optimistically, however, she stresses the generational difficulties Hillary Clinton faced reaching young voters with as much impact as Barack Obama did. In an op-ed for the *New York Times* in January, 2008, Gloria Steinem hypothesized a female version of Barack Obama. She then asks the reader: "Be honest: Do you think this is the biography of someone who could be elected to the United States Senate? After less than one term there, do you believe she could be a viable candidate to head the most powerful nation on earth? If you answered no to either question, you're not alone. Gender is probably the most restricting force in American life, whether the question is who must be in the kitchen or who could be in the White House."[5]

Sarah Palin, another prominent national political figure continues to make the most of the celebrity-driven nature of American politics as Fox news pundit, one-time TLC network reality show star and active public speaker. Her "mama grizzly" mantra and neo-Republican motherhood have strong support from a segment of American voters and even former President Bill Clinton described Palin as "someone to be reckoned with."[6] In June, 2011, she told reporters she "hasn't decided yet"[7] if she would jump into the 2012 Republican race for the presidency as she traveled the country on a "Freedom Tour" that highlighted historical American sights.

Michele Bachmann, a member of the U.S. House of Representatives, representing Minnesota's 6th congressional district, a supporter of the Tea Party movement and founder of the Tea Party Caucus gained momentum with her strong performance in the second national Republican debate in June 2011 when she announced that she filed paperwork with the Federal Election Committee. Her official announcement speech later that month in her birthplace, Waterloo, Iowa, was largely biographical and offered her approach to governing. She said:

> In Washington I am bringing a voice to the halls of congress that has been missing for a long time. It is the voice of the people I love and learned from growing up in Waterloo. It is the voice of reasonable, fair-minded people who love this country, who are patriotic, and who see the United States as the indispensable nation of the world.
>
> My voice is part of a movement to take back our country, and now I want to take that voice to the White House. It is the voice of constitutional conservatives who want our government to do its job and not ours and who want our government to live within its means and not our children's and grandchildren's.[8]

Appearing on the news program "Fox News Sunday," host Chris Wallace welcomed Bachmann as he noted how her campaign had "taken off" after her impressive performance in the debate. He went on to ask her: "Are you a flake?"[9] Initially, she seemed insulted by the question, but she went on to provide evidence that she was not only not a flake, but a serious candidate. She said, "I think that would be insulting to say something like that because

I'm a serious person. He interrupted her again and she continued, "Well, I would say, I'm 55 years old. I've been married 33 years. I'm not only a lawyer, I have a post-doctorate degree in federal tax law from William and Mary. I've worked in serious scholarship. . . . My husband and I have raised five kids, we've raised 23 foster children. We've applied ourselves to education reform. We started a charter school for at-risk kids. I've also been a state senator and member of the United States Congress for five years."[10]

Wallace's question drew criticism from women's media groups and later he apologized to Bachmann. In August 2011 a *Newsweek* cover showed Bachmann with a penetrating, wild-eyed look with the headline "Queen of Rage" prompting even Jon Stewart to comment "shame on you *Newsweek* and your editor Tina Brown."[11] He suggested that to make Bachmann look crazy a photo of her constructed of her words would be more appropriate, and showed one to the audience. He asserted that she is nothing if not photogenic, and then showed a wide-eyed, erratic appearing image of Tina Brown.

A lengthy *New Yorker* profile of Bachmann revealed that her staff does not want photos of her taken in casual clothes, evidence of the careful construction of image that faces women candidates that simply doesn't confound most male candidates. Although the midterm elections of 2010 showed a reduction in women in Congress, it yielded a gain of two Republican women governors: Nikki Haley in South Carolina and Mary Fallin in New Mexico. With Michele Bachmann the only woman in the pack of presidential hopefuls for 2012, once again there is still a collective hesitation about a woman being cast as a possible future United States president.

All around the world women are presidents and prime ministers. Margaret Thatcher was elected prime minister of Great Britain three times. Women presidents have led Argentina, Iceland, the Philippines, Nicaragua, Sri Lanka, Bangladesh, Ecuador, Finland, Ireland, Liberia, Chile, Bermuda, New Zealand, and Latvia.

After the 2010 midterm elections, there were nine female governors and seventeen women senators. One would think that more women would be mentioned as having presidential potential and that more women would boldly announce their desire to be president, but they have not. Is it the harsh media treatment of women that is keeping them from entering the ultimate political fray? Is it the double-binds? Are women psychologically holding themselves back with their own negative illusion about their ability to be elected? There are more women than men in the United States. This statistic would suggest that more women would be running for president even if it cannot guarantee that more women would vote for women.

According to several studies conducted by the White House Project, an organization dedicated to advancing women's leadership across all sectors, including the United States presidency, the public is overwhelmingly comfortable with women in most positions of leadership across all sectors, and that comfort level is growing.

In polls conducted in 2007, 2005, and 2002, the overall comfort level of Americans with women as leaders has increased from 77 percent in 2002 to 89 percent in 2007. Three-quarters of Americans say they would feel comfortable with a woman as president of the United States, and 82 percent with a woman as vice president. More than 90 percent of the American public is comfortable with women as members of Congress, leaders of universities, charities, newspapers, television and film studios, heads of large companies of various types, and law firms. About 80 percent feel comfortable with a woman as head coach of a professional sports team and as a minister or other religious leader. The lowest ranking in the poll was a 70 percent comfort level with female generals in the media.[12] David Paul and Jessi Smith examined the influence of the gender of presidential candidates on perceptions of candidate qualification. They found that women presidential candidates were viewed as significantly less qualified to be president when compared with male candidates with similar credentials. (2007).[13] In another study, Jane Hall discovered that the reporting on Elizabeth Dole and Hillary Clinton in Campaign 2000 illustrates old and new trends in the coverage of candidate's for high office. She contends that while Dole was taken seriously as a candidate for president, Hillary Clinton was mistreated in her senate campaign because her celebrity received more attention than her stances on issues.[14] The role-model effect is also of interest in the quest to see more women elected president. The lack of strong women role models in either American myths or culture doesn't help the plight of would-be women presidents, suggests Laura Liswood, secretary general of the Council of Women World Leaders. America is filled with stories that suggest the "princess should wait for the prince. Charming men has been promoted by much of the American culture as the single greatest way for women to improve their positions in life."[15]

DO YOUNG WOMEN BELIEVE IN MADAM PRESIDENT?

The idea that we are "getting closer" to a woman in the White House forces those of us who have written about women and the U.S. presidency to consider the obstacles that may face women as presidential candidates. Why haven't more seemingly qualified women candidates run for president of the United States? It would seem that in a world without gender bias, more women would be top contenders for the presidency.

The question of whether or not young women believe that a woman will be president is a pertinent one. Presumably it is the college-educated women who will seek elected office and one of them will ascend to the Oval Office. For years, scholars of women and leadership have contended that the mere presence of women leaders will create a more positive environment for future leaders and that seeing a group of women in leadership roles helps remove a psychological barrier.

Research on the prospects of a woman president often considers the leadership potential of young women and girls. The reasoning is that if future leaders believe that they could be successful, more girls will grow into women who will enter elections and the more women who run, the more women will win. For example, the program Take our Daughters to Work and the leadership conferences and institutes springing up for girls as young as age seven are evidence that training girls and young women early to think of themselves as leaders may increase their chances of becoming leaders later. For example, the Girls Leadership Institute in Pittsfield Massachusetts, "inspires girls to be true to themselves," and offers "the skills and confidence to live as leaders." And at the Women's Media Center, girls' voices have been added to the conversation about women in the media in several ways. For example, a multimedia series called Girls Investigate: Our Views on Media that explores girls' ideas about popular culture, social media, and the intersections between the two.

A poll titled "Believing or Not Believing in Madam President" surveyed college women to learn whether or not they were encouraged by the presidential and vice presidential bids of Hillary Clinton and Sarah Palin to believe that a woman would be president in their lifetime.

"Believing or Not Believing in Madam President" has been administered to college women, age eighteen to twenty-five and after a little over 500 surveys were returned, there is evidence to show that more young women were encouraged by the presidential race of Hillary Clinton than by the vice-presidential bid of Sarah Palin and that the effort of both women were more encouraging than discouraging to their belief in a future woman president.

The poll asked young women to reflect about whether or not the campaigns of these national female politicians made them believe that there would be a woman president in their lifetime. Out of 518 surveys, 291 women said "yes" that the presidential bid of Hillary Clinton encouraged her to believe that a woman would be president in her lifetime. One hundred twenty were encouraged by the vice-presidential bid of Sarah Palin while fifty-seven respondents were not encouraged by either woman and fifty women thought that both women's efforts turned them into believers.

Some comments about Hillary Clinton from respondents include: "She was one of the first women who looked like she could win" and "She made me believe that a woman will be a strong candidate." Another respondent said, "I knew she wouldn't win." As for Palin, students wrote: "She made women sound stupid" and "The media focused too much on her personal

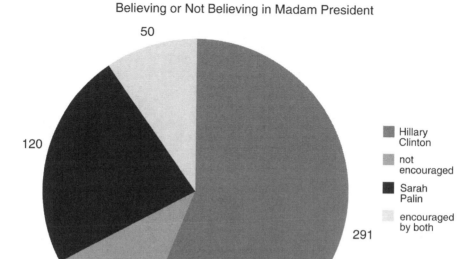

Believing or Not Believing in Madam President

life and not enough on her politics." Another respondent said Palin made her a believer in a woman president in her lifetime because "as soon as Obama won many people were already campaigning for Palin in 2012." Some respondents were encouraged by both Clinton and Palin. One wrote: "Both Clinton and Palin are evidence that women are beginning to climb the ladder in education, work and politics. It is still a struggle, for many reasons, but it is much better than it was."

This poll indicates that young women have noticed the efforts of Clinton and Palin and for the most part more young women are encouraged by their efforts than turned off by them. By a considerable margin, the bid of Hillary Clinton was even more encouraging than that of Sarah Palin's.

ADDING TO THE GROWING LITERATURE

Interest in women and the American presidency has never been more intense than it is now. Several books have been published that are more focused on the presidency and that add to the older writings that explore women, politics, and leadership. *Washington Post* reporter Anne E. Kornblut took copious notes as she covered the campaigns of Hillary Clinton and Sarah Palin in 2008 and wrote: *Notes from the Cracked Ceiling: Hillary Clinton, Sarah Palin, and What It Will Take for a Woman to Win.* Leslie Sanchez cast a more negative tone in her book, *You've Come a Long Way, Maybe: Sarah, Michelle, Hillary, and the Shaping of the New American Woman.* Rebecca Traister offers her own joys and frustrations about the cultural shifts brought on by the 2008 election in *Big Girls Don't Cry: The Election That Changes Everything for American Women.* Rhetorical scholars tackled the topic of women and the United States presidency in several new volumes including editor Janis Edwards's *Gender and Political Communication in America: Rhetoric, Representation, and Display* (Lexington Studies in Political Communication). Theodore Sheckels edited a volume dedicated to Hillary Clinton's bid: *Cracked but Not Shattered: Hillary Clinton's Unsuccessful Bid for the Presidency.* Marie C. Wilson's *Closing the Leadership Gap; Why Women Can and Must Help Run the World* recounts her experiences as one of the founders of the White House Project. Gail Collins, in her work *America's Women: 400 Years of Dolls, Drudges, Helpmates and Heroines,* traces the lives of more than four centuries of women and shows the tension surrounding the expectations for women. Linda Witt, Karen M. Paget, and Glenna Matthews's *Running as a Woman: Gender and Power in American Politics* orients the reader about the challenges women candidates face. Catherine Whitney, et al., *Nine and Counting: The Women of the Senate,* and Kim Fridkin Kahn, *The Political Consequences of Being a Woman,* also bring attention to the nuances experienced by female candidates. Kathleen Hall Jamieson's book, *Beyond the Double Bind, Women and Leadership,* offers insight into the unique constraints facing women candidates. Eleanor Clift and Tom Brazaitis tell the story of women angling for the White House and engage the reader with *Madam President, Blazing the Leadership Trail.* Robert P. Watson and Ann Gordon, editors of *Anticipating Madam President,* focus more specifically on the obstacles facing female presidential hopefuls. Brad Koplinski 's book *Hats in the Ring Conversations with Presidential Candidates* ambitiously offers interviews with many presidential candidates and similarly Mary S. Hartman edited a collection of interviews with powerful women, called *Talking Leadership: Conversations with Powerful Women.* In their own words, women leaders describe the situations they have faced in their quest for leadership equality.

Maria Braden in *Women Politicians and the Media* examines the media's role in women politician's careers. Jo Freeman's *A Room at a Time: How Women Entered Party Politics,* chronicles how women have made progress slowly in the political process. In *American Women Speak,* editors Doris Earnshaw and Maria Elena Raymond offer the reader a collection of speeches and short biographies of nineteen women politicians. The introduction by Ruth B. Mandel of the Eagleton Institute of Politics at Rutgers University warns that "as a society, we must yet learn how to listen and really hear the varied voices of American women." In *American Political Rhetoric, A Reader* (fifth edition), editors Peter Augustine Lawler and Robert Martin Schaeffer offer a chapter on gender as it relates to civil rights. In that chapter, Barbara Jordan's 1992 speech, "Change: From What to What" includes the hopeful wish that "what we see today is simply a dress rehearsal for the day and time we meet in convention to nominate . . . Madame President."

Autobiographies by women politicians offer insights about their lives, and they include *It's My Party, Too* by former New Jersey Governor Christine Todd Whitman, and *24 Years of Housework and the Place is Still a Mess* by Patricia Schroeder. Geraldine Ferraro's *Ferraro, My Story* and Hillary Clinton's *Living History* offer readers firsthand experiences of the lives of women politicians. In *Lives of Their Own: Rhetorical Dimensions in Autobiographies of Women Activists,* Martha Watson describes the value of studying biography as a useful tool in scholarship. James Olney's *Studies in Autobiography* offers a similar perspective on the advantage of studying autobiographies. In the span of just two years national newcomer Sarah Palin published two best-selling books, *Going Rogue* and *America By Heart.*

Books that focus on the rhetoric of women leaders have been important in the effort to chronicle women's political progress, since, as Thomas Hollihan points out in *Uncivil Wars: Political Campaigns in a Media Age,* "politics is communication." Brenda DeVore Marshall and Molly A. Mayhead, eds., *Navigating Boundaries, the Rhetoric of Women Governors* offers insight into the challenges faced by five female governors. In *Governing Codes: Gender, Metaphor and Political Identity,* Karrin Vasby Anderson and Kristen Horn Sheeler examine the political identity of four contemporary female politicians. *The Rhetoric of First Lady Hillary Rodham Clinton: Crisis Management Discourse* by Colleen Elizabeth Kelley describes the unique rhetorical position of Hillary Clinton. Nichola Gutgold followed up her 2008 book *Paving the Way for Madam President* by offering her take on the presidential bid of Hillary Clinton in *Almost Madam President, Why Hillary Clinton 'Won' in 2008.* She argued that rhetorically speaking Clinton did win. Karlyn Kohrs Campbell's edited volumes *Women Public Speakers in the United States* still serve as valuable reference tools as they profile many of the prominent women speakers of our time.

Deborah Alexander and Kristi Andersen surveyed voters to determine gender role attitudes toward women candidates in an article titled "Gender as a Factor in the Attribution of Leadership Traits" in *Political Research Quarterly* in September, 1993, Stephen Stambough and Valerie O'Regan asked whether the "Year of the Woman" in 1992 changed how women candidates are covered in the press in a chapter for a book called *Campaigns and Elections,* edited by Robert P. Watson and Colton C. Campbell. In the same volume, Gary Aguiar examined women's under-representation in elective office. Jane Blakenship and Deborah C. Robson unveiled a "feminine style" in women's political discourse in an exploratory essay in Communication Quarterly article in 1995. Karlyn Kohrs Campbell discussed the feelings phenomenon of "hating Hillary" that has swept the nation in her 1998 article in Rhetoric and Public Affairs.

In addition to a growing number of books, scholarly and popular press articles or news stories continue to explore the campaigns of individual women and larger issues related to women candidates and office holders. There is no doubt that the 2008 presidential campaign and the growing number of women in governors' seats and in the U.S. Senate make it difficult to ignore the growing question of why more qualified women have not made it to a national ticket and what it will take to have a woman in the White House or a heartbeat away.

NINE PRESIDENTIAL WOMEN

Gender and the American Presidency: Nine Presidential Women and the Barriers They Faced invites the audience to consider nine women qualified enough to be president and explores reasons why they have been dismissed as presidential contenders. The women profiled in this book include: Barbara Mikulski, Nancy Pelosi, Nancy Kassebaum, Kathleen Sebelius, Christine Gregoire, Linda Lingle, Elizabeth Dole, Dianne Feinstein, and Olympia Snowe.

Senator Barbara Mikulski and Representative Nancy Pelosi have emerged from the thick of Baltimore, Maryland, politics to serve the voters of Maryland (Mikulski) and California (Pelosi) well in the U.S. Congress. Both are thought to have disqualified themselves because of an overly aggressive manner of conducting legislative business as well as liberal stances on most issues. In addition, their personal appearances have been judged either not especially presidential or rather comic. All political personae are the product of both reality and media coverage with the latter emphasizing the personae. The question then is has the media so emphasized these two women's non-presidential personae that voters know them only as "cartoons"? A related question is, to what extent do audience attitudes toward female aggressiveness, liberal views, and certain physical characteristics play a role in how easily these political women have been "cartoon-ized" and, then, dismissed? Answers will be premised on an extensive survey of media coverage of Mikulski and Pelosi and relevant research in communication and cognate disciplines on attitudes toward the personality and physical traits they allegedly possess. These chapters will demonstrate to which extent media coverage has tapped certain negative audience attitudes and thereby trapped Mikulski and Pelosi in no-win-the-presidency personae.

Kansas politics produced two women whose names found their way into vice presidential speculation games. Nancy Kassebaum was the first woman in the U.S. Senate who did not follow a husband to the halls of Congress upon his death. Unlike her father, 1936 Republican presidential candidate Alf Landon, Kassebaum made it to Washington, but admittedly riding on her father's coattails. Kassebaum's eighteen years in the U.S. Senate were marked by a committee chair position—the first woman to hold one—and several important appointments on foreign relations subcommittees. She was a temporary co-chair of the RNC's 1980 convention and was often mentioned as a potential vice presidential running mate. As the only woman in the Senate for several years, she learned how to bridge feminine and masculine communication styles to probe those testifying before committees and to defend votes that broke with her party. Kathleen Sebelius, the current secretary of Health and Human Services, is the daughter of a former Ohio Democrat governor, the daughter-in-law of a long-time Kansas Republican Congressman, and a savvy politician in her own right. She served in the Kansas legislature, as insurance commissioner, and was elected twice as governor—doing all of this as a Democrat in a predominantly Republican state. She appeared on the White House Project's list of women presidential contenders and was often mentioned as a vice presidential candidate for Barack Obama. While an excellent one-on-one campaigner, Sebelius's public communication style was considered deadly dull by many political observers in Kansas and nationally. Both women compared favorably to many of the men who entered presidential primaries and even had more political experience than some who received nominations, but neither became running mates for very different reasons.

And though political scientists often direct attention to governors when determining who will emerge as presidential candidates, like Sebelius, neither Christine Gregoire nor Linda Lingle have been seen as presidential material. Still, from a communication perspective, the governorship gives a candidate a platform that showcases leadership ability while distancing them from legislative intricacies, which can complicate their presidential possibilities. Governorships frequently serve as a proving ground for presidential hopefuls. A governor rises above partisan legislative actions, which increases her ethos as a presidential contender.

Democratic governor of Washington, Christine Gregoire is enjoying the same high approval ratings during her second term that marked her first. A compelling personal narrative, Gregoire was raised by a single mother and was the first woman elected attorney general in Washington. As governor, she balanced the budget and expanded health coverage. Like Gregoire, former Republican governor of Hawaii Linda Lingle enjoyed success and popularity in her second term. She was the first mayor elected governor of Hawaii and the first female governor of Hawaii. During the 2004 Republican National Convention in New York City, Lingle took to the national stage when she served as chairman of the convention during the absence of permanent chairman Dennis Hastert from the convention. Most recently she held court in Honolulu as Republican leaders met and she received thunderous applause when she declared a Democratic majority as "toast." Considering a run for the Senate, as Republicans actively seek a new fig-urehead, why not former Governor Lingle? Despite her success at offering Hawaii a "new beginning" by making state government more open, and her high approval ratings throughout her two terms, she, like Chris Gregoire, is not mentioned as presidential timbre.

Suggestions that Elizabeth Dole should run for president were in the press starting in the 1980s. At the 1984 Republican National Convention, buttons that depicted "Dole in '88" over cameo pictures of Bob and Eliza-beth Dole were everywhere. Some articles speculated that since Elizabeth Dole campaigned so lovingly for her husband they made an agreement that she should have the next shot at the presidency. Though she was the very picture of a candidate's spouse, she continued to be on the short list of can-didates herself. But the press buzz about the presidential potential of Eliza-beth Dole hit an all-time high after her rousing speech at the 1996 G.O.P. Convention. And though she insisted she had no intention of running in March 1999 she made an exploratory bid for the presidency. She placed third in the August 1999 Iowa straw poll, but dropped out of the race in October when she admitted she could not compete with the unprecedented personal fortunes of George W. Bush and Steve Forbes.

Dianne Feinstein, a member of the Senate since 1992 and ten-year mayor of San Francisco, negotiated the double binds fairly well. In an interview in 2000, she notes that "the glass ceiling has been chipped, but it hasn't been broken by a long shot." She doesn't admit it, but she might have been able to do considerable damage to that ceiling, given how well she had been able to negotiate the double binds that had trapped other women. But those double binds were not ultimately her problem. Ultimately, her problem was that she was not in tune with the prevailing Democratic Party ideology all the time. Her independence and her self-confessed tendency to stake out middle ground made her less attractive presidential material than many men who had (arguably) weaker credentials but "the right politics."

Olympia Snowe, currently one of Maine's two Republican women in the U.S. Senate, is an interesting blend of several other women in the book. She has an independent streak like Kassebaum and extensive Washington expe-rience like Mikulski and Pelosi. Like Sebelius she is not considered a great orator. She is also compared to the first woman elected to the U.S. Senate from Maine, Margaret Chase Smith, who also had presidential qualities. Snowe's first office, like Smith's, resulted from her husband's death. Snowe replaced her late husband in the Maine House of Representatives in 1973.

She later served in the Maine Senate before being elected to the U.S. House where she served for sixteen years before being elected to the Senate. She was the youngest Republican woman and first Greek-American woman to enter Congress. While Hillary Clinton was the first First Lady to run for office, Snowe held the distinction of serving as Maine's First Lady while she was in Congress as a result of her marriage to Maine's governor, John McKernan. Snowe's committees in both houses of Congress provided an excellent background for anyone seeking a place on a presidential ticket. She has served on the House Foreign Affairs Committee, Senate Select Committee on Intelligence, and the Armed Services Committee, where she was the first woman to head a subcommittee. In addition to international policy experience, Snowe's Finance Committee and Commerce, Science and Transportation Committee work provided her with important economic policy experience. Snowe's moderate label, willingness to work across the aisle, and pro-choice stance are usually appealing to voters in the middle where presidential races are won. However, those same traits—which are clearly in evidence in her rhetoric—are exactly what prevented her from rising to a national ticket during an era of conservative political choices by her party.

These essays offer analyses of political women who seem to have all the right qualifications to be president. Although Hillary Clinton put 18 million cracks in the glass ceiling, that dramatic showing as a presidential candidate remains elusive for any other political women, even the most qualified. The 2012 election is evidence of just how far women in political culture have not come. Only one woman, Michele Bachmann, is officially in the 2012 race and is facing many of the double binds offered as obstacles in this book. Will she be tough enough? Is motherhood a qualification for the presidency? Is she attractive or too attractive? Is she a flake? What does her husband do? Would she be submissive to him as president? These questions often overshadow women's core ideology in the press. Gender barriers, media coverage, communication style, geography, and other factors are examined to determine why seemingly qualified powerful politicos failed to make presidential impact. This book endeavors to create awareness of what might need to be done to foster a more positive environment for female candidates.

NOTES

1. Chris Cilizza, "The Fix," July 27, 2009, http://voices.washingtonpost.com/the-fix/eye-on-2012/a-woman-in-the-white-house.html?referrer=emaillink (accessed April 28, 2010).

2. Susan Page, "Majority Says They'd Vote for Clinton," *USA Today*, May 26, 2005, www.usatoday.com/news/washington/2005-05-26-hillary-poll_x.htm (accessed April 4, 2011).

3. Paul Steinhauser, "Clinton Has High Job Approval," CNN, March 25, 2009, www.cnn.com/2009/POLITICS/03/25/clinton.poll (accessed May 3, 2011).

4. Rebecca Traister, *Big Girls Don't Cry: The Election That Changed Everything for American Women* (New York: Free Press, 2010), p. 3.

5. Gloria Steinem, "Women Are Never Frontrunners," *New York Times*, January 8, 2008, www.nytimes.com/2008/01/08/opinion/08steinem.html (accessed December 22, 2010).

6. Lucy Madison, "Don't Underestimate Sarah Palin," CBS News, September 21, 2010, www.cbsnews.com/8301-503544_162-20017091-503544.html (accessed December 13, 2010).

7. "Sarah Palin Criticizes Romney on Health Care during Freedom Trail Tour," Boston.com, June 8, 2011, www.boston.com/Boston/politicalintelligence/2011/06/sarah-palin-criticizes-romney-health-care-during-freedom-trail-tour/bQB6ZvLjvu-SUMWipTbRSlL/index.html.

8. Michele Bachmann Presidential Announcement Speech, C-Span, June 27, 2011, www.c-spanvideo.org/program/300204-1 (accessed August 9, 2011).

9. Fox News Sunday with Chris Wallace transcript, June 27, 2011, www.foxnews.com/on-air/fox-news-sunday/transcript/rep-michele-bachmann-talks-earmarks-obamacare-and-gay-marriage-sen-kyl-debt-talks (accessed August 10, 2011).

10. Ibid.

11. The Daily Show Official website, www.thedailyshow.com/watch/tue-august-9-2011/glazed-and-confused (accessed August 9, 2011).

12. The White House Project, "Benchmarking Women's Leadership, 2009," www.benchmarksthewhitehouseproject.org. (accessed April 28, 2010).

13. David Paul and Jessi L. Smith, "Subtle Sexism? Examining Vote Preferences When Women Run against Men for the Presidency," *Journal of Women and Politics*, Vol. 29, No. 4 (2007), p. 451.

14. Jane Hall, "Hillary and Liddy," *Media Studies Journal*, Vol. 14, No. 1 (Winter 2000), p. 68.

15. Assunta Ng, "Women Still Face Many Hurdles on Way to Presidency," *Northwest Asian Weekly*, Vol. 16, No. 10 (May 1997), p. 7.

2

Nancy Landon Kassebaum: The Junior Senator from Kansas with a Mind of Her Own

I frequently encourage women to run for public office because I believe that greater political participation by women adds an important perspective to governmental actions.[1]

—Nancy Landon Kassebaum

When Nancy Landon Kassebaum was elected to the United States Senate in 1978, the *London Daily Mail* expressed shock—not so much because a woman was invading what was traditionally a male bastion but because she was "not from a trendy East Coast or West Coast state, but from conservative Kansas, where a man's a man and a woman's his cook!"[2] Had the writer done some research on Kansas history, the result might have been to extol the state's long tradition of women's firsts or near firsts when it comes to U.S. politics.

In 1861, the year Kansas entered the Union just ahead of the start of the Civil War, Kansas women were granted the franchise in school board elections. Two years after the Civil War's end, Kansas considered a constitutional amendment to give full suffrage to women. It failed despite visits from women's suffrage luminaries such as Susan B. Anthony, Elizabeth Cady Stanton, and Lucy Stone. However, in 1887 women were given the right to vote in municipal elections, and three weeks later Susannah Medora Salter was elected mayor of Argonia, Kansas—the first woman mayor in the United States Within thirteen years, fourteen more women would hold the title of "mayor," and two cities would have all-female city councils. Kansas was the eighth state to grant full suffrage in 1912—eight years before the passage of the 19th amendment. In 1974, four years prior to Kassebaum's election to the Senate, Martha Keys was elected to a House seat where she served two terms. Between 1887 and 1978, hundreds of women were elected to city, county, and state offices.[3] Kassebaum attributed her success in part to these pioneering women when she said, "I've always believed one reason Kansas could accept a woman in politics was because women, from the very beginning, have always been involved in a major way in our state. . . . There's a certain openness and a tolerance in Kansas—if you prove yourself."[4]

While Nancy Kassebaum followed a long line of Kansas women politicians into office, she, like Nancy D'Alesandro Pelosi and Kathleen Gilligan Sebelius, followed a father into politics as well. Her primary election victory over eight opponents in August 1978 was often credited to the use of her maiden name. She brushed aside remarks about riding former Kansas governor and 1936 Republican presidential nominee Alf Landon's coattails by noting that "It has been said that I'm riding on the coattails of my dad, but I can't think of any better coattails to ride on."[5] Winning an election and succeeding in the U.S. Senate required more than coattails, however. In her eighteen years in the Senate, Kassebaum proved worthy of the trust Kansans placed in her as she garnered national attention for her political independence, willingness to tackle tough issues and bipartisanship on many issues. She was considered a rising star in the Republican Party soon after taking office and many were talking about her as a possible presidential or vice presidential candidate. Her political pedigree may have been well established, but her entry into electoral politics and the mark she made in her own right were not probable for many, including Kassebaum.

CHALLENGING HER FATHER'S EXPECTATIONS OF WOMEN

Nancy Landon was born on July 29, 1932, in Topeka, Kansas, less than four months before her father, Alfred Mossman Landon, was elected governor in a close three-way race.[6] Her mother, Theo Cobb Landon, was Landon's second wife, and was known for her interest in music—harp and piano—rather than politics. Landon's first wife, Margaret Fleming, died in 1918, and their daughter, Margaret (Peggy Ann), was sixteen years older than Nancy. A brother, Jack, completed the family a year and a half after Nancy's arrival.

Landon was a successful businessman with interests in banking, oil, and radio. His interest in politics was long-standing and his run for governor was preceded by service as county chair for Teddy Roosevelt's third party candidacy in 1912, secretary to Governor Henry Allen, and Republican state chairmanship in 1928. He was associated with the progressive wing of the Kansas Republican party—a legacy he would bequeath to his daughter. He was the only Republican governor re-elected in 1934. That distinction along with his reputation for balancing the state budget while putting a moratorium on foreclosures, supporting tax reductions, and introducing banking reform catapulted him into national prominence. In 1936 he accepted his party's presidential nomination on the State Capitol's steps and took on Franklin Roosevelt and Social Security in a race that left him winning only two states—Maine and Vermont.

After 1936 Landon never again sought public office, but he remained active as a Republican elder statesman until his death at one hundred in 1987. In that role, he introduced his daughter to politics through visitors to their Topeka home—including William Howard Taft—and political dinner talk. Kassebaum explained that her interest in politics stemmed from "growing up in a political family and at the dinner table, whether I was a participant or just listening, and in our house I listened more than I was a participant."[7] Kassebaum also listened in on late night political conversations through a vent in her room that was above her father's den. Landon's support of other candidates had her and her brother Jack out distributing campaign material when she was as young as ten.[8]

Although Kassebaum had an early interest in politics and majored in political science at her father's alma mater, the University of Kansas, she did not grow up with a political campaign agenda of her own. Early on she considered a career as a journalist and described her attempts to hone her skills through a neighborhood newspaper using a toy typewriter: " 'The kind where you have to turn the type ball for every letter. I was the political columnist,' she recalled with a laugh."[9] She did admit that "there were times in high school and college when I mused about becoming actively involved as a candidate,"[10] but she considered those thoughts "only daydreams, fantasies."[11] She did give consideration to a career in the foreign service, but instead of heading east to pursue that goal she went to work for Hallmark Cards as a receptionist after graduating in 1954. She frequently quotes her father as asking her, "What can you do with a political science degree?" Being a typical male of his generation, Landon questioned his daughter's interest in having any job and vetoed her desire to go to New York to find one.[12]

Instead of New York, Nancy Landon pursued a course a year after graduation that was typical of many women of her generation—she got married—to John Philip Kassebaum who she met at the University of Kansas. Phil Kassebaum was studying law at the University of Michigan, and Nancy took advantage of her time in Ann Arbor to pursue a master's degree in diplomatic history, which she earned in 1956. She then had an eye toward teaching at the college level since she lacked certification to teach elementary or secondary education and married women couldn't be in the foreign service at that time.[13]

In the end, there was no teaching career in her future. Instead she moved with her husband to Maize, Kansas, near his Wichita legal practice, and raised four children. She eventually held the position of vice president of Kassebaum Communications, which owned several radio stations, again following in her father's footsteps. It was during her years as a traditional mother and homemaker that she developed skills that served her well in her runs for office and as a senator. She was involved in community activities and was a 4-H leader. Community service gave her an appreciation for grassroots connections. She ran for and won a seat on the Maize School Board and served as its president. She held state appointments on the Kansas Committee on the Humanities and the Kansas Government Ethics Commission. These positions contributed to her ability to serve on and chair Senate committees. Her trajectory into elective politics was described by Ruth Mandel, director of the Eagleton Institute of Politics at Rutgers, as "a typical profile of a woman going into politics at that point [in time]. . . a lot of experience as a volunteer in local civic groups and a general interest in politics."[14]

With the exception of the nonpartisan school board race, Kassebaum was not seriously involved in politics—either nationally or in the state. It was Phil Kassebaum who was the political activist.[15] Her husband supported Nelson Rockefeller in 1968 and they attended the nominating convention. He was involved in Wichita politics and supported Senator James B. Pearson's campaigns. As for the State's then junior senator, Bob Dole, she indicated that she "never really followed that much when he was in the House of Representatives."[16]

In 1975 after separating from her husband (they were divorced in 1979) and sending her oldest child off to college, she decided to pack up her other three children and give all of them a Washington, D.C., experience. For ten months she was a liaison between constituents and federal agencies for Senator Pearson. The casework and Washington bureaucracy were often frustrating and she had no intention of extending her stay in Washington. She was "really glad to come home."[17] When Pearson decided not to run for re-election in 1978, "a friend [of Kassebaum's] said they thought it was a good time for a woman and I ought to think about it."[18] Her mother and mother-in-law also encouraged her as did her estranged husband, with whom she was on good terms. In fact, he served as an advisor and told her, "You have to want it enough to have a gnawing in the pit of your stomach that won't let you sleep. If you have that you can put up with the strenuous campaign."[19] Pearson also encouraged her. During her decision-making period, the only firm naysayer was her father. According to Kassebaum, her father's first reaction was "sheer incomprehension" based partially on "a generational difference toward women in politics"[20] and a genuine concern that the campaign would be physically and financially demanding.[21] One of Landon's friends, Lew Ferguson who worked for the Associated Press for many years, remarked that Alf "was petrified of her running for the U.S.

Senate. . . . A lot of it was personal. . . . At the start, he didn't think she could possibly win, and he thought it would just reinforce the image of the Landons being big political losers because he had lost the presidency."[22]

Kassebaum described her entry into the crowded 1978 Republican primary with nine candidates, many of whom had considerable political experience, as "in a way I'm sure that looked like Mary Poppins dropping out of the sky with her umbrella."[23] The only woman in the Kansas Senate, Jan Meyers, was in the field so the novelty of a woman was mitigated. Meyers would go on to serve in the U.S. House of Representatives and chair a House committee in 1995 when Kassebaum became the first woman to chair a major Senate committee. Kassebaum's decision to run was based on her belief that "I could contribute something, that I had something to offer."[24] And what she had to offer was touted in her campaign slogan "A fresh face—a trusted Kansas name" and her approach to campaigning from one neighbor to another. Kassebaum relied on several women friends to keep her campaign office going and two of her children to drive her to events and serve as surrogates. She recruited friends across the state whom she knew at the University of Kansas to help her in their counties and to enlist their friends.[25] Kassebaum won the primary with 31 percent of the vote, but Kansas does not have a runoff system so she looked to the November election and a race against former Congressman Bill Roy, a medical doctor with a law degree, who narrowly lost to Bob Dole in 1974. It was assumed it would be a tough and close race, and it was.

The major issues were the economy, farm subsidies, and the Panama Canal treaty. Abortion, which was a deciding issue in the 1974 Dole-Roy race, played no part in this campaign. As Kassebaum explained years later, she and Roy agreed.[26] Kassebaum's refusal to release her tax returns became a major issue after Dr. Roy released his. Her argument was that she and her husband were estranged but not divorced and it was unfair to him to release his personal information. Kassebaum's ratings dropped during the controversy and she was referred to as an "injured wren" by the *Kansas City Star.*[27] Roy, however, made a strategic error in continuing to harp on the tax issue after Kassebaum had explained and moved on to asserting that Roy would be "beholden to the 'big spenders' in Congress and to the labor unions that supported him."[28] She observed several years later, "I don't think he [Roy] quite knew how to run against a woman. Running against a woman, if you got too aggressive, you were accused of being too tough."[29]

The "fresh face" strategy was emphasized in the final weeks and "Bob Dole trumpeted this theme around the state. He assured audiences that Nancy would become an instant celebrity and have immediate clout in the Senate, unlike other freshmen senators."[30] Kassebaum's strategy of turning her lack of experience into an asset resulted in a series of television ads in which she was shown working in her kitchen, walking out of a grocery store, and pumping gas—just like other Kansans—and talking about the issues on their minds such as high grocery and gas prices, farm prices, and concerns about family. Her approach worked. When the votes were counted, Nancy Landon Kassebaum bested Roy 403,354 votes to 317,682 and she was headed for Washington as the first woman elected to the Senate who had not earned her way into Congress as a widow.

James Pearson provided her with an opportunity to get a head start on the all-important Senate commodity of seniority by stepping down early so that the governor could appoint her to Pearson's unexpired term. That edge helped her win her chairmanship in 1995. She was sworn into office December 23, 1978. The practice of giving a new senator an edge on seniority was later ended by the man she would marry in 1996, Howard Baker, when he became majority leader. A fact that causes Kassebaum to laugh and emit a sigh when relating the irony.[31] She won reelection handily in 1984 and 1990 and elected to not seek a fourth term in spite of her 82 percent approval rating. Her position as the only woman in the Senate until Paula Hawkins's election in 1980, her independence, her bipartisanship, and her tackling of key foreign policy and domestic issues gave rise to talk of her as a vice presidential candidate briefly in 1980 and more seriously in 1984 and 1988. Her major policy initiatives were the Kennedy-Kassebaum Health Insurance Portability and Accountability Act, sanctions against South Africa to protest apartheid, campaign finance reform, legislation to limit liability for general aviation aircraft manufacturers, and extending the minimum time for new mothers to remain in the hospital after childbirth. She chaired the Labor and Human Resources committee during her last two years in office—she was the first woman to chair a major Senate committee. In 1996 she retired from the Senate and married Howard Baker. She accompanied him to Tokyo in 2001 when he was appointed ambassador and finally had her foreign service dream realized. She has served on numerous boards and special committees since retiring from the Senate and currently divides her time between Tennessee and Kansas.

After her election, the *New York Times* wrote that she "defies stereotypes,"[32] and over the course of her career she proved them right. In analyzing Senator Kassebaum's rhetoric, it is important to remember that a senator has fewer opportunities for epideictic speeches or major speeches that reach large audiences. The majority of a senator's rhetorical choices are related to committee work, negotiating with other senators, and public statements via various media. Eleanor Holmes Norton observed that "women in legislative office are afforded many occasions to take command of a subject or situation. In the House and Senate, for example, women both lead and speak in committees and on the floor about the broadest range of complicated subjects and difficult policy choices."[33] Thus, the analysis that follows focuses largely on Kassebaum's communication in the Senate or publicly about legislation or committee activities through a variety of sources. Her journalistic tendencies resulted in occasional op-ed pieces and a scholarly article. Letters in her files provide insight into her thinking about the role of women in politics. Her two addresses in the public policy lecture series that bears her father's name are also included.

THE KASSEBAUM STYLE: STRAIGHT TALK IN PUBLIC, QUIET PERSUASION IN PRIVATE

A general description of Kassebaum's rhetorical style would have to include the words "straightforward," "colloquial," "measured," "witty," "logical," "tough," "instructive," and "principled." Ted Kennedy, with whom she collaborated on health care legislation, described her as "one of the ablest and most caring senators of our time."[34] In an article anticipating her retirement she was described as adhering "to the old virtues of graciousness and civility. She has earned a reputation for moderation and consensus-building."[35] Her colleague from Kansas, Bob Dole, with whom she disagreed more than once in eighteen years, complimented her this way: "Nancy's record of intelligence, integrity and independence have ensured she will always be remembered as one of the true giants in Kansas political history."[36]

Kassebaum combined feminine and masculine communication traits in ways that enabled her to disagree with someone and to encourage disagreement without sacrificing respect and civility. James J. Kilpatrick described her as having "the steel spine of a Margaret Thatcher and the warm smile of a Helen Hayes."[37] She fully understood "the double bind" Kathleen Hall Jamieson explored in which women are penalized if they are "too tough" or "too traditionally female." Jamieson relates that Kassebaum "quip[ped] that someday she was 'going to hit someone over the head for calling me diminutive and soft-spoken.' "[38] Kassebaum touted Margaret Chase Smith's congratulatory statement that she "ran as a candidate first, and a woman second."[39]

The most blatantly feminine aspect of her strategic approach to working in the Senate was her emphasis on relationship building, and terms that clustered around that concept were common in her rhetoric. From her first campaign until she left Washington eighteen years later, she espoused the philosophy that "to be a good Senator, you need to be willing to work with people. You don't need to be a professional politician."[40]

She was described as pressing "for consensus to resolve complex issues."[41] In her Landon Lecture on her father's 100th birthday in 1987 she identified "two of the central challenges that face our nation as we move toward the twenty-first century. One of these challenges is our relationship with the Soviet Union as it attempts to achieve a watershed change in its economy."[42] She went on to project possible outcomes of the Gorbachev regime with an emphasis on the one that eventually brought an end to the Soviet Union. Throughout this section of the speech she emphasized language of collaboration and trust building—key principles in relationship building. She called for the U.S. to

> take the Soviets at their word and seek to build an era of active cooperation between the superpowers. In saying this, I am not suggesting that we accept Soviet statements and promises at face value.
>
> I hope we soon will take a small step in this direction by signing a new arms control agreement with the Soviets to eliminate all short- and medium-range missiles. This will have the obvious and important benefit of reducing military tensions. It also could be the first step toward an improved and perhaps markedly different relationship.
>
> Beyond this step, I believe we must become more creative and more thoughtful about managing our end of the superpower equation, and we must constantly seek reciprocity from the Soviets.[43]

Ten years later on what would have been her father's 110th birthday she gave a lecture in commemoration of the series' thirtieth anniversary. The subject matter focused more on domestic issues, but her concern with relationships as a partial solution to the complex social issues facing the country in a technological age was equally apparent. Rather than calling for improved relationships between governments, she called on citizens and elected officials to improve the relationship between Americans and their government:

> The second force reshaping America is the growing disconnection between the people—the ultimate source of power in a democracy—and the government at all levels but particularly the federal government. Ironically while more Americans than ever before are informed about and active in our federal affairs, many of our citizens have concluded that Washington is more remote to them than ever before, and growing more annoying by the day. . . .
>
> I believe we must revive an old approach from the early days of our democracy—a genuine federal-state-local-and private partnership in which government seeks the best match of needs, resources, and accountability.[44]

Kassebaum did not just talk about the need for relationships, she used them to break stalemates and craft legislation. She explained the fundamental problem with Congress as "How we look at issues is often in terms of how we're going to play on the evening news. Everything gets telescoped. . . . What we have today is 100 people going their own way, each with their own little sound bite. What we lose is the willingness to work together . . . to use leverage in a way that won't make headlines."[45] Instead of making headlines, Kassebaum's approach was to work across the aisle to reach consensus on major issues such as health care and campaign finance reform. In an interview with PBS's Margaret Warner, Kassebaum explained that "compromise is viewed as somewhat a word that we don't want to use these days, but it does take that in order to accomplish good, solid end results."[46]

One of her greatest accomplishments was partnering with Ted Kennedy—someone at the opposite end of the political spectrum from most Republicans—to devise some type of health care reform. Throughout the process, her quiet, private persuasive skills came into play:

> After President Clinton's health care disaster of 1994, insurance reform seemed impossible. Yet the problems remain for millions of Americans.
> Quietly, Kassebaum and Kennedy set out to find a solution. Working behind closed doors, they found enormous agreement among insurance companies, doctors, consumers and businesses. Only then did they unveil their bill, which would make health insurance portable for workers who change jobs and ban insurers from canceling coverage for sick people.[47]

Along with reaching across the aisle, Kassebaum also reached out to the public for support, especially when she exhibited her independent streak. She and fellow Republican Richard Lugar from Indiana wrote an opinion piece explaining their position to override President Reagan's veto of legislation imposing sanctions on South Africa. An excerpt from the op-ed piece is a final example of consensus building skills and a genuine concern for developing policy that promotes social justice. They began by explaining that they "sought to work with the administration" to no avail, but they blunted their criticism and also demonstrated a pragmatic approach to reaching consensus by acknowledging that they "share some of the president's reservations about parts of this bill. It is not a perfect product. However, we are convinced that this legislation provides an important and necessary departure from our policy toward South Africa, based on a bipartisan consensus." After defending their position, they also offered an olive branch: "Whatever the outcome, however, we pledge to renew and redouble our efforts to work with the administration on the issue. We believe it is particularly important to focus attention on the next step," and then they proceeded to outline the real problems facing South Africa and called on allies to assist.[48]

The approach Lugar and Kassebaum took to exercise their responsibility to South Africa and simultaneously maintain their relationship with a president from their party with whom they disagreed is rooted in a more feminine approach to moral reasoning explicated by Carol Gilligan. It demonstrates "the reality of relationships . . . in which individual lives [are] . . . connected and embedded in a social context of relationship. . . . Responsibility now includes both self and other, viewed as different but connected rather than as separate and opposed."[49] Countless other examples of Kassebaum's work in the Senate demonstrate this approach and provide an insight into her successes. Gilligan and Sally Helgesen[50] wrote about webs

of influence that provide interconnectedness rather than the more traditional view of power being based in hierarchy with those at the top standing alone. Kassebaum's rhetoric reflected an awareness of the delicate webs
to which she and others were a part whether they wove them or not. In an
article about the changing role of women in society she concluded that "in
the final analysis, the basic web of relationships and responsibilities that all
women experience makes it impossible for any one of us to avoid making
some contribution to the progress that lies ahead. We couldn't sit out the
dance if we tried."[51]

Kassebaum discussed her position in the Senate as the only women for
eight years, the role of women in politics and society, and women's issues,
but she described herself more as being a "moderate feminist, but felt that
humanist was a more accurate label."[52] Often her comments about being
a woman politician demonstrated her sense of humor and her ability to
not take her historic role too seriously. She explained her unique position
this way: "There's so much to do: the coffee to make and the chambers to
vacuum. There are Pat Moynihan's hats to brush and the buttons to sew
on Bob Byrd's red vests, so I keep quite busy."[53] Harriett Woods, who had
served as the president of the National Women's Political Caucus, agreed
that Kassebaum was a senator first and a woman second but that "you're a
product of your life experience, so she brought to her role those qualities
which she gained by being a mother and a woman. She never put herself
forward as primarily an advocate for women. She just was."[54] Woods's
analysis is reflected in a letter Kassebaum wrote to a student, Ann Porch, in
Madison, WI, who wrote to her as part of a school assignment. In responding to a question about her unique position and the relationship between
gender and policy, she wrote:

> Since my election, I have been asked many times what it is like to be the
> only woman in the Senate. Of course, I do believe that I have a special con-
> stituency and am concerned about issues that especially affect women. If
> you have followed the conventions and the surrounding activities, you will
> have noted that I have been repeatedly asked about my views on "women's
> issues." I do not, however, believe that one's role in Congress should be de-
> fined or limited by gender or that any contributions I may make should be
> so restricted. I do hope my perspective as a woman will add a new dimension
> to the Senate, but I do not want my ability to serve to be limited by any one
> characteristic.[55]

The dimension Kassebaum added was better described as shining a light
on how issues affected women as opposed to issues being women's. In an
article she penned for *Newsday* in 1982, she once again defined the nature
of the issue as a way of sorting out what should be considered in explaining
the differences in views of policy by men and women and preferences for

one party over another. She made it clear that it had nothing to do with the number of key appointments a president gives to women because

> neither party has been particularly sensitive to women's views and concerns. . . . This sort of argument misses the point. . . . It is not possible to offer a definitive explanation of the emergence of disparities in political opinion between men and women. . . . Initially, however, it appears that divergent viewpoints on economic and military issues play a large role.[56]

Kassebaum went on to explain the disparities from women's experiences as being more likely to live in poverty and having lower salaries. She enumerated budget priorities on military rather than domestic spending, fear of sending male relatives to war, and women's involvement in communities suffering from the economic crisis as other causes. Scattered throughout these explanations were historical references to women's roles and lessons from her own experiences and interactions with women constituents. Basing arguments on life experiences whether hers or others was a common characteristic of Kassebaum's rhetoric and it demonstrated her connections to constituents—both women and men.

A final characteristic of Kassebaum's rhetoric was how she structured arguments. While not educated in legal argument, Kassebaum was known to approach preparation for floor speeches and examination of witnesses at hearings with lawyer-like inquiry. In preparing she also showed her penchant for collaboration. The chief of staff for the Senate Budget Committee on which Kassebaum served for eight years contrasted Kassebaum's approach on issues with that of other senators he has worked with:

> There are senators that if you would say that we shouldn't have legal aid (free legal services for poor people) because it just was not the right thing to do, would go along.
>
> But Sen. Kassebaum would say, "Well how much do we spend on it? What does it do? How well is it doing it?" and after you'd answered all of her questions, she'd study it and check with some other folks outside government and then she'd come back and tell you whether she thought the program needed to be reformed, cut altogether, or left alone.[57]

During a floor debate after which she broke with her party to vote for President Clinton's crime legislation that included gun control on semi-automatic weapons, Kassebaum argued, "I rise not as a legal scholar or a lawyer. I rise as a mother of sons who like to hunt. . . . I frankly cannot imagine any legitimate hunting or sporting purpose for this kind of weapon. No hunter, certainly, in Kansas, in his right mind, would go after a deer or a pheasant with this firepower."[58] In making the argument Kassebaum exhibited her trademark common sense, plain talk, and life experiences as a woman and mother as Harriett Woods noted—much as she did in her first campaign—to reach a logical conclusion. The article went on to say, "For the next five minutes she countered, point by point, the arguments of pro-gun senators. And when the vote came, the ban on semiautomatic guns was approved, 51–49."

One of the best examples of how she constructed her arguments is found in an opinion piece she wrote for the *Washington Post* syndicate in 1992 discussing the state of the Republican Party after the 1992 election. Kassebaum believed that her party was no longer true to its principles and through the use of definition and representative anecdotes, she outlined how the party had strayed from true conservatism. She defined the three basic tenets of the Republican Party through the use of anaphora: "We are the party of fiscal responsibility. . . . We are the party of limited government. . . . We are the party of American leadership in foreign affairs." She criticized Republicans in the 1980s who "willingly exchanged the tax-and-spend policies of Democrats for borrow-and-spend policies that quadrupled the national debt . . . [and] discarded the basic principle that government should live within its means." When it came to the issue of limited government she capitalized on Republican claims to support "family values" by differentiating her pro-choice position as one based the political philosophy of limited government rather than on the more common argument of a woman's right to choose. She used the contentious abortion issue as a means to call for a return to the conservative value of reducing government intrusion into our lives and personal decisions. She argued:

> Individual responsibility cannot be replaced by government fiat. . . . Nowhere is this topsy-turvy thinking more evident than in the divisive debate regarding abortion. Individuals who have believed that the traditional values of personal freedom and individual responsibility should be addressed in the home and the church now find themselves under attack within the party for objecting to government intrusion into this area. . . . It is big government at its worst.
>
> Unless we face up to this contradiction, our party will continue to be drained of its energy and enthusiasm, and many Republicans, including me, will no longer feel at home in our party."

By separating the moral issues from the political, Kassebaum sought to take the issue out of politics and pave a way for more party unity. She was unsuccessful, however, and her position would affect her personally.

Finally, on leadership in world affairs, she questioned growing isolationism "at the time when the world and our own national security most need American leadership. If our bumper-sticker philosophy—Peace Through Strength—no longer resonates with voters, it is because we have failed to redefine 'strength' in terms of current circumstances."[59]

Kassebaum's rhetoric was pragmatic and devoid of most rhetorical flourishes. It did get the job done, and that is what she believed was what Kansans expected her to do. Because she was successful, highly respected, and the only woman for eight years and one of two for most of her last ten years, it was impossible for her name to not appear on speculative lists of potential candidates for the executive branch.

WHY NOT MADAM (VICE) PRESIDENT?

Even before she was sworn in as a U.S. senator, the question of presidential aspirations was raised with Nancy Landon Kassebaum's father by a *New York Times* reporter. Given his concern over her Senate run, Alf Landon's characteristically blunt response was not surprising: "That's ridiculous. Why ask me that question? It's a great honor for her to be elected a United States Senator without talking about the national ticket." The chastised reporter went on to admit that "Mrs. Kassebaum brushed aside the same question with a similar astonishment that it was asked. She has other things on her mind."[60]

Correspondence in the senator's files indicates that young journalists were equally interested in seeing Kassebaum in higher office. The *Viking Saga* staff from North Arlington High School in New Jersey informed Kassebaum less than fourteen months after taking office that she was selected "one of our top ten favorite women for President of the United States. We would like to know how you would feel if a national campaign was started to draft you for the Republican party's nomination for president?"[61] Kassebaum responded:

> I am flattered to have been selected by the North Arlington High School as one who is qualified to be President of the United States. From the outset however, I must say that I do not intend to seek this office. I have more than enough to do in mastering the workings of the Senate and effectively representing the interests of my state.

She went on to discuss the future prospects of a woman president and in doing so was true to her belief that a woman should be elected based on merit not gender:

> Since each year sees greater acceptance of women in what were once considered non-traditional roles, we are getting closer to the time when we could have a woman president. . . . Because of the importance of the office and the gravity of the issues before us, anyone considered for the presidency should be so considered because of intelligence, education, experience, and a host of other qualities. Any woman on the presidential ticket should be there because of the qualities and insights she can bring to the office.[62]

As the 1980 presidential race heated up, Kassebaum's name was occasionally mentioned as a possible vice presidential nominee should her
colleague Bob Dole not win the nomination. Senator S. I. Hayakawa of
California suggested her as a person to "heal the rifts in the G.O.P. on the
abortion and the Equal Rights Amendment issues."[63] Kassebaum dismissed
all such talk by claiming that she was too new and needed to learn how
to be a senator first. She did, however, use the 1980 Republican National
Convention as a way to further her visibility within the party and on the
national stage when she "aggressively sought the position" of temporary
chair. She learned, to her surprise, that John J. Rhodes, the House minority
leader from Arizona who as a native Kansan, was in line to be chair and
that she should talk to him about wanting a role. The temporary position
became hers.[64]

In 1984 when there was talk as to whether or not Reagan would run for
a second term, her name was mentioned again as one of the women to
consider for a number-two slot, and the most serious consideration was
given in 1988. When asked about her ambitious for higher office in a recent
interview, she responded:

> Frankly, I would not have wanted to and as close as it ever came perhaps was
> in 1988 when George Bush was running. And my name was on a short list,
> and I really didn't think anything about it and then I heard it being circulated
> in a couple of places. Jack Kilpatrick had done a piece in the paper. I wouldn't
> want to do it and it wouldn't work. I didn't know where it was coming from
> and now one of the things I think is that they always want to have a woman
> on the list and I think that was true then.
>
> But I talked to Lisa Myers at NBC. She's been there for years and she came
> to Kansas to cover part of the [1978] campaign prior to being with NBC—
> and I said, "What is this all about?" And she said there were some polls
> and yours was a name that resonates and I said, "Oh Lisa, I can't believe it
> and I don't want it to go any further." And so I called at that point Jim Baker
> and I said, "Please take my name off of any list while you're at it. It wouldn't
> work and I don't want to do it." I didn't want it to get serious and be out
> there.[65]

But it was out there, even after she asked to be taken out of consideration. The talk began seriously in a 1984 *Christian Science Monitor* article
that profiled Elizabeth Dole, Anne Armstrong, and Kassebaum with a look
toward 1988.[66] Kassebaum said at that time that she had no interest and
she was still sticking to her campaign promise to retire after a second term if
re-elected in 1984. She did "lay claim to being qualified, however, an asser-
tion she would not make in 1980."[67] On January 11, 1987, Richard Roeper
wrote in the *Chicago Sun-Times*, "It is my firm belief that the next president

of these United States should be a woman. That's right, the sooner the better."[68] Among the women he would vote for was Kassebaum. In June Kassebaum won over Iowans during a speaking engagement, but she dismissed vice presidential talk since she predicted that Bob Dole would be the nominee.[69]

As the 1988 campaign progressed and George H. W. Bush sewed up the nomination, talk turned to the number-two position. In April, Kassebaum made light of the possibility saying, "You know, there are going to be 500 (possible) tickets between now and August. . . . Part of the game will be for (Bush) to keep throwing out a lot of names and speculation on who will be the vice presidential nominee. . . . It's presumptuous to think you'd even be asked."[70] A month later while on a campaign swing in California for colleague Pete Wilson's reelection campaign, Republicans who heard her began seeing her as someone who could wrest California away from the Democrats in the fall. The vice president of the California Republican League saw her as "an ideal choice for vice president," with her "low-key but thoughtful approach to foreign affairs."[71] On the same California trip she told Young Republicans that Bush needed a "loyal running mate much like himself. . . . You can't have any division there. We have to be unified."[72] The following day the *Topeka Capital Journal* reported "Kassebaum, the junior Kansas Republican senator, did not say she would refuse a vice presidential nomination, but she said George Bush had not approached her on the subject and she did not expect him to. Kassebaum said she did not think she would provide the right balance on the Republican ticket."[73] Two weeks later, with Michael Dukakis showing a 54–38 percent lead over Bush, a Gallup poll suggested that Kassebaum or Sandra Day O'Connor would strengthen the party's ticket.[74]

The speculation continued into late July. By that point Kassebaum had long since quietly pulled herself out of the race and was beginning to do two things: dismiss the choice of a woman simply to close the gender gap and promote Bob Dole. During a weekend in Kansas she told reporters, "Just to put a woman on the ticket doesn't answer any gender gap problems. I resent putting a woman on the ticket just for that. . . . I would not be the best balance for George Bush on the ticket. I'm a strong supporter of Bob Dole. He adds a lot of strength to the ticket." She also touted Elizabeth Dole as a strong contender and made it clear that her record in the Senate would not endear her to the conservative wing of the party.[75] Even after these statements, syndicated columnist James J. Kilpatrick wrote a glowing endorsement of Kassebaum while acknowledging her negatives with the far right,[76] and Gerald M. Boyd of the *New York Times* included Kassebaum and Elizabeth Dole as two possibilities and touted Kassebaum's potential help in the Midwest.[77]

On "Meet the Press," July 31, 1988, Kassebaum responded with an emphatic "No" when asked if she wanted the vice-presidential spot. When further pushed as to whether or not she was "ruling out if he called and said, 'Senator, Nancy, I need you,'" she responded, "I don't expect him to call."[78] And he didn't. Instead, Bush selected a little-known senator from Indiana, Dan Quayle, who was described as "a younger version" of Bush by Sandy Grady of the *Philadelphia Daily News*. Kassebaum was quoted in the same article as saying "it best" when she opined, "I think George was trying to find a person he'd be comfortable with."[79]

In the April 28, 2011, interview with Kassebaum, she explained why "it wouldn't have worked." Quite simply it was her stand on the abortion issue more than anything else. Kassebaum's independence and split with Reagan on many issues during his eight years also could have contributed to a lack of comfort. Kassebaum discussed reasons why she was not interested in the position and why it is difficult for women to break through one of the last glass ceilings. For one thing, she believed she could accomplish more as a senator than vice president. She attributed her ability to work across the aisle to the fact that she wasn't "any threat." In part that was due to her lack of blatant political ambition and the power realities within the Senate. With the senior senator from her state running for the presidency in 1980, 1988, and 1996, Kassebaum realistically couldn't set her sights on that office. While the rumors of her being on "lists" of potential candidates for vice president were rampant, she and most likely others in the Senate knew that she would never appeal to the party's right wing.

Kassebaum also discussed her own lack of desire to put herself and her family through a grueling presidential campaign. She said, "You have to really want to be out there and have your life continually examined. It wasn't a question that I didn't want to do that, and I think many other women don't either." While Kassebaum didn't have young children at the point she was being considered for vice president, she often said that she would have never considered running for Senate if her children had been younger or she were still married. McGlen, et al.,[80] identify five barriers to women's participation in elective and appointive offices and one of them is family demands. Like Kassebaum, many women postpone electoral politics until children are older with the result being less time to move up the ladder. A spouse's business interests, as Geraldine Ferraro and others discovered, can make a spouse less likely to want the type of scrutiny to which Kassebaum alluded. The overall loss of privacy, no matter how dedicated one is to public service, is something Kassebaum believes is considered more by women than men.

Another factor she ruminated about was the challenge women have being seen in the commander in chief role. She laughed as she said, "I'm short and can't you just see me standing next to those generals? A woman has to radiate confidence that she can take troops into war and some women can." Perhaps that's why ABC cast the six-foot Geena Davis as president in the short-lived series "Commander in Chief." However, the issue of foreign policy competence is one that is destined to hold women back, even when it doesn't affect male candidates, such as governors, who have little or no military or foreign policy experience. Kassebaum related this to gender stereotypes that are unfair to both sexes when she noted that

> when some of my male colleagues have suggested that I know nothing about national defense issues because I am a woman, I have been offended. In the same vein, I have to assume that many of my male colleagues are offended by the notion that they cannot begin to understand the seriousness of sexual harassment or the anguish of its victims.[81]

Some of the barriers to women's success at the highest levels that Kassebaum identified were discussed by J. McIver Weatherford, a Congressional staffer, who examined Congress as an anthropologist might who "lived among any tribe in the world." His book *Tribes on the Hill* was written during Kassebaum's early years in Washington. In examining the peculiar Congressional rituals and "masculine styles of interaction in locker rooms and men's clubs" to which women are not privy, he concluded that lack of access can partially explain women's lack of political power. However, he also acknowledged an advantage women such as Kassebaum or Margaret Chase Smith had as a result of "not being a part of clan politics." And that is their ability "to violate normal congressional standards and perform some extremely unconventional actions that no insider could have done."[82] To a large extent, that is why Nancy Kassebaum's independent approach, which allowed her to break with her party's president and senate leader, confounded political observers and pundits but accomplished much.

Nancy Landon Kassebaum may never have been on a national ticket, but she did put cracks in political glass ceilings. She may have ridden into the Senate partially on her father's coattails, but she left walking out much taller than her five feet two inches. And when it comes to glass ceilings her attitude is that "I don't worry about glass ceilings. There are women who have broken them in extraordinary ways, and there always will be."[83]

NOTES

1. Nancy Landon Kassebaum, untitled statement written for U.S. Jaycee Women, September 1984, from Papers of Nancy Landon Kassebaum, Kansas State Historical Society.
2. Quoted in Celia Morris, "Changing the Rules and the Roles: Five Women in Public Office," in Paula Ries and Anne J. Stone (eds.), *The American Woman 1992–93: A Status Repor,* (New York: W.W. Norton & Company, 1992), p. 95.

---

3. For a discussion of Kansas's long tradition of women political activists see Joanna L. Stratton, *Pioneer Women: Voices from the Kansas Frontier* (New York: Simon and Schuster, 1981), pp. 251–267; Stacy Morford, "From Settlers to Screen Stars, Pilots to Politicians, Kansas Women Have Embodied Pioneering Spirit," the *Topeka Capital-Journal*, September 7, 1999, www.highbeam.com/doc/1P2-7389122.html/print on (accessed August 29, 2011); and Teresa Lindquist, "Women in Office," 2001, http://skyways.lib.ks.us/genweb/shawnee/library/KSHSvol12/women.txt (accessed September 4, 2011).

4. Morford, pp. 1, 2.

5. Eleanor Marshall-White, *Women, Catalysts for Change: Interpretive Biographies of Shirley St. Hill Chisholm, Sandra Day O'Connor, and Nancy Landon Kassebaum* (New York: Vantage Press, 1991), p. 91.

6. Biographical information about Nancy Landon Kassebaum is a summary of material found in all of the referenced sources. Only exact quotations from the source are endnoted.

7. Linda Witt, Karen M. Paget, and Glenna Matthews, *Running as a Woman: Gender and Power in American Politics* (New York: The Free Press, 1994), p. 106.

8. Paul Hendrickson, "His Daughter, the Senator-Election from Kansas: Alf Landon Aimed for Washington, Now Nancy Kassebaum Is Going," the *Washington Post*, November 30, 1978, G1, www.lexisnexis.com.www2.lib.ku.edu:2048/hottopics/lnacademic/?verb=sr&csi=8075 (accessed September 5, 2011).

9. Witt, Paget, and Matthews, p. 86.

10. Women in the Congress, "Nancy Landon Kassebaum, Senator, 1978–1997, Republican from Kansas," http://womenincongress.house,gov/member-profiles/profile.html?intID=125 (accessed April 28, 2011).

11. Eleanor Marshall-White, p. 85.

12. Paula Ries and Anne J. Stone (eds.), *The American Woman 1991–93: A Status Report* (New York: W. W. Norton & Company, 1991), p. 95.

13. Dave Kendall, "Nancy Kassebaum Baker: Personal Reflections on Her Years in the Senate," http://ktwu.washburn.edu/journeys.scripts/1305c.html(accessed April 28, 2011).

14. Alissa Rubin, "A Republican with a Mind of Her Own," *Wichita Eagle*, July 15, 1990, accessed from Files of Nancy Landon Kassebaum, Kansas Historical Society, Box K, BB, Clipp, v.193, Kassebaum, N.L.

15. Nancy Landon Kassebaum Baker, interview with Brien R. Williams, April 16, 2009, www.c-spanvideo.org/program/295445-1 (accessed September 4, 2011).

16. Nancy Landon Kassebaum, interview with Brien R. Williams.

17. Kendall, "Nancy Kassebaum Baker."

18. Kendall, "Nancy Kassebaum Baker."

19. *Current Biography* in "Women in Congress."

20. Witt, Paget, and Matthews, p. 106.

21. Paul Hendrickson and Martin Tolchin, " 'Dynasty' Washington Style: Fishes, Longs, Pells," *New York Times*, September 18, 1984, www.nytimes.com/1984/09/18/us/dynasty-washington-style-fishes-longs-pells.html? (accessed April 28, 2011).

22. Bill Blankenship, "Government Becomes a Family Affair," *Topeka Capital-Journal*, April 6, 2003, www.highbeam.com/doc/1P2-7325807.html (accessed August 29, 2011).

23. Julia Malone, "Three Leading Republican Women Discuss Why Their Party May Be the First to Run a Woman for Vice-President. But All Three Say They Have Little Interest in Being the One," *Christian Science Monitor*, March 28, 1984, accessed from Files of Nancy Landon Kassebaum, K, 329.6, v. 18, Kansas State Historical Society.

24. "Nancy Landon Kassebaum," *Current Biography*, (New York: H.W. Wilson and Company, 1982), p. 191. Quoted in Office of History and Preservation, office of the clerk, *Women in Congress, 1917–2006* (Washington, DC: U.S. Government Printing Office, 2007.) http://womenincongress.house.gov/memberprofiles/profile.html?intID=125 (accessed July 20, 2011).

25. Malone, "Three Leading Republican Women."

26. Brien R. Williams interview with Nancy Kassebaum Baker.

27. Kendall, "Nancy Kassebaum Baker."

28. Ann R. Wilner, "Nancy," *The New York Times*, November 13, 1978, A23, http://query.nytimes.com/mem/archive/pdf?res=F50E12F63D5511728DDDAA099 4D9415B888BF1D3 (accessed July 20, 2011).

29. Kendall, "Nancy Kassebaum Baker."

30. Wilner, "Nancy."

31. Nancy Landon Kassebaum Baker interview conducted by Diana B. Carlin, April 28, 2011.

32. Douglas E. Kneeland, "Senate's Only Woman Defies Stereotypes," *The New York Times*, November 29, 1978, A18, www.lexisnexis.com.www2.lib.ku.edu:2048/hottopics/lnacademic/?verb=sr&csi=8075 (accessed August 24, 2011).

33. Eleanor Holmes Norton, "Elected to Lead: A Challenge to Women in Public Office," in Deborah L. Rhode (ed.), *The Difference "Difference" Makes: Women and Leadership* (Stanford, CA: Stanford University Press, 2003), p. 112.

34. Tom Webb, Knight Ridder/Tribute News Service, "Sen. Kassebaum Ending Career on High Note," August 21, 1996, www.highbeam.com/doc/1G1-18605121.html (accessed August 29, 2011).

35. Tom Webb, Knight Ridder/Tribune News Service, "Sen. Kassebaum to Announce Whether She Will Retire or Run for Fourth Term," November 15, 1995, accessed August 29, 2011, http://highbeam.com/doc/1G1-17610286.html.

36. Associated Press, "Kansas' Kassebaum Opts for Retirement," *Los Angeles Daily News*, November 21, 1995, www.highbeam.com/doc/1)2-25027033.html (accessed August 29, 2011).

37. James J. Kilpatrick, ". . . Nancy Kassebaum Would Be a Fine Choice," *Chicago Sun-Times*, July 27, 1988, www.highbeam.com/doc/1P2-3896636.html (accessed August 29, 2011).

38. Bella Abzug, *Gender Gap* (Boston: Houghton Mifflin, 1984), p. 171, quoted in Kathleen Hall Jamieson, *Beyond the Double Bind: Women and Leadership* (New York: Oxford University Press, 1995), p. 129.

39. Hendrickson, "His Daughter, the Senator-Elect from Kansas."

40. *Current Biography*, 1982, p. 192 in *Women in Congress*.

41. Knight Ridder/Tribune News Service, "Kassebaum and Schroeder will be missed," December 7, 1995, www.highbeam.com/doc/1G1-17822040.html (accessed August 29, 2011).

42. Nancy Landon Kassebaum, "The Challenge of Change," September 9, 1987, in Diana Prentice Carlin and Meredith A. Moore (eds.), *The Landon Lecture Series on*

Public Issues: The First Twenty Years, 1966–1986 (Lanham, MD: University Press of America, 1990), p. 851.

43. Kassebaum, "The Challenge of Change," p. 853.

44. Nancy Landon Kassebaum, "The Intersection of Hope and Doubt," September 9, 1996, http://gos.sbc.edu/k/kassebaum.html (accessed April 28, 2011).

45. Angelia Herrin, "A Senator Out of the Limelight: Kassebaum Plugs Away to Get Results, Not Attention," *Wichita Eagle-Beacon*, July 5, 1987, accessed from Files of Nancy Landon Kassebaum, K, BB, Clipp.; 193, Kassebaum, N.

46. Margaret Warner, "Interview with Nancy Kassebaum," November 29, 1995, www.pbs.org/newshour/bb/congress/congress_11-29.html (accessed September 12, 2011).

47. Webb, "Sen. Kassebaum to Announce."

48. Richard Lugar and Nancy Kassebaum, "S. Africa Sanctions: 2 Opposing Views: 'It Is time to Send a Blunt Message to President Botha," *Chicago Sun-Times*, October 2, 1986, www.highbeam.com/doc/1P2-3788298.html (accessed August 29, 2011).

49. Carol Gilligan, *In a Different Voice* (Cambridge, MA: Harvard University Press, 1982), p. 147.

50. Sally Helgesen, *The Female Advantage: Women's Ways of Leadership* (New York: Doubleday), 1990, pp. 49–50.

51. Kassebaum, untitled article for U.S. Jaycee Women.

52. "Nancy Kassebaum (Baker)," *Encyclopedia of World Biography*, www.bookrags.com/printfriendly/?p=bios&u=nancy-kassebaum (accessed April 28, 2011).

53. Interview, *Working Woman*, October 4, 1979, p. 62 in *Women in Congress*.

54. Webb, "Sen. Kassebaum to Announce."

55. Files of Nancy Landon Kassebaum, Letter to Ann Porch, August 18, 1980, Kansas State Historical Society, BAS, Women, Porch, Ann.

56. Nancy Landon Kassebaum, "Women Emerge as Force in Party Politics," Newsday, August 29, 1982, accessed from Kansas Historical Society, News Files.

57. Rubin, "A Republican with a Mind of Her Own."

58. Rubin, "A Republican with a Mind of Her Own."

59. Nancy Landon Kassebaum, "Republican Party Has to Reinvent Itself," *Buffalo News*, November 15, 1992, www.highbeam.com/doc/1P2-22438913.html (accessed August 29, 2011).

60. Douglas E. Kneeland.

61. Letter from Robert Barto, February 5, 1980, papers of Senator Nancy Landon Kassebaum, Kansas State Historical Society, File BAS Women, Barto, Robert.

62. Letter to Robert Barto, March 21, 1980, papers of Senator Nancy Landon Kassebaum, Kansas State Historical Society, File BAS Women, Barto, Robert.

63. Associated Press, "Kassebaum Not Spurning VP Talk," *Topeka Capital-Journal*, April 5, 1988, accessed from Files of Nancy Landon Kassebaum, K, 329.6, v. 18, Kansas State Historical Society.

64. Nancy Landon Kassebaum Baker interview with Diana B. Carlin.

65. Ibid.

66. Julia Malone, "Three Leading Republican Women."

67. Ibid.

68. Richard Roeper, "What This Country Needs Is a Woman as the President," *Chicago Sun-Times*, January 11, 1987, www.highbeam.com/doc/1P2-3805028.html (accessed August 30, 2011).

69. Hood, "Kassebaum Gaining Fans."

70. Associated Press, "Kassebaum Not Spurning VP Talk."

71. Rich Hood, "A Bush-Kassebaum Ticket Sounds Good to Californians," *Kansas City Star*, May 1, 1988, accessed Files of Nancy Landon Kassebaum, K, BB, Clipp., 193, Kassebaum, N6.

72. "Kassebaum Speaks on Vice Presidency," *Boston Globe*, May 4, 1988, www.highbeam.com/doc/1P2-8060472.html (accessed August 29, 2011).

73. Kathy Bartelli, "Kassebaum Says Spot on Ticket Unlikely," *Topeka Capital-Journal*, May 5, 1988, accessed Files of Nancy Landon Kassebaum, K, BB, Clipp., 193, Kassebaum, N.L., Kansas State Historical Society.

74. Diane Alters, "Gallup Shows Dukakis with 14 Point Lead," *Boston Globe*, May 18, 1988, www.highbeam.com/doc/1P2-8062461.html (accessed August 30, 2011).

75. Harris New Service, "Kassebaum Won't Seek VP Position," *Hutchinson News*, July 26, 1988, accessed from Files of Nancy Landon Kassebaum, K, BB, Clipp., 193, Kassebaum, N.L.

76. Kilpatrick, ". . . Nancy Kassebaum Would Be a Fine Choice."

77. Gerald M. Boyd, "Bush Is Lining Up Prospects for No. 2 Spot on the Ticket," *New York Times*, July 28, 1988, www.nytimes.com/1988/07/28/us/bush-is-lining-up-prospects-for-no-2-spot-on-the-ticket.html?scp=1&sq=&st=nyt (accessed August 29, 2011).

78. Associated Press, "Senator Kassebaum Insists She Doesn't Want No. 2 Job," *New York Times*, August 2, 1988, accessed August 29, 2011, http://www.nytimes.com/1988/08/02/us/senator-kassebaum-insists-she-doesn-t-want-no-2-job.html?scp=1&sq=&st=nyt.

79. Sandy Grady, "Quayle: A Younger Version of Bush," *Post-Tribune* (IN), August 18, 1988, www.highbeam.com/doc/1N1-1085382F75AFDE39.html (accessed August 30, 2011).

80. Nancy E. McGlen, et al., *Women, Politics, and American Society*, 4th ed. (New York: Longman, 2002), p. 90.

81. Timothy Phelps and Helen Winternitz, *Capitol Games* (New York: Hyperion, 1992), p. 411, quoted in Kathleen Hall Jamieson, *Beyond the Double Bind: Women and Leadership* (New York: Oxford University Press, 1995), p. 194.

82. J. McIver Weatherford, *Tribes on the Hill: The U.S. Congress Rituals and Realities*, revised ed. (Westport, CT: Bergin & Garvey, 1985), p. 251–252.

83. Morford, "From Settlers to Screen Stars."

3

Dianne Feinstein: The Loneliness of a Moderate Voice

From her youth, Dianne Feinstein learned to hide her emotions and work hard.[1] Her mother was abusive (later diagnosed with a mental disorder), and Dianne hid from various publics how her mother's behavior made her feel. Her father was a very hard-working and successful surgeon, and Dianne emulated him, always working harder than others with a determination to succeed. He succeeded despite being Jewish at a time when anti-Semitism was common. Feinstein rarely spoke about the obstacles that stood in her path to success, but being Jewish and being a woman were two. The ultimate obstacles, however, were less ethnicity and gender and more her independent, moderate politics as well as the way she sometimes non-verbally communicated her wealthy status. The former made her not quite the Democrat progressive Democrats were seeking in a candidate; the latter made her suspicious among the rank-and-file, who felt that she was too well-off to understand the plights of the workers, the poor, and those suffering from AIDS. She, through her actions as a public servant, could overcome the latter obstacle; the former, however, would prove to be *the* barrier between Feinstein and the highest office in the land, one that she once said she aspired to.[2]

PROVING HERSELF IN SAN FRANCISCO

Like Mikulski and Pelosi, Feinstein's commitment to public service is rooted in her early Catholic education, for young Dianne Goldman, although Jewish, was sent to San Francisco's Sacred Heart Academy. There, the nuns emphasized both social grace and social service. The Sacred Heart pedigree meant a great deal in educational circles, for it—and perhaps Dr. Goldman's connections—led Dianne to Stanford University despite academic credentials that were not as stellar as those of most admitted to the prestigious school. There, she became involved in campus politics, learning what would and what would not work in a campaign.

What followed Stanford was a short-lived fiery marriage and, then, an enduring one to an older, wealthy man. Her post-graduate employment, aided by an out-of-the-blue appointment by California Governor Edmund G. Brown, was in criminal justice. She sat on a board that investigated women convicted of crime, determining their sentences and whether or not they might be paroled. This work exposed her to the less desirable side of life in her city (and state). Her lifestyle, however, was among the privileged of San Francisco. So, with rather pronounced views on "law and order" and with the white gloves of an elite San Franciscan woman, Dianne—still with a young daughter from her first marriage to raise—turned to politics. She, a political unknown, decided to run for the City of San Francisco Board of Supervisors.

Out of nowhere, aided by the fact that she looked so unlike the other candidates (the sole woman) that she was memorable to voters, she not only won elected office, but came in first, entitling her to not only serve on the Board but be its president. Some thought she would defer to others with more city experience, but she did not. She would serve on the Board for many years, winning reelection despite being "the darling" of neither the political right nor the political left. The job she really wanted, however, was not the legislative one she had. She preferred to be in charge, not wrestle with the statute-making process. So, she wanted to be mayor.

Feinstein would run for mayor and lose three times. Sometimes she lost because of her campaign blunders; sometimes she lost because of her opponents' ingenuity and energy; sometimes events would intervene. In general, however, she was disadvantaged in her mayoral campaigns because she could be out-flanked on both the right and the left. She had positions on issues that both extremes disliked, and her attempts at moderation were portrayed as revealing indecision and lack of confidence. She was also hurt by the assumption, held by voters male and female, that a woman was not tough enough for the job. Her "white gloves" image fed that assumption: she, in particular, was not tough enough because of her privileged background.

Tragedy would give Feinstein the office that elections would not. Dan White was a conservative-leaning supervisor. In retrospect, several, including Feinstein, recalled observing signs that he was struggling under a great deal of stress. That stress was at least partially because he was torn between serving his constituents and providing for his family: with the salary a supervisor received, providing was difficult. Finally, he resigned. Then, he quickly changed his mind. Mayor George Moscone was willing to tear up White's resignation letter; however, legal opinion held that, since White had officially resigned, he had to be officially reappointed by the mayor. Then, politics kicked in. Many lobbied Moscone not to reappoint White, including ultra-liberal supervisor Harvey Milk; and Moscone ultimately decided not to do so. The morning he heard the news, White snuck into City Hall, walked into Moscone's office and shot him dead. Then, he walked down the hall into Milk's office, and shot him dead as well.

Feinstein, as Board president, became mayor, offering the public a compassionate but strong speech within hours of the double assassination. She thus began her nine-year term as San Francisco mayor communicating a firm but compassionate message. During those years, there would be ups and downs. Her moderation would anger those at the political extremes, but, in general, she maintained high ratings from the city's residents for the job she was doing. Yes, she was subject to an embarrassing recall vote, but she turned that to her advantage when those calling for her ouster because of her stance on gun control came across to voters as very much out of the political mainstream. They were renounced by so large a margin as to make Feinstein formidable if not invincible as a mayoral candidate in future races.

Her service as mayor brought her considerable national attention. This attention was most evident when *Time* magazine put her on its cover along with New York Congresswoman Geraldine Ferraro. The cover accompanied a story about the 1984 Democratic vice presidential nomination. *Time* successfully predicted both that presidential nominee Walter Mondale would select a woman and that Feinstein and Ferraro would be the two finalists. Feinstein may actually have been Mondale's first choice, but, at the last minute, Ferraro's appeal to the working-class was thought to trump Feinstein's appeal to moderates. Nonetheless, Feinstein received a great deal of national visibility, perhaps whetting her appetite for a public office higher than mayor.

So, when the office of governor of California became available, Feinstein announced her interest. Her opponent, Republican U.S. Senator Pete Wilson, proved formidable. Ultimately, his ability to appeal to fiscal conservatives and social progressives trumped her moderation. She may also have failed in the campaign to project a sufficiently positive image: polling showed that many of those voting against her disliked or distrusted her.[3] The campaign, however, did get Feinstein out of the cocoon San Francisco had been: she had to discover the rest of the state. In addition, the campaign marked a drift leftward in Feinstein's self-positioning. She found that she needed to appeal to liberal voters to win statewide. Whereas her relationship with liberal groups was uneasy in this campaign, it was stronger when, two years later, she ran for the U.S. Senate. There were still issues on which she and liberals parted ways—for example, capital punishment; however, in her Senate race she will campaign as a fairly progressive candidate.

The year she ran for the Senate, 1992, saw two U.S. Senate races in California. Retiring Democratic Senator Alan Cranston's seat was up for grabs as was the seat Pete Wilson had vacated when he became governor. Feinstein ran for the Wilson seat, allowing liberal Democratic Congresswoman Barbara Boxer from Marin County (just North of San Francisco) to run for Cranston's seat and the full six-year term. This gracious act signaled a rapprochement between the San Francisco Bay area women. In mayoral campaigns and in the 1990 gubernatorial campaign, Boxer had supported liberal challengers to Feinstein. Now, they campaigned occasionally together, and, with Feinstein's victory secure, she urged donors to help Boxer win in a somewhat tougher race. Feinstein's campaigning with Boxer may also have in itself helped Boxer win, for Feinstein attracted moderate voters to both Democratic candidates. They both won and were part of the swell of women in 1992 who took the total number there from just two to seven. Some even characterized the two as the "Bobbsey Twins," although it would not have required much investigation to discern both their differing political views and their differing political styles.[4] Twins of any sort they were not (although it is instructive to compare them).

Feinstein has served in the U.S. Senate since. Occasionally, the press and political pundits have speculated about her candidacy for higher office. Meanwhile, she has gained a reputation as a Democrat Republicans can work with because of her centrist political views.

RHETORICAL STYLE

Senate debating rarely gets media coverage for a variety of reasons, most noteworthy being the facts that such debates are frequently long and that they often have rather boring stretches. Nonetheless, it is through this communication venue that senators often exhibit their rhetorical style. The debate over the retirement rank of Admiral Frank Kelso showcased the differing rhetorical styles of Feinstein and Boxer, as well as the styles of the other women who were objecting to an honorary rank of four-star admiral for Kelso because he was the admiral in-charge at the time of the notorious 1991 Tailhook Convention in Las Vegas. The showcasing was the result of the debate being bannered by the media and the Senate women alike as a stand the women in that body were taking in response to systemic sexism in the U.S. Navy and beyond.[5]

Boxer's style was quite feminist, as she repeatedly told the stories of women assaulted at the Tailhook '91 aviators' convention. This style she would exhibit even more dramatically later in a lengthy debate over a bill to ban a medical procedure labeled "partial birth abortion" by opponents. Feinstein's style contrasted starkly with Boxer's, suggesting to observers that these two California women were politically very different.

The attempt to deny Kelso a four-star retirement united the seven women in the Senate, but it was very much a liberal cause. Thus, Republican Senator Nancy Kassebaum of Kansas did not speak, and Republican Senator Kay Bailey Hutchinson of Texas spoke only briefly. The lead was taken by the liberal quartet of Boxer; Barbara Mikulski (Maryland), who was the floor leader for those opposed to the four-star rank; Carol Moseley-Braun (Illinois); and Patty Murray (Washington). In between the reluctant Republican duo and the liberal quartet was Feinstein. Her approach contrasted with that of the more liberal women.

She began by saying that she had "listened very carefully to what Senator Sam Nunn (D, Georgia) and Senator John Warner (R, Virginia) had to say."[6] She acknowledged her "great respect" for them and praised them for their knowledge of the military. Then, she politely disagreed saying, "I must say that I look at this a little differently." She grounded that disagreement by noting that "she took the time to read the IG [Inspector General's] report as well as *The Navy Policy Book.*" That book defines "accountability," and Feinstein used that definition as the key to her decision to oppose an honorific retirement rank for Kelso. She noted his accomplishments, but she also noted how sexual harassment cannot be ignored by naval officers who know it is occurring. This was, in her view, the case with Kelso: not only did Tailhook have a reputation that Kelso must have been aware of, but Kelso was present at the 1991 gathering.

Feinstein said, referring to the Tailhook convention, that she did "not want to rehash that entire incident," but then proceeded to summarize the events that occurred at that meeting. Unlike her California colleague Barbara Boxer who used her time on the Senate floor to tell the stories of particular victims, Feinstein refrained from talking specifically about certain "incidents" because doing so would not, in her judgment, be "appropriate" in a Senate debate. Her summary, then, focused on Kelso's "accountability" and very often quoted the IG report. Her pattern was to comment, to quote at length, and to transition quickly to another quotation. The pattern is lawyerly (even though she is not a lawyer), and, in keeping with this pattern, she concluded with a summation:

> So, Madam President, what I believe we women are saying is it cannot be business as usual in the U.S. military. Women are taking their places in the ranks of the military, defending our Nation proudly, and they must be treated with respect. They are not property. They are not to serve people who view themselves as women haters. They are individuals. They are there to serve one entity, and that is their country, the United States of America, and they are to be treated with respect, their minds as well as their bodies.

Her language here drifted in what one might term a feminist direction. Sensing that perhaps, she retreated to middle ground:

> I hope this is not looked at as any—at least it is not on my part, and I know it is not on the part of my female colleagues—any kind of female need to speak out. What it is is that we have suddenly come head on with the whole ethic, a whole mentality, a whole period of decades condoning activity of people at official conventions, official behavior at conventions, and in their personal lifestyle as well.

She then recounted briefly what occurred at Tailhook '91 and characterized the events as representing "failed leadership." Kelso, in her view, failed, but her last paragraph stated that conclusion in very moderate language:

> So I hope that our votes are viewed in this light. I believe a man should not be judged by the last thing he did. He should be judged in his life by the best thing he did. Nonetheless, the issues here have been joined, and the Senate simply cannot sanction these kinds of activities at officially sponsored conventions of the U.S. military.

One might even argue that, in straining to moderate her position and differentiate it from that some might have been ascribing to the other women, she offered a contradictory position: one should judge Kelso's entire career; however, we are not going to do so.

Consider her style in another Senate debate. This one occurred a few years later over the very controversial issue of what pro-life forces had labeled "partial-birth abortion." This debate, which occurred over several days, became more of a duel or endurance test between Senator Bob Smith, a Republican from New Hampshire, and Senator Barbara Boxer, a Democrat from California.[7] Perhaps sensing her fatigue, colleagues did come to Boxer's aid. Among them was Feinstein.

She began by citing what she had learned from the hearings conducted by the Senate Judiciary Committee. Then, like a lawyer or like an academic debater, she presented her brief:

> I wanted to speak today on what I learned from the hearings and my reasons for opposing this bill. Let me summarize those reasons up front, and then go into each one specifically.
>
> First, I believe that this bill attempts to ban a specific medical procedure which is called, in this bill, a "partial-birth abortion," but there is no medical definition for what a "partial-birth abortion" is.
>
> Second, the language in the bill is so vague that I believe it will affect more than any one single medical procedure.
>
> Third, the bill presumes guilt on the part of the doctor, so that every physician may have to prove that in fact he did not perform this procedure, or justify his reasons for so doing if he did.

This bill could be an unnecessary, I think an unconscionable complication to families who face many tragic circumstances involving severely deformed fetuses. I also believe it is an unnecessary Federal regulation, since 41 States have already outlawed post-viability abortions, except to save a woman's life or health.

Finally, I hope to make a case that this bill is very carefully crafted to provide a direct challenge to Roe versus Wade.[8]

She, then, proceeded argument-by-argument, citing source after source, quoting some at length. Whereas Boxer spent her time telling the stories of women whose lives were saved by procedures that the bill might ban, Feinstein ended up talking about the "commerce clause" in the U.S. Constitution and how, under its terms, the proposed law might well only apply to physicians who cross state lines in order to perform an abortion. Their rhetorical styles could not be more different.

Feinstein then offered her summation, which states the position of many who voted against the ban and the position of U.S. president Bill Clinton, who eventually vetoed the legislation, in calm but strong terms:

The point is, that this legislation, I believe, has little or nothing to do with stopping the use of some horrific and unnecessary medical procedure performed by evil or inhumane doctors. If that were simply the case, we would all be opposed. I believe this legislation's major purpose is the camel's nose under the tent to get at second-trimester abortions and to put a fear over all legitimate physicians, obstetricians who do perform an abortion when an abortion is necessary—a fear that they could be hauled into court and have to defend themselves and prove that they did not perform whatever a partial-birth abortion is eventually adjudicated to be.

So the legislation is vague, it is flawed, and it presumes guilt on the part of the doctor. It ignores the vital health interests of women. I believe these are strong reasons to vote against this bill.

Feinstein's style fits the image she brought with her to the Senate. Her approach revealed a careful examination of the relevant documents. That examination, of course, meant that Feinstein, assisted perhaps by aides, had labored long and hard to master a large body of sometimes-tedious reading material. Feinstein worked hard, worked carefully, and analyzed issues systematically. Whereas others involved in this debate told stories or expressed outrage or showed pathos-evoking diagrams (Smith) and pictures (Boxer), Feinstein offered a restrained approach that both accepted and rejected claims made by both sides. She modeled moderation as she explained what, in her judgment, made the partial-birth abortion bill unacceptable. In this case, she joined pro-choice liberals in seeing in the legislation a larger assault on women's reproductive rights, but she voiced that view in less inflammatory language than others. Similarly, as in the former

Tailhook case, she tried to distance her position from a more radical interpretation that some might attempt to give it. Her rhetorical style was, then, a model of careful thought and careful restraint.

Two other moments during her U.S. Senate career are worth noting in an attempt to describe her style. One shows the careful restraint; the other that, beneath that restraint, was passion that could be provoked. The first was her attempt, in concert with Republican Senator Robert Bennett from Utah, to craft censure language during the Senate trial of President Clinton that was "strong enough to woo Republicans and soft enough to keep Democrats on board."[9] She spent many hours revising and revising, trying to find just the right language that a bipartisan group might ascribe to. The second was her dramatic retort to Idaho Republican Senator Larry Craig in 1993. Feinstein had added a ban on semiautomatic assault weapons to a crime bill; in defense of her amendment, she had cited a 1984 mass killing at a McDonald's in San Ysidro, California. Craig argued (in error) that the weapon used there was a shotgun, not an Uzi. He said, "The gentlelady from California needs to become a little bit more familiar with firearms and their deadly characteristics." Feinstein responded:

> I am quite familiar with firearms. I became mayor as a product of assassination. I found my assassinated colleague [Harvey Milk] and put a finger through a bullet hole trying to get a pulse. I proposed gun control legislation in San Francisco. I went through a recall on the basis of it. I was trained in the shooting of a firearm when I had terrorist attacks, with a bomb at my house, when my husband was dying, when I had windows shot out. Senator, I know something about what firearms can do.[10]

Her passion prevailed, overcoming considerable lobbying by pro-gun interests; her amendment passed 51 to 49.

In Feinstein's case, her rhetorical style then mirrors her political style. The rhetorical style might have made her only a moderately effective stump speaker during a presidential campaign. The word "might," however, is key, for Feinstein could exhibit less restraint when campaigning or even one-on-one during an interview. Campaigning in 1990, for example, she sounded traditional Democratic themes strongly: "I want to be the governor who protects the pocketbooks of working men and women, because we've had enough of tax cuts for the rich and tax hikes for everyone else"; "The right to choice in this country is now threatened . . . threatened by the vagaries of male-dominated legislatures," by "a male body of politicians lay[ing] down the rules for us."[11] And she sounded other themes strongly as well. In a published debate with Wilson, she characterized California as "a coke capital, the methamphetamine lab, the PCP lab and heroin importation capital of America," and, in calling for action against drugs, she used the words "war," "muscle" (two times), and "fight" (four times).[12]

So, her style outside the halls of the legislature might—as one would expect—occasionally have a degree of rhetorical fire, but, should she enact the moderate persona as is her wont, people might have walked away from a rally feeling less than inspired. This rhetorical style may well have been one factor that kept her from becoming "a player" in the presidential sweepstakes, but it was the political style the rhetorical style reflected that was the major problem for Feinstein. She could, if pushed, ratchet her rhetorical style up beyond the moderate mark; her political style, however, was fixed at that mark.

Early in her political career, commentators noted her issues—"good schools, clean air, safe streets, a woman's right to choose"—and her carefully cultivated persona—"tough and caring."[13] She would fight crime with police presence and capital punishment as tools, but she would also provide "some mothering," for, in her words, "the state can't be hurt by somebody who cares, who can add some closeness to the people, who can provide the kind of inspiration a mother does to a family."[14]

Those were words from 1990. Although "tough and caring" might well be an apt description for the entirety of her political career, after 1990, "moderate" would be a better adjective. Two years after 1900, political scientist Eric Schockman described Feinstein as "a Democrat of a different stripe," noting how she was booed by Democrats for her support of the death penalty and how she had proved herself repeatedly to be "a friend of the business community."[15] A decade later, in an interview, she recalled how she was thought to be a quasi-Republican when mayor and declared that "the center of the political spectrum is the best place to govern" and characterized herself as "a very passionate believer in the center of the political spectrum."[16] In 2005, *San Francisco Chronicle* reporter Zachary Coile described her as "a pragmatist who is willing to work with Republicans" and stressed her "centrist stance" and "cooperative approach."[17] Two years later, *San Francisco Chronicle* writer Bob Egelko described her as "the Democrat most likely to cross party lines," "a moderate," and "the most conservative Democrat" on the important Judiciary Committee. Egelko noted how she was conservative on immigration and crime but liberal on women's rights and gun control.[18]

She was then that rare political creature—a genuine moderate. And in her case, being a moderate meant that that her positions on issues ran the gamut and, thus, some posed problem for Democratic Party power brokers and, probably, some Democratic Party voters. During the primary phase of a presidential campaign, there is a tendency for candidates to tack to the party's extremes because voters in the primaries tend to be more ideological and, thus, conservative for Republican primaries and liberal for Democratic primaries. Given this phenomenon, Feinstein would have struggled in a primary. If she had gotten beyond the primaries and won the party nomination, she might have found that her moderation had appeal, especially for independent and crossover voters. Early in a campaign season, however, she would likely have been thought not Democratic enough.

WHY NOT MADAM PRESIDENT?

Earlier in her political career, Feinstein was indeed trapped in some of the double binds Kathleen Hall Jamieson discusses in her important 1995 book.[19] These binds, by definition, trap women in leadership roles, no matter which direction they choose. The womb/brain bind she overcame by rarely emphasizing the fact that she was a mother. On a few occasions, Feinstein would bring daughter Katherine into the political picture. More usually, Feinstein acted as if she did not have children. Her workday schedule was as long and tiring as that of her surgeon father. She was wealthy enough to afford at-home childcare and did not to have to drop city business to pick up her daughter from a daycare center (at a time when daycare centers were still rare); she was able to pursue that business as long as necessary. The only people noticing that she was not home addressing Katherine's needs were Katherine and, perhaps, her husband. He was very supportive of Feinstein's career; daughter Katherine was not, until many years later, warm to it.

The silence/shame bind she overcame—in large measure—by adopting a speaking style that was neither wordy nor emotional. Her words were not the sometimes angry, sometimes crusading ones that other women in politics—at least Democratic Party politics—often uttered. There is plenty of evidence that, one-on-one, in the day-to-day management of her office, she could be demanding. Mayor Moscone's office had been characterized by a casual atmosphere. Hers was characterized by a sometimes-stiff formality, and, undoubtedly, when one did not do the job expected or did not do the job as thoroughly as Feinstein would have done herself, the guilty aide felt a degree of verbal wrath. This strong style, however, was largely out of sight. That Feinstein could be verbally aggressive was circulated in political gossip, so the style was not unknown. However, it was not widely known because it was not part of her public persona. Therefore, Feinstein might be said to have negotiated the silence/shame bind fairly effectively. She was far from silent, but her style was such that few had difficulties when she spoke. She was castigated as neither witch nor bitch.

The feminine/competent bind posed problems for her early in her career. She was frequently described as strikingly attractive; and her attire, usually chosen from the best and most stylish available, was almost always noted in press coverage.[20] She thus was sometimes thought too feminine to tackle the tough jobs of city government. She was also, because of the quality of her wardrobe and where in the city she lived, thought too privileged to understand the problems facing many people in San Francisco. Her work ethic, which has her at the job long, demanding hours, helped her overcome the first prejudice; some of her acts in service of the less privileged in the city helped her overcome the second. She was, nonetheless, very aware of the need to project a strong image when she spoke to the public. That need was in her mind as she planned her first address to the people after the Moscone and Milk assassinations. That time, she succeeded in appearing strong, yet compassionate, giving her material years later for "the ad" that made her, overnight, a significant political figure in California.[21] The need was in her mind as she tried to cope with the "White Night" riots that followed the lenient sentencing Dan White received for the double murder. That time, she failed by taking the advice of her security team and, thus, separating herself as mayor from the police chief who dealt with the riots (arguably) first too leniently and second too brutally. She ended up safely, weakly on the sidelines.

Daniel B. Sullivan has studied Feinstein's statewide campaign advertising in considerable detail. In a 1998 *Women's Studies in Communication* article, he reported that "consistency characterizes the images Feinstein promoted across her three campaigns."[22] These images reflect a desire on her part to blend toughness with two different dimensions that women often emphasize in their campaigns: first, being a political outsider to the male-dominated establishment; and, second, being caring. She stressed her "tough" position on issues such as capital punishment, budget trimming, anti-drug enforcement, law enforcement more broadly, and anti-immigration enforcement. She also stressed how she was an outsider to "politics as usual" and her arguably more "caring" position on reproductive freedom, day care, and affirmative action. Her ads, which were both argumentative and attacking, contained 39 percent outsider themes, 28 percent leadership themes, 20 percent toughness themes, and 7 percent caring themes. Thus, one would conclude that she stressed stereotypically masculine traits in her self-presentation and, when taking a tack common among female candidates, she chose, as Cheryl Sullivan discovers in an 1988 interview, the outsider persona much more than the caring one.[23] She did, however, in 1990, run a series of ads posing with young children, and, in 1992, she ran an ad entitled "Eileen," in which she posed with her infant granddaughter.[24] That ad, however, is as overtly maternal as Feinstein ever gets. Usually, she stresses the "tough" in her recurring "tough and caring" slogan.

Her desire to project "toughness," however, did not cause her to harden her oft-noted (in the media) good looks and fashion sense, but, as she aged, they matured. So, the Dianne Feinstein who might have been considered presidential material had stately good looks accentuated by her height and grooming that screamed corporate boardroom, not debutante beauty and high fashion. Stately and corporate a female president might well be. She was said to look like the Disney character "Snow White" in 1990[25] That striking resemblance to "Snow White" was still noted as late as 2004, when there was talk of a Feinstein presidential campaign and the seven men thus far in the race were thought to be without stature.[26] The "Snow White" resemblance notwithstanding, she had a stately demeanor that did not entirely obliterate her femininity while, at the same time, suggesting a high level of competence.

The age/invisibility double bind also seems to have affected Feinstein less than other political women. When Walter Mondale considered her for his running mate in 1984, she was turning fifty-one, but, when Al Gore considered her in 2000, she was turning sixty-seven. And when there was speculation about her becoming the "Snow White" to the seven dwarfs in 2004, she was nearing seventy-one. News stories note her age; however, they do not dwell upon it.[27] Why? One might suggest that her stately appearance allowed her overcome the negatives usually associated with aging women. Like older men, she had the ability to look distinguished.

One last matter needs to be raised in discussing Feinstein as a presidential aspirant: her religious, ethnic heritage. She is Jewish. Before 2000, this may have been an issue with some. John F. Kennedy made it possible for Roman Catholics to seek the presidency without evoking a great deal of prejudice, but his groundbreaking may not have extended to candidates who were Jewish, even to ones such as Feinstein who had attended Catholic school. After 2000, the choice of Connecticut Senator Joseph Lieberman as Democratic vice presidential nominee may have made it easier for subsequent Jewish politicians. Still, prejudice undoubtedly remained.[28] There seems, however, to be a degree of consonance between her gender and her religious heritage in evoking prejudice: those who dislike her for the one dislike her for the other.[29] In addition, many who would reject a candidate because he or she is Jewish are highly likely to reject the Democratic candidate regardless of his/her religious background.[30] Thus, her being Jewish probably did not add to her electability problems.

So, in general, Feinstein negotiated the double binds fairly well. In an interview in 2000, she notes that "the glass ceiling has been chipped, but it hasn't been broken by a long shot."[31] She doesn't admit it, but she might have been able to do considerable damage to that ceiling, given how well she had been able to negotiate the double binds that had trapped other women. But those double binds were not ultimately her problem. Ultimately, her problem was that she was not in tune with the prevailing Democratic Party ideology all the time. Her independence and her self-confessed tendency to stake out middle ground made her less attractive presidential material than many men who had (arguably) weaker credentials but "the right politics."

In fact, she drew more negative commentary from fellow Democrats than from Republicans. Civil libertarians have criticized her desire to restrict the Internet and her tolerant attitude toward racial profiling, her Green Party opponent in 2000 claimed she was "moving further and further to the right," and back in 1990 Bay Area feminists, Barbara Boxer among them, criticized her record on women's issues, preferring her male Democratic primary opponent to her in the gubernatorial race, while Ralph Nader attacked her as "a Republican in Democratic clothing."[32] She supported Condoleezza Rice's nomination for Secretary of State, while liberals opposed it; she supported George W. Bush's tax cuts, while liberals opposed them; she supported the use of military force in Iraq, while liberals opposed it.[33] Thus, she is not a favorite among those in the liberal wing of the party despite the fact that her ADA (Americans for Democratic Action) ratings and AFL-CIO (American Federation of Labor and Congress of Industrial Organizations) ratings are usually very high.[34] As noted earlier, the conventional wisdom is that parties—and candidates who want the parties' nominations—tilt to the extremes in primary season, only to move to the center after Labor Day. Feinstein could so tilt, but only on certain issues. On others, she would be centrist long before the party faithful would want her to be. Her centrism, then, would be her downfall. And it should be noted that her centrism is a curious brand. It is not that Feinstein is moderate on issues; rather, it is that Feinstein is liberal on some issues but conservative on others. She is independent, voting on matters as she sees them, not as party leaders tell her to do. So, perhaps it is more accurate to say that her independence, not her centrism, has barred her from the presidential sweepstakes.

NOTES

1. Biographical information is heavily gleaned from Jerry Roberts, *Dianne Feinstein: Never Let Them See You Cry* (New York: HarperCollins, 1994).

2. Cheryl Sullivan, "Dianne Feinstein's Future; From Mayor to . . . President," *Christian Science Monitor*, January 8, 1988.

3. Jay Matthews, "Wilson Pushing Image as a Caring Conservative; In TV Spots and California Stops, GOP Candidate Places Emphasis on His Personal Side," *The Washington Post*, September 18, 1990.

4. See Carolyn Lochhead and Susan Yoachum, "Boxer, Feinstein Blaze Separate Trails," *San Francisco Chronicle*, June 9, 1993; Carolyn Lochhead, "Feinstein and Boxer Explain Dismissal Vote; Opposing Tones in Defending Clinton," *San Francisco Chronicle*, January 28, 1999; Marc Sandalow, "Boxer, Feinstein Offer Democrats 2 Paths; Distinct Approaches for Party as GOP Loses Control of Senate," *San Francisco Chronicle*, June 3, 2001.

5. For full discussion of this Senate debate, see Theodore F. Sheckels, *When Congress Debates: A Bakhtinian Paradigm* (Westport, CT: Praeger, 2000), pp. 51–66.

6. The text of the debate is that found in the *Congressional Record* for April 19, 1994, on pp. S4431–34.

7. For a full discussion of this debate, see Sheckels, *When Congress Debates* pp. 67–85.

8. The debate is quoted from the *Congressional Record* for December 5, 1995, p. S18002–03.

9. Carolyn Lochhead, "Feinstein Puts Her Powers to the Test; Timing, Wording Key to Passing Censure," *San Francisco Chronicle*, February 9, 1999.

10. Carolyn Lochhead, "Feinstein's Retort Stuns Senate; During Crime Bill Debate, a Dramatic Defense of Weapons Ban," *San Francisco Chronicle*, November 12, 1993.

11. Jerry Roberts, "Feinstein Tells College Students She's '100 Percent Pro-Choice,'" *San Francisco Chronicle*, October 31, 1990; Jerry Roberts, "Feinstein Appeals for the Women's Vote," *San Francisco Chronicle*, May 31, 1990.

12. Susan Yoachum and Jerry Roberts, "How Feinstein, Wilson Stand on Criminal Justice Issues," *San Francisco Chronicle*, October 1, 1990.

13. John Lichfield, "US Elections 1990: The Rise of Tough and Caring Dianne; Next Week a Woman Could Become Democratic Governor of California," *The Independent* (London), November 1, 1990.

14. This persona was well-captured in "the ad" that arguably made her political career. It featured footage from Feinstein's remarks in the wake of the Moscone/Milk assassination, and it catapulted her from also-ran to victor in the 1990 Democratic gubernatorial primary. See Jerry Roberts, "Feinstein's Road to Victory: Airing TV Spot in January Proved to Be Turning Point," *San Francisco Chronicle*, June 8, 1990.

15. Sally Ann Stewart, "The Senate: California, Here They Come; Voters Send Two Women to Senate," *USA Today*, November 4, 1992.

16. Carolyn Lochhead, "Feinstein Seizes the Middle Ground; Senator Finds Allies on Both Sides of the Aisle," *San Francisco Chronicle*, June 2, 2003.

17. Zachary Coile, "Where Feinstein Woos, Boxer Wallops; Democratic Party Also Must Picks Its Fights, or Cut the Best Deals it Can," *San Francisco Chronicle*, January 24, 2005.

18. Bob Egelko, "Feinstein's Votes on Bush's Judges Blur Party Lines," *San Francisco Chronicle*, November 19, 2007.

19. Kathleen Hall Jamieson, *Beyond the Double Bind: Women and Leadership* (New York: Oxford University Press, 1995).

20. Tom Wicker, "Dianne Feinstein Brings a New Style to California Politics," *Seattle Post-Intelligencer*, June 5, 1990.

21. Jerry Roberts, "Feinstein Proves She Has the Stomach," *San Francisco Chronicle*, March 31, 1990.

22. Daniel B. Sullivan, "Images of a Breakthrough Woman Candidate: Dianne Feinstein's 1990, 1992, and 1994 Campaign Television Advertisements," *Women's Studies in Communication*, Vol. 21, No. 1 (Spring 1998).

23. Sullivan, "Dianne Feinstein's Future.

24. Jerry Roberts, "How Dianne Feinstein Has Defied the Odds; From Stiff Stranger to Front-Runner," *San Francisco Chronicle*, May 10, 1990.

25. Lichfield, "US Elections 1990."

26. The "Snow White" image probably stuck because Feinstein maintained an image of principle and probity. See Richard Rapaport, "The Snow White Factor; Why Dianne Feinstein Is the Democrats' Best Hope to Win the 2004 Presidential Election," *San Francisco Chronicle*, November 10, 2002.

27. See Daniel Borenstein, "Vice President Feinstein? Not Likely; She's One of Al Gore's Best-Respected Potential Running Mates, but There's a Long List of Reasons to Rule Her Off the November Ticket," *Contra Costa Times*, May 28, 2000; Rapaport, "The Snow White Factor."

28. Sidney Zion, "Not So Fast on Jewish Veep," *Daily News* (New York), June 20, 2000.

29. Rapaport, "The Snow White Factor."

30. Lars-Erik Nelson, "Pick Won't Cost Gore; Anti-Semites Not Likely to Pull Lever for Al, Anyway," *Daily News* (New York), August 8, 2000.

31. Phillip Matier and Andrew Ross, "Feinstein Won't Rule Out Future Presidential Run," *San Francisco Chronicle*, August 14, 2000.

32. For civil libertarians' criticism, see Marc Sandalow, "Feinstein Throws Hat in Ring for 2000; She Brushes Aside Notion of Vice Presidential Nomination," *San Francisco Chronicle*, December 4, 1998, and Zachary Coile and Diana Walsh, "Feinstein Says Racial Profiling Fears Hinder FBI; Admit That Nationality is Key, She Says," *San Francisco Chronicle*, June 3, 2002. For Green Party's criticism, see Steve Capps, "State's U.S. Senate Candidate Hard to Define Dianne Feinstein Says She Stands in Middle of the Road," *Modesto Bee*, October 16, 2000. For feminists' criticism, see Jerry Roberts, "Some Feminists Question Feinstein's Commitment to the Cause," *San Francisco Chronicle*, May 26, 1990. For Nader's criticism, see Jerry Roberts, "Feinstein Appeals for the Women's Vote," *San Francisco Chronicle*, May 31, 1990.

33. Zachary Coile, "Where Feinstein Woos, Boxer Wallops; Democratic Party Also Must Pick Its Fights, or Cut the Best Deals It Can," *San Francisco Chronicle*, January 24, 2005.

34. Lochhead, "Feinstein Seizes the Middle Ground."

4

Barbara Mikulski:
Wrong Style, Wrong Appearance

To this day, U.S. Senator Barbara Mikulski is a "Baltimore girl." Every day, she boards commuter rail and journeys south to Washington, D.C., to do her job. Then, it's back to the neighborhood where she grew up and still resides. This strong identification with the city has been through the years Mikulski's political insurance policy, for, like her liberal politics or not, Baltimoreans have voted overwhelmingly for their "Baltimore girl." As *Washington Post* reporter Tom Kenworthy noted in his coverage of her successful 1986 U.S. Senate campaign, "Affection for the Baltimore congresswoman is a common sentiment in the working class areas at the city's borders." There and elsewhere in the state, "Mikulski has broad support among blue-collar and conservative Democrats, an appeal that seemingly has little to do with ideology."[1] So, put in sports or entertainment terms, Mikulski has quite a fan base, and they cheer for her in the role of U.S. senator. But what if she wanted to play a very different role, or what if she wanted to try her hand, as Michael Jordan did, at another sport? Would they still cheer? The answer would seem to be that, although cheered—that is, re-elected—as a self-described brawler in the legislature, she would not be so cheered should she seek a higher office such as president because she just doesn't fit the new role.

CRUSADING AGAINST "THE ROAD,"
CRUSADING THEREAFTER

From her early days, Mikulski steered a path toward public service. She attended Notre Dame Academy a few miles from her home neighborhood, a school noteworthy for both its strong education for girls and its commitment to service. She was drawn to serve as a nun; she was drawn to serve as a social worker. During her college days at Baltimore's Mount St. Agnes College, the latter won out. She pursued a graduate degree in social work at the University of Maryland after receiving her B.A. Then, she set out to serve the people of her city, working initially for Catholic Charities and, then, the Baltimore City Department of Social Services.

A superhighway intervened. I-83, the Jones Falls Expressway (or JFX), leaves I-695 (the Baltimore Beltway) just west of Towson and meanders its way downtown. There, it was supposed to intersect with I-95, coming in from the South, as well as with I-70, coming in from the West. The resulting intersection—touted at the time as something tourists from all over would flock to Baltimore to see—and the roads feeding it from three directions would have prevented the redevelopment of the city's Inner Harbor and would have destroyed several neighborhoods, including Mikulski's east Baltimore neighborhood. She played a major role campaigning against the road's construction because of the damage she knew it would do to her community. At a rally, she stood on a table—given her short stature, she probably had to—and proclaimed, "The British couldn't take Fells Point, the termites couldn't take Fells Point, and, goddamn, the State Roads Commission can't take Fells Point."[2] She won the battle: I-70 now terminates west of the city, I-95 now sweeps south of downtown, and I-83 now terminates in city streets just east of downtown. She also found that she enjoyed the political crusade she had embarked upon. Perhaps—she asked herself—she could serve her community in politics as well as in social work.

Mikulski then ran for and was elected to the Baltimore City Council. At that point in time, Baltimore politics was dominated by two political "bosses"—Irvin Kovens and Jack Pollack. Most politicians were beholden to the one or the other.[3] Mikulski, although supported in her quest for office by Kovens, tried to steer a course independent of him. She would allow herself to be bossed only so far.

Her independence as a member of the Baltimore City Council was striking. It caused many to promote her candidacy for the Democratic Party's U.S. Senate nomination in 1974. Whoever won the primary was highly unlikely to win the seat, however. Although Maryland is indeed a state in which Democrats usually have a marked political advantage, Mikulski would be facing the very popular moderate Republican incumbent Charles "Mac" Matthias. Therefore, no well-known Democrat was seeking the nomination. The contest was among a handful of relative unknowns, and, at least as the press handicapped the race, the nomination was very much up for grabs. Mikulski won the primary by a large margin, demonstrating her (surprising) political clout, although not setting her up for a victory over Matthias in November. Matthias, scorned by many Republicans as a virtual

Democrat, was unbeatable. That she came within single digits of Matthias commended her to the Maryland Democratic Party: she was someone to reckon with in races to come.

She made those races in the Maryland 3rd Congressional district, the district in which she had long resided. As 1986 approached, Matthias was finally ready to retire, and, this time, many Democrats did line-up to replace him. Notably, outgoing Maryland Governor Harry Hughes wanted the Senate seat, as did popular suburban Washington, D.C. Congressman Michael Barnes. The battle was supposed to be between them; Mikulski was supposed to be the third-place finisher. When she gained on them, they attacked her, suggesting that her aggressive manner, while appropriate for the sometimes-raucous House of Representatives, was not genteel enough for the Senate. There was perhaps a backlash against these attacks. That backlash, plus other problems that beset Hughes and Barnes, helped gain Mikulski the nomination. Some saw a veiled sexism in the Hughes and Barnes comments. Would they have said the same thing about a male candidate whose style was sometimes brash?

The negative attacks Mikulski endured during the primary served as preparation for what was to come from her Republican opponent, former Reagan aide Linda Chavez. Chavez began her campaign by denouncing Mikulski as a "San Francisco-style Democrat." Chavez implied that Mikulski was liberal, which was arguably true; Chavez also implied that Mikulski was a lesbian, which was only rumored. The Republican then ran positive television advertisements stressing that she was a wife and a mother—that is, had traditional values and was straight. Chavez then sent a direct-mail piece to Maryland voters that associated Mikulski with Marxist feminism and sleazy sexuality. The piece told Maryland voters that, if they elected Mikulski, they would be "kissing their traditional values goodbye."

Some voters responded to Chavez's advertisements: Mikulski's negative rating went up. However, there was such a backlash against Chavez that her negative rating went up even more. After an ugly campaign, Mikulski found herself a U.S. senator.[4] As such, she began working for both her Maryland constituents and especially for women. Her committee assignments and her legislative record reflected this dual commitment. She is remembered for helping Baltimore harbor, federal government retirees, and the Space-related agencies and enterprises throughout Maryland; and she is remembered for promoting the careers of women in politics and in the workplace more generally.

When Mikulski joined the U.S. Senate, she joined Republican Nancy Kassebaum, bringing the total number of women in that body to two. Mikulski will see the number increase to seven in "The Year of the Woman," 1992. After that, the number will steadily increase. Besides publishing *Now We Are Seven* and subsequent editions celebrating higher numbers,

Mikulski played a major role mentoring the additional women, regardless of political party, who joined the revered body. Mikulski very clearly saw advancing the standing of women in politics as her cause. As Maine Republican Senator Susan Collins has noted, "Barbara takes all of the new women senators under her wing."[5] And the women who join the U.S. Senate are strong in their praise of Mikulski's non-partisan mentoring. California Senator Barbara Boxer, in a letter to *Roll Call*, commended Mikulski: "For the women of the Senate, Mikulski has generously given of her time, experience, and expertise. We look to her for leadership, and we value her insights." Boxer called Mikulski "one of my heroines" and noted that "she did not become the 'near-permanent fixture on Capitol Hill' that you [i.e., *Roll Call*] describe without being a formidable force." In Boxer's judgment, *Roll Call* had slighted Mikulski, not noting that she held an important leadership position, secretary of the Democratic Conference.[6] California's other senator, Dianne Feinstein, said in 2011 that Mikulski "is really sort of the dean of the women": she orients them, and she organizes dinners for them every sixty days or so about which there are "no memos" and "no leaks" and at which there is "no staff."[7]

Mikulski was able to provide such non-partisan mentoring of Senate women because she was not vulnerable come reelection time. Relying on heavy support in Baltimore City, she coasted to reelection in 1992, 1998, 2004, and 2010. She was never popular in the more conservative regions in the state, sometimes losing there to Republicans with very minimal credentials. However, her support in Baltimore City, as well as in other liberal-leaning jurisdictions, was sufficient to provide Mikulski a sequence of comfortable reelection victories. Those victories have given her seniority and a degree of clout, although perhaps not as much as one might expect.

When Mikulski is on the stump in Maryland, especially in Baltimore, she comes across as friendly, open. One on one in the Senate, some report a similarly friendly Mikulski. Senator John Warner of Virginia, for example, feared what the Senate might be getting as he watched the 1986 campaign from just across the Potomac River. "I thought, 'Oh, my goodness, are we getting another Bella Abzug?' But I was astonished at how quickly I established a warm relationship with her."[8] However, Mikulski clearly had another style that sometimes served her political ends at the cost of losing her staff members as well as—arguably—chances for advancement within the party leadership in the Senate. A former staff member noted how "she would flip out" if arrangements were not perfect; another reported that she could "rip your face off," yelling at you in a manner described as "brutal" and "humiliating." I should quickly note that not all of her staff members agreed with this picture. Lynne A. Battaglia, Mikulski's chief of staff for two years before leaving to become the U.S. Attorney for Maryland, said Mikulski had high expectations for her staff and "some [didn't] hear that clearly."

Battaglia also noted that many Capitol Hill offices have a high turnover rate, that Mikulski's was far from unique.[9] Still, there was a style, evident in Mikulski's dealings with staffers as well as in Mikulski's public presentations. This style might be termed "assertive" if one wishes to characterize it positively or it might be termed "aggressive" if one wishes to characterize it negatively. And the fact that the style can be described in either a positive or a negative way suggests Mikulski's rhetorical problem. Whereas many applaud her sometimes brusque, assertive approach, many also do not appreciate it.

RHETORICAL STYLE

Mikulski's rhetorical style was displayed dramatically not long after the number of women in the U.S. Senate swelled to seven. The occasion was an action reported out to the floor by the revered Senate Armed Services Committee. Upon the recommendation of President Bill Clinton, the Committee had recommended that Admiral Frank Kelso retire at the rank of four stars. Two would have been normal; four was a special honor that required Senate approval.

Why would such a matter raise the ire of a Maryland senator? Well, Kelso had been nominally in charge at the time the notorious Tailhook '91 Convention took place in Las Vegas. This annual gathering for naval aviators had a history of excess, and the 1991 version perhaps went farther with excessive drinking, pornography, strippers, and the sexual assault (arguably) of female naval officers. One of those went public with what had happened to her as she was forced to run a gauntlet of groping, grabbing aviators, and, then, quickly, what the Navy had kept to itself became a scandal prompting two investigations.

The seven women in the Senate united in opposing four stars for Kelso because he knew about and tolerated the Tailhook gathering, was there in Las Vegas for the 1991 rendition, and then (arguably) bungled one of the two investigations, an investigation that resulted in minimal disciplinary action against naval personnel. The women—and the men in the Senate who supported them—were given a six-hour slot during which they might debate whether Kelso merited the four-star retirement.[10] Those in favor of four stars would, during their three hours, cite Kelso's accomplishments and, knowing who was opposing them, Kelso's initiatives that helped women in the Navy. Gradually, some on the four-star side would grow testy, resulting, late in the debate, in an angry confrontation between Illinois Senator Carol Moseley-Braun and Alaska Senator Ted Stevens. What seemed to irk the men who wished to honor Kelso was the tone of some of the women during their three hours.

Most of the seven women spoke against four stars, some at length. Some men did too, usually briefly. The men usually just lent their support. The women took very different tacks. California Senator Dianne Feinstein and Texas Senator Kay Bailey Hutchinson sounded like attorneys whereas the other California Senator, Barbara Boxer, told the stories of the assaulted women. Moseley-Braun and Washington Senator Patty Murray offered what one might term a more common woman's assessment of what had transpired in Las Vegas and during the inquiries. This polyphony was orchestrated by Mikulski, who served as floor manager for the women (and supporting men) who were opposing the extra honor for Kelso.

Being floor manager in a Senate debate does not mean you are just the stage manager; rather, it means you take the lead for your side. Thus, Mikulski spoke several times during the debate—once, to present the case against four stars; later, to rebut opposing speakers; and, at the end, to defend Moseley-Braun against attack by Stevens and sum up the debate for her side. These speeches exhibit three slightly different Mikulski styles, although there are commonalities.

In the first instance, Mikulski announces her position, reviews the law governing retirement ranks in the military services, and acknowledges Kelso's accomplishments. She then asks:

> So then why am I opposing a four-star retirement? Madam President, I am opposing the two additional because of, No. 1, the Tailhook matter; No. 2, the failure of leadership at all levels of the U.S. Navy related to sexual harassment and sexual assault and scandal in general; and No. 3, the unchanged culture of the Navy regarding these matters. And I believe that if we do not take action to change the culture, as well as the law and the rules, this type of activity that went on at Tailhook and other forms of sexual harassment will happen again and again and again.[11]

Her style here is orderly but also casual. It continues:

> The Tailhook matter is a sordid sleazy stain on the U.S. Navy. All are familiar with what happened there. During a 1991 convention, what was supposed to be a convention of Navy aviators, there was a series of actions that no one disputes in which several women were sexually harassed, sexually battered, and sexually assaulted. It was a scene of drunkenness, debauchery, vulgarity, and violence.[12]

Her style acquires a touch of ornamentation with the alliteration in the first sentence and the double alliteration in the third. This ornamentation is coupled with the emphasis she gives what happened at Tailhook by repeating "sexually." The style, however, retains its studied informality despite these touches of artistry. It is apparent in her wit when she says, "It is the U.S. Navy and the men who served under Kelso that torpedoed the career of Frank Kelso."[13] It is also apparent in her off-hand but quoted recollection of her call to men to speak up after Anita Hill's testimony before the Senate Judiciary Committee fell on too many unbelieving ears and in her off-hand but quoted recollection of what her words of encouragement to women were at that time.

This is the style Mikulski uses when she is largely scripted. The unscripted Mikulski can be personal and calm, but can rise to sarcasm:

> Later on this evening, I know we will be doing our wrapup and rebuttal prior to the vote. It is very hard to debate this on the Senate floor. The reason it is hard is that when one reads what happened in Tailhook, and when one hears about the chants that Admiral Kelso allegedly heard and turned his back on, it is so vulgar that I cannot bring myself to even read from the report on the Senate floor. I will not do that to the Senate. But let me say to the American people and to everyone watching on C-SPAN, because that is where it is, it is pretty bad. In fact, it is so bad that we, the women of the Senate, do not wish to use the type of language that is described.
>
> But I am going to talk about some things. For example, pornography. Some squadron hospitality suites did feature pornography. . . .
>
> There were other things that went on there that created an atmosphere of degradation to women, and actually degradation to all men who regard themselves as officers and gentlemen.
>
> For a lot of people who saw "Top Gun," that is what they thought it was all about, being an officer and a gentleman. And what is this that we expect of the officers? We expect them to be gentlemen, just as we would expect the female officers to be gentleladies.[14]

After talking about the bad behavior at Tailhook, she talks about the poorly conducted Navy investigation of the events there. She quips:

> Here we have a whole U.S. Navy, it equipped itself with night optics, but it has myopia when it goes to investigate this matter. Well, put your goggles on, guys. It is time to look and see what is going on.[15]

At the end of this debate, sarcasm becomes anger. Coming to her colleague Illinois Senator Carol Moseley-Braun's defense when she was attacked by a question by Alaska Senator Ted Stevens, Mikulski says, "And this is not about whether Senator Moseley-Braun gets it. It is whether the rest of the Senate gets it."[16]

She then speaks directly about why the women in the Senate are opposing the higher rank. She addresses, first, those who are criticizing the women:

> There are those who say that somehow or other we are the problem for raising this. I must bring to everyone's attention it is not the Senate pulling Admiral Kelso down. It is the U.S. Navy that let Admiral Kelso down. It is the U.S.

Navy that had the Tailhook incident in the first place. It is the U.S. Navy that bungled the investigation. It is the U.S. Navy that had the buddy system over the honor system. It was the U.S. Navy that torpedoed Admiral Kelso. It was not the women of the Navy, and it was not the women of the U.S. Senate.[17]

Then, she addresses not only the matter at hand but larger issues—in very strong terms:

We hope we win this. But whether we win the vote or not, we feel that we have won a victory here today because we have raised this issue to show that from now on when we look at what is going to happen in promotions and in retirements and in rewards, the issues will be raised, and they will be raised not only about the United States military, they will be raised about the FBI, they will be raised about the Bureau of Alcohol and Firearms, they will be raised about Social Security, they will be raised about the gender discrimination going on at the National Institutes of Health. They will be raised.[18]

WHY NOT MADAM PRESIDENT?

Mikulski can be casual and conversational; but she can turn sarcastic and turn angry. Her rhetorical style, regardless of which register, is not understated. A recognition of Mikulski's style leads directly to a discussion of the silence/shame double bind Jamieson outlines in *Beyond the Double Bind* (1995) as well as to a related matter, the media coverage Mikulski has received.[19]

Mikulski's style qualifies her as outspoken, regardless of whether she technically speaks often or not in the Senate. Thus, she is far from silent. Her style could quite easily result in some "shaming" her with some unflattering label. She seems very aware of this potential problem as evidenced in how she characterizes herself when she campaigns. She presents herself to the voters as a fighter, someone who is aggressively working on behalf of Maryland as well as particular constituencies, such as women, who extend beyond the state's boundaries. In her *Communication Quarterly* study of how Mikulski tries to overcome some of the negative stereotypes women in politics fall prey to, Deborah Robson stresses this twist on aggressiveness in Mikulski's commentary on herself.[20] *Washington Post* writer Doug Struck comments on how "her speeches are laced with the gunpowder terms of combat: She is forever 'doing battle,' a 'scrapper,' waging war along with other 'tough fighters.'"[21] Mikulski seems then to be trying to keep this "fighting for Maryland" image in people's mind.

Media coverage of her campaigns reflects this self-characterization. In 1986, during her first Senate campaign, the *Washington Post*, the newspaper of record for many of Maryland's counties, characterized her as "volatile," "outspoken" (two times), "tart-tongued," "combative," "aggressive," "blunt" (two times), "forceful," and "hell-rais[ing]." The newspaper repeated characterizations her opponent Linda Chavez had offered: "feisty," "loud," and "rough," which refer to Mikulski's communication style; and "ultraliberal," "San Francisco style" (nine times), "too liberal" (two times), "out of step (five times), "radical," and "anti-male." The relevance of these latter characterizations is that they definitely color Mikulski's aggressiveness, transforming her from being a fighter to being a fighter for specific political causes. In that same election, the *Baltimore Sun* characterized Mikulski as "outspoken," "feisty" (two times), "bellowing," "bullying," "seeming[ly] mean," "tough-talking," "blustery," "too threatening for male voters," "fight[ing]," "rude," "abrasive," "aggressive," and "sometimes raucous." A few more positive characterizations slipped in—"genuine," "surprisingly marketable," "hometown" (two times), "warm," and "funny"—but the descriptions that coincided with her "fighter" persona dominated. The *Sun* also repeated others' assessments of Mikulski, referring to her as "zip[py]," "feisty," "outgoing," "not afraid," "loud" (two times), "boisterous" (two times), "outspoken," "spunk[y]," "fight[ing]" (four times), "dynamic," and "abrasive." Some were positive, some were negative, and some were neutral. In addition, there was repetition of Chavez's attacks: "San Francisco style" (four times), "radical[ly] feminist," "extreme left," "out of step" (two times), "anti-male" (three times), "Marxist," and "feminist."

Curiously, media coverage in general of her style declines from election to election. This decline is partially because her reelection campaigns were never that newsworthy insofar as she was always a heavy favorite to win. In 1992, the *Post* characterized her as "progressive," "as strong of voice as she is short of stature," "composed," and "folksy"; the *Sun* noted her focus in her first term on women's issues and repeated her opponent's charge that she is "soft on crime," but, otherwise, ignored the Senate campaign. In 1998, the *Post* characterized her as "thunder-voiced," "notoriously blustery," "in your face," "brash," "outspoken," and "difficult to work with," while the *Sun* once again said little, noting that she is "generally liberal" on issues and repeating her weak opponent's attack on Mikulski because she was "unmarried." The decline may also reflect a recognition on the part of the media that Mikulski and her style are already well-known among voters, especially those in her native Baltimore. So, Marylanders may well have in their minds a rather fixed image of her. Few imagine her silent, but whether they imagine her outspokenness as negative or positive may well depend on party allegiance. A fighter she is, but whether it was for "ultraliberal" causes or "progressive" or "generally liberal" ones was a matter of opinion. Also, in the Baltimore media, she was also characterized as "never forget[ting her] roots" and as "our Barbara." These phrases certainly softened somewhat any hard-edged image she might have had.

The reaction to Mikulski on "The Hill" seemed just as polarized. Thus, her advancement was slowed. Others, better at being gracious to those with long tenure, won leadership positions before she did. Not—because of her style—good at playing the political games necessary to advance, she focused on issues important to her constituents, although they were neither glamorous not likely to attract national news coverage. She also committed herself to mentoring other women, regardless of party, who would come to the Senate. In this role, as noted earlier, she earned respect and acclaim. In general, however, she did not escape the silence/shame double bind in the eyes of a sufficient number to either rise in prominence in the Senate or become a presidential contender.

Mikulski also seemed to be aware of what Jamieson refers to as the Womb/Brain double bind. The double bind traditionally offers women a choice, as if being a successful mother and a successful careerist were impossible. Sequencing is, as we will see in the chapter on Nancy Pelosi, one way of negotiating the double bind: pursuing motherhood first and then a career. Mikulski's way is by claiming the first metaphorically while pursuing the second in reality.

In her campaign rhetoric, Mikulski refers to herself as "Aunt Barb." She is, she says, like that maiden aunt who takes care of the elderly parents and is there to pitch in whenever anyone in the extended family needs help. She will serve, she says, as "Aunt Barb" to the people of the state. This persona seems to have been embraced by at least the voters of Baltimore City, perhaps because Mikulski maintained her connections to—and her residence in—the Baltimore neighborhood she had grown up in. People in Baltimore could then see her in a social context that made the "Aunt Barb" persona understandable and admirable. Or, if not as "Aunt Barb," they still saw her as playing the maternal role in politics not in a family. As Jeanne Rand, a Dundalk resident, commented in 1986, "Mikulski's been Maryland; that seems to be her husband and her baby."[22] Outside of the city, the persona perhaps did not resonate as well because people did not know as well Mikulski's Baltimore story. Also, the persona may well be one that ties her to the local. That persona might work in the context of the federal legislature and might work in the context of state government. In both, representatives have a local constituency. But the persona probably would not work in the context of the presidency, an office with national and international, not local, resonance. Do we want a stereotypical maiden aunt in the White House? Maybe in a legislature, where we can call upon her for constituency service, but the White House seldom functions in that quasi-maternal/paternal manner.

Mikulski may also have other characteristics that make her undesirable as a presidential candidate. Jamieson notes, in describing the feminine/competence double bind, that an extremely feminine appearance can be detrimental to a woman's success because femininity is associated with incompetence. Thus, women in politics try to be more masculine or at least strike a balance between stereotypically feminine and masculine traits. The problem, of course, is that a woman, striving to avoid being too feminine, will end up coming across as steely cold. Mikulski, who is not feminine in her appearance, has run this risk. That risk, however, has been overwhelmed by those associated with two other physical characteristics: she is short, and she is overweight.

Media coverage did occasionally focus on these physical characteristics. Again, just examining newspaper coverage during election campaigns, we find the *Post* in 1986 describing her as "ample" and the *Sun* that same year describing her as "plump." In 1992, the *Post* characterized her as "short of stature" and in 1998 as "fire-plug shaped." The number of print references is certainly not overwhelming, but one must add to them the visual impression Mikulski made in person and when videotaped for television news. She is short, and she is overweight.

To understand the effect this characterization might have on one's political career, we must consider the growing body of work on discrimination based on appearance. Deborah L. Rhode's 2010 *The Beauty Bias: The Injustice of Appearance in Life and Law* documents discrimination based on appearance.[23] She notes that it is widespread in general, citing studies by Landy and Sigall (1974) and Quereshi and Kay (1986).[24] She notes that it is true in politics, citing Robert B. Cialdini's *Influence: The Psychology of Persuasion* (2007) as well as popular discussions appearing in the *Economist* in December 2007 and the *New York Times* in December 2008.[25] The research and commentary reveal that the discrimination cuts both ways: the unattractive are discriminated against; the attractive are advantaged. Rhode notes also that attractiveness is heavily sexualized for women, even in politics. So, attractive male political figures must be handsome while attractive female political figures must be sexy.

Height and weight are the two variables on which there is substantial research. On the first, the taller the better.[26] This variable, however, seems to affect males more than females. So, whereas Jimmy Carter and Michael Dukakis might have been disadvantaged by not being especially tall, women in politics have more leeway. One might suggest, however, that Mikulski, at four foot, eleven inches, is outside that leeway and suffers discrimination based on height when being thought of for such an elevated office as the presidency.

On weight, there is even more research. Those who are overweight are frequently socially stigmatized.[27] Furthermore, that stigmatization leads to outright discrimination.[28] Females seem to experience this stigmatization and discrimination more than males.[29] Discrimination based on weight is especially debilitating because of the assumptions people seem to make about those who are overweight. They are thought to lack self-control and intelligence; they are also often judged to be unhappy, uninteresting, unlikeable, and not especially well-adjusted.[30] Mikulski, never trim during her long political career, admits to struggling more and more with her weight as the years have passed. Her being overweight has never stopped her from dancing at campaign stops; however, that weight (especially when coupled with her height) may well make her appear as non-presidential.

Perhaps making matters worse, but perhaps making matters better, have been her own references to her height and weight while campaigning. In 1974, she quipped about her height. During the Congressional races that followed, she termed herself "roly-poly." These light-hearted comments seemed sufficient in campaigns in which opponents did not try to use her appearance against her, and, in 1986, her campaign ran an early September "image ad" in the same light-hearted manner that joked about her weight. In October, the opposition decided to make Mikulski's appearance an issue. That month, retiring Republican Congresswoman Marjorie Holt struck a comparison between the short, heavy Mikulski and the attractive Linda Chavez. A few weeks later, Mikulski played-off this comparison, jokingly (still light-heartedly) terming Chavez "glamorous" and herself "attractive." A week later, she responded to opponents' continuing comments on her "fit" for the Senate and remarks that she "doesn't measure up" to the job, by frankly noting her size—and insisting that she did fit and did measure up. The tone was still light-hearted, but there was a pronounced indignant "edge" to Mikulski's comments.

In 1992, her campaign ran an ad in which Washington Bullets center Wes Unseld endorsed her: it depicted the two of them, standing side-by-side. Unseld said, "When you pick players, height isn't the only thing that counts. You know Maryland's a team, and we don't have any better player than Barbara Mikulski. She may not win the slam-dunk competition, but she's a heck of a playmaker. She's the little giant who fights for Maryland."[31] And in 1998, she cracked jokes about her height, noting that, when she was in the chair in the Senate, her feet did not touch the floor. In the political novels she co-authored with *Los Angeles Times* reporter Marylouise Oates, she even created a female character (very much Mikulski's alter ego) who is height-challenged. One might argue that Mikulski, since she could not hide from her appearance, defused it as a prejudicial factor by joking about it. After 1986, one might suggest that there was a degree of inoculation in Mikulski's remarks: she brought the negative out in the open before opponents might, and she defused it by joking about it. However, one might also argue that she focused attention on appearance issues that made her look not just less "senatorial," but not at all "presidential." She could joke about these issues as long as it was the U.S. Senate she would be standing up in. There, she did not look the role, but, for the most part, few would observe the miscasting. However, if she were seeking the higher office requiring greater stature—that is, the presidency—she would have far, far greater visibility.

As Deborah Robson has noted, humor is a strategy Mikulski uses to overcome negative stereotypes and doublebinds.[32] She jokes about her height, she goes to Senator Edward Kennedy's sixtieth birthday party dressed as Jackie Kennedy, she entertains guests at a fund-raiser by doing an imitation of Lily Tomlin's telephone operator character in NBC's *Laugh-In*, she characterizes herself as "a little stealth rocket, a heat-seeking missile," she observes how she is just like Princess Leia in *Star Wars*, and she—sharing her family recipe for crabcakes on Maryland Public Television—terms herself "Mayo Mikulski" (McQueen; "Maryland Senator"; Struck; Jones).[33] The question to ask of her humor, much of which is self-deprecating, is, of course, rhetorical: does she deflect attention from characteristics that might be negative or does she draw attention to them? Related to that rhetorical question is another: if she succeeds in deflecting attention, does she simultaneously reduce her *gravitas* and, thus, her suitability for a high political office such as the presidency?

Another personal characteristic needs to be discussed, but carefully. As already noted, Linda Chavez, Mikulski's 1986 opponent, struck a contrast between herself and Mikulski based on appearance. She also struck a contrast based on her being wife and mother and Mikulski neither. That contrast added to Chavez's constant references to Mikulski's "San Francisco" liberalism and her indictment of some of the political ideas that the future senator had entertained during her House service as "radical," "Marxist style feminist." Without saying it directly, Chavez was telling voters that Mikulski was a lesbian. The comments by opponent Ross Z. Pierpont in 1998 focusing on the incumbent senator's marital status (unmarried) also implied her sexual orientation.

We do not know what Mikulski's sexual orientation is. Although she has responded to the accusation that she is anti-male, jokingly noting that her brothers and the "boys down at Bethlehem Steel" she was talking at length with while campaigning would be surprised by the claim, she has not directly addressed the question of her sexual orientation. She has, however, joked about it, noting that when she goes to a Washington social event alone she is described as gay but when she goes with a married male friend she is attacked as a "home-wrecker." The joking demonstrates her awareness of the issue, so her silence on the matter must be deliberate. She either feels the matter is private, or she feels her sexual orientation might hurt her politically. Or both. In a presidential campaign, of course, very little can be withheld from media scrutiny or even, after the Senator Eagleton debacle in 1972, the party vetters. In an American society that is in some measure homophobic, the rumor and/or the fact would probably eliminate her from presidential consideration. One would, of course, hope that this prejudice among the electorate might be overcome as others have. Nonetheless, political calculations would in the short-term have to consider her rumored or real sexual orientation.

Mikulski's case is, then, a complex one. Her ways to circumvent the double binds may only succeed to a point—enough to get her reelected repeatedly to the Senate but not enough to gain her consideration for the presidency. Her ways—primarily humor—to overcome the prejudice she experiences as short and overweight may only succeed to that same point. She has also been aided in circumventing and overcoming by a popularity in certain parts of Maryland that are rooted in her strong local Baltimore identity. In addition, her sexual orientation might be a time bomb, ready to explode should she seek an office for which the scrutiny is intense. In general, Mikulski seems to have found ways to succeed that work in the House of Representatives and even in the Senate but would not work in a campaign for the presidency. She has been able to lift the glass ceiling; however, it is still present, limiting her ability to go beyond the high offices she has obtained and held.

NOTES

1. Tom Kenworthy, "Mikulski's Kind of People: Many Blue-Collar Conservatives Like Her," *Washington Post*, October 8, 1986.
2. Doug Struck, "Barbara Mikulski, Fact vs. Fiction; Senator-Novelist's Style on Hill Clashes with Populist Image," *Washington Post*, September 8, 1998.
3. Bossism in Baltimore was in decline. Because he was older and because of illness, Pollack's influence faded before Koven's.
4. For a full discussion of this campaign, see chapter 6 in Theodore F. Sheckels, *Maryland Politics and Political Communication, 1950–2005* (Lanham, MD: Lexington Books, 2006).
5. Ben Pershing, "Longest-Serving Female Senator Wears Down the Skeptics," *Washington Post*, January 5, 2011, pp. B1, 8.
6. Barbara Boxer, "Her Name is Barbara," *Roll Call*, March 31, 1997.
7. Pershing, "Longest-Serving Female Senator."
8. Struck, "Barbara Mikulski, Fact vs. Fiction."
9. Ibid.
10. For a full discussion of this debate, see Theodore F. Sheckels, *When Congress Debates: A Bakhtinian Paradigm* (Westport, CT: Praeger, 2000), pp. 51–66.
11. Quotations are from the *Congressional Record* for April 19, 1994. This one is from p. S4422.
12. Ibid.
13. Ibid, p. S4423.
14. Ibid, p. S4444.
15. Ibid, p. S4445.

16. Ibid, p. S4453.

17. Ibid.

18. Ibid.

19. Kathleen Hall Jamieson, *Beyond the Double Bind: Women and Leadership* (New York: Oxford University Press), 1995.

20. Deborah Carol Robson, "Stereotypes and the Female Politician: A Case Study of Senator Barbara Mikulski," *Communication Quarterly,* Vol. 48, No. 3 (2000), pp. 205–222.

21. Struck, "Barbara Mikulski, Fact vs. Fiction."

22. Kenworthy, "Mikulski's Kind of People."

23. Deborah L. Rhode, *The Beauty Bias: The Injustice of Appearance in Life and Law* (New York: Oxford University Press, 2010).

24. David Landy and Harold Sigall, "Beauty Is Talent: Task Evaluation as a Function of the Performer's Physical Attractiveness," *Journal of Personality and Social Psychology,* Vol. 19 (1974), p. 299; M. Y. Querishi and Janet P. Kay, "Physical Attractiveness, Age, and Sex as Determinants of Reactions to Resumes," *Social Behavior and Personality,* Vol. 14 (1986), p. 103.

25. Robert B. Cialdini, *Influence: The Psychology of Persuasion* (New York: Harper Collins, 2007), p. 171; "To Those That Have, Shall Be Given," *Economist,* December 19, 2007; Michael Luo and Cathy Horyn, "Three Palin Stylists Cost Campaign More Than $165,000," *New York Times,* December 6, 2008, p. A9, A11.

26. Sidney Katz, "The Importance of Being Beautiful," in James M. Henslin (ed.), *Down to Earth Sociology: Introductory Readings* (New York: Prentice-Hall, 1997), p. 312; Gordon L. Patzer, *The Physical Attractiveness Phenomena* (New York: Plenum, 1985), p. 164–165.

27. Janet D. Latner, Albert J. Strunkard, and G. Terence Wilson, "Stigmatized Students: Age, Sex, and Ethnicity Effects in the Stigmatization of Obesity," *Obesity Research,* Vol. 13 (2005), p. 1226; Esther D. Rothblum, "The Stigma of Women's Weight: Social and Economic Realities," *Feminism and Psychology,* Vol. 2 (1992), p. 61.

28. Greg Crister, *Fat Land: How Americans Became the Fattest People in the World* (London: Penguin, 2003); Michael Fumento, *The Fat of the Land: The Obesity Epidemic and How Overweight Americans Can Help Themselves* (New York: Viking Press, 1997); J. Eric Oliver, *Fat Politics: The Real Story Behind America's Obesity Epidemic* (New York: Oxford University Press, 2006), p. 102; Rebecca Puhl and Kelly D. Brownell, "Bias, Discrimination, and Obesity," *Obesity Research,* Vol. 9 (2001), pp. 788–790.

29. American Psychological Association, *Report of the APA Task Force on the Sexualization of Girls* (Washington, D.C.: American Psychological Association, 2007), pp. 32–33; Sondra Solovay, *Tipping the Scales of Justice: Fighting Weight-Based Discrimination* (New York: Prometheus Books, 2000), p. 105 ; Janna Fikkan and Esther Rothblum, "Weight Bias in Employment," in Kelly D. Brownell et al. (eds.), *Weight Bias: Nature, Consequences, and Remedies* (New York: Guilford Press, 2005), p. 16; Kate Soblosky, "'Probative Weight': Rethinking Evidentiary Standards in Title VII Sex Discrimination Cases," *New York University Review of Law and Social Change,* Vol. 30 (2006), pp. 333–335.

30. Rhode, *The Beauty Bias,* pp. 26–27.

31. "Unseld Lends Mikulski a Hand," *Washington Post,* October 15, 1992.

32. Deborah Carol Robson, "Stereotypes and the Female Politician: A Case Study of Senator Barbara Mikulski," *Communication Quarterly*, Vol. 18, No. 3 (2000), pp. 205–222.

33. Michael McQueen, "An Evening with Lily Tomlin, Starring Barbara Mikulski," *Washington Post*, October 8, 1986; "Maryland Senator Shows Off Her Culinary Skills," *The Hill*, January 28, 1998; Struck, "Barbara Mikulski, Fact vs. Fiction"; Mary Lynn F. Jones, "Lawmaker-Novelists Exploit Their Hill Experience," *The Hill*, June 2, 1999.

5

Elizabeth Hanford Dole: A Star Surrogate

Suggesting that the slate of candidates for president, and the condition of the country had left her no choice but to run for president, Elizabeth Dole began her speech on March 10, 1999, in Iowa by reminding voters, "I'm not a politician, and frankly, I think that's a plus today."[1] In a narrative style that has become her trademark, she recounted her "lifetime" in public service, which she believed qualified her to be president. She highlighted her "governing" work as secretary of transportation, a job focusing on "material resources" where she argued that "you had to be an anti-trust lawyer, a rail expert and an investment banker" to get assignments done. As secretary of labor, a post she held in the George Herbert Walker Bush administration, she described her work in dealing with "human resources," which enabled her to "turn young lives around." Finally, as president of the American Red Cross, she built her ethos for the presidency by explaining to the audience that it is a job that focused on "inner resources." She added: "You notice I still speak in the present tense about the Red Cross; I guess it'll always be a part of me and very much in my heart."[2]

Earlier that year in January, when she resigned the presidency of the American Red Cross, the press predicted she would make a bid for the office that so long eluded her husband, former Kansas senator and majority leader, Bob Dole. In her Red Cross resignation speech, the ever-prepared Elizabeth Dole teased: "I have not made definite plans about what I will do next. I didn't feel it was right to spend the time I owed to you thinking about anything but our work together. Soon, I will begin to consider new paths and there are exciting possibilities."[3] Elizabeth Dole did explore the viability of a presidential campaign in an exploratory campaign that lasted from March 1999 to October 1999 and during that time she consistently ran second in the polls to George W. Bush and well ahead of John McCain, Steve Forbes, Gary Bauer and Alan Keyes. She also had high favorability ratings and consistently beat Al Gore in hypothetical head-to-head match ups.[4] While she was a newcomer as a candidate, she was hardly a Washington outsider, since her career started in the Lyndon B. Johnson administration.

BACKGROUND

Mary Elizabeth Alexander Hanford came into the world on July 29, 1939, a welcomed only daughter for John and Mary Hanford, who thirteen years earlier had a son, John, Jr.[5] By the age of two, the precocious toddler had nicknamed herself "Liddy." The name stuck and friends, family, and colleagues knew her as Liddy for many years in both Salisbury and Washington, D.C., until she made known that she preferred the more elegant "Elizabeth."

Elizabeth grew up in Salisbury, in the Piedmont textile country between Charlotte and Greensboro. Her father was a local floral wholesaler, who built his company into a well-known entity, especially noted for its beautiful "Hanford" roses. The comfortable lifestyle protected the Hanford family from the hardship of the Depression. In addition to his floral company, John Hanford also owned real estate, including apartment buildings and rented apartments to area residents. Her mother, an accomplished musician, happily sacrificed the opportunity to study music at Julliard for marriage and a family. Elizabeth said, "Having abandoned her own career pursuit early on, she poured all the more love and energy into the lives of her children."[6] Until Mary Hanford's death in 2004, at the age of 102, Elizabeth described her mother as her "best friend," whom she called daily and visited often.

The Hanford's comfortable lifestyle afforded Elizabeth the opportunity of travel and her family took train trips across country. These trips fostered Elizabeth's love of learning and encouraged her to aim high in her education and career goals. In high school, she was active in student government and made an unsuccessful bid for its presidency when she was a senior. Elizabeth ran for senior class president at Boyden High School and although she didn't win, her effort gave her a "lesson in how to lose," a lesson that she says is something "no one likes but from which most of us can benefit."[7] Elizabeth's potential as a leader was noticed by her classmates and she was voted "Most likely to succeed."

After Elizabeth graduated from high school, she followed in her brother's footsteps and enrolled at prestigious Duke University. Although social opportunities abounded at Duke, and Elizabeth enjoyed some, her focus was more on her studies and she took courses in political science, which was her major, which was also unusual at the time. As a freshman, she unsuccessfully ran for class representative, but in 1957 she was elected president of the Women's Student Government Association. Her campaign skills and leadership ability were so apparent, that even her opponent voted for her. "She was so well spoken, so thoughtful, so poised—I had to support her," recalled Karen Black Miller who remembers the Duke election.[8] In her campaign speech, Elizabeth forecasted that "with our changing world, it was and is necessary for us to change in order to adapt, even in our university life. We must remember that our influence is far reaching."[9] She developed her public speaking skills by taking a course in speech, which was rare for women at the time, and she also learned parliamentary procedure. In her senior year, 1958, she was named "Leader of the Year" by both the men's and women's campuses. At the same time she was elected May Queen and came out as a debutante in Raleigh. Duke University was a wonderfully, positive experience for Dole, who "found the deans to be strong mentors, like her mother and grandmother."[10]

She graduated Phi Beta Kappa from Duke University and then moved to Boston, Massachusetts, where she became secretary to the head librarian at the Harvard Law School Library. She also enrolled in the Master of Arts degree program in Harvard University's School of Education, with a dual major in government. She was an engaging student teacher, but she decided that teaching wasn't the career path she wanted to pursue. She completed the master's program in 1960, and then moved to Washington, D.C., where she found a position as a secretary, working in the office of North Carolina Democratic Senator B. Everett Jordan. Elizabeth's mother said that her daughter was drawn "like a magnet" to Washington, D.C., and while Elizabeth was there she consulted Maine Senator Margaret Chase Smith for professional guidance. Senator Smith encouraged Elizabeth Hanford to earn a law degree if she wanted to contribute more to a job in public policy.

Elizabeth returned to Cambridge in September 1960 and began her studies at Harvard Law School. Despite her academic excellence and her considerable experience in the library of the law school and in Washington, D.C., Elizabeth was less prepared for the rigors of law school than she thought. Like other women of her era, Dole's experience at Harvard was "thoroughly unpleasant" mostly because of the sexism that she faced as one of only twenty-four women in a class of 550 students.

Upon her graduation from Harvard Law School, twenty-nine-year-old Elizabeth Hanford moved to Washington, D.C., where she found a temporary position with Health, Education and Welfare (HEW), organizing a conference on deaf education. After passing the D.C. Bar Exam, she spent a year as a defender in night court. Her next position was with the Johnson Administration, working for the White House Office of Consumer Affairs under the direction of commercial spokeswoman Betty Furness. After

Nixon became president, Elizabeth kept her position, under a new supervisor, Virginia Knauer, who had been head of the Pennsylvania Consumer Protection Bureau. The office was renamed the President's Committee on Consumer Interests, and Elizabeth was promoted to deputy. The committee was responsible for ensuring proper labeling on food items and enforcing expiration dates. Elizabeth excelled in the position and more and more her boss Virginia was relying on her to go out and make speeches on behalf of the organization. In 1972, Virginia Knauer introduced Elizabeth to Republican Senator Robert Dole from Kansas, who was also serving as the national chairman of the Republican Party. Several months after they met, they began dating and three years later on December 5, 1975, they married; he was fifty-two and she was thirty-nine.

The newlyweds didn't have much time to grow accustomed to a prosaic route as a couple, since just eight months later, Gerald Ford, who had replaced Nixon after his resignation, won the Republican nomination for president and asked Bob Dole to be his vice presidential candidate. While the new couple reveled in the thrill of the campaign, Elizabeth wondered what her husband's political aspirations meant to her career at the Federal Trade Commission (FTC). Elizabeth resolved the dilemma of a possible conflict of interest, by taking a leave of absence from her position on the FTC, but not before Elizabeth Dole received criticism from reporters who wondered why she would interrupt her career for her husband. Elizabeth Dole discovered she loved campaigning. She spent only one week on the campaign trail with her husband and then proposed going on the road alone, putting to use the public speaking skills she had fostered over the years. Despite the efforts of both Doles, the Ford-Dole ticket lost to the Democratic ticket of Jimmy Carter and Walter Mondale.

In 1979, Bob Dole announced that he would be a candidate for the presidency in the 1980 election, and in March, 1979, Elizabeth resigned from the FTC to devote her full attention to Bob's campaign.[11] She campaigned so much for Bob, that some confused voters thought that she was running. He dropped out of the race in the spring of 1980, saying with humor, "at about the time Elizabeth passed me in the polls."[12] Elizabeth Dole, who was now known as a viable campaigner in the Republican Party, campaigned vigorously for Ronald Reagan and George H. W. Bush. When Ronald Reagan won the presidency, he appointed Elizabeth head of the Office of Public Liaison. In that position, it was Elizabeth's job to marshal grass roots and organization support for the president's policies. In 1983, President Reagan invited Elizabeth to serve as Secretary of Transportation, a cabinet position responsible for a 100,000 employees nationwide with a budget of $27 billion. As Secretary of Transportation, Dole made safety her priority and she instituted the third brake light, which came to be known as the "Dole light." She served in that position for almost five years, until she stepped down to campaign for her husband for the presidency in the 1988 election. Once George H. W. Bush won the nomination, both Elizabeth and Bob were rumored to be on the short list of vice presidential candidates, but the choice was young Indiana Senator Dan Quayle. Once elected, Bush asked Elizabeth to serve as secretary of Labor where she targeted at risk youth, women and minorities. She left her work at the labor department to become president of the American Red Cross in 1991. She described her work at the American Red Cross as a "glorious mission field." In 1995, however, she took a one-year leave of absence to assist her husband in his bid for the presidency when Bob Dole won the Republican nomination. Elizabeth Dole was a tireless campaigner. Her years of campaigning seemed to culminate with this election's yeoman's effort on her part to help her husband get elected. The presidency was handily won, however, by incumbent Bill Clinton.

In 1999, Elizabeth Dole resigned from the American Red Cross to "consider new paths." In March 1999 she announced her exploratory bid for the presidency and withdrew from the race in October, citing a lack of funds. In her withdrawal speech, Elizabeth Dole promised that she was a "long way from the Twilight," which proved true when, in 2002, she won a Senate seat from her home state of North Carolina. In 2008 she failed in her bid for re-election to Democrat Kay Hagan. A particularly nasty campaign television ad, run by the Dole campaign, accused Hagan of being "godless" and buoyed support for the Hagan campaign.[13]

Suggestions that Elizabeth Dole should run for president have been in the press since the 1980s. At the 1984 Republican National Convention, "Dole in '88" over cameo pictures of Bob and Elizabeth Dole were everywhere. During Campaign 1984, Bob Dole said, "There are a lot of people around here talking about 1988. . . . They're not talking to me, they're talking to Elizabeth." In 1988, one article speculated, "One wonders, if her husband doesn't win this time, have they made an agreement that she gets the next crack at it?"[14] When Bob Dole withdrew from the 1988 race, the press focused on which one of them would be tapped for vice president. Columnist Ellen Goodman opined that one of Elizabeth's assets as vice president in 1988 was her appeal to both liberals and conservatives, and the kind of "lady like women's rights advocate that passes muster in Republican circles."[15] And the *Washington Post* reported that "Elizabeth Dole is the very picture of a candidate's spouse, despite the fact that she continues to be on the short list of candidates herself."[16] Press buzz about the presidential potential of Elizabeth Dole hit an all-time high after her rousing speech at the 1996 G.O.P. Convention. At the conclusion of her speech, *CBS* anchor Dan Rather announced, in tones you associate with the early space launches, "What you have witnessed here tonight is the birth of a new form of campaigning and a new standard for convention speeches by which others will likely be judged for a long time." Tom Brokaw, *NBC* anchor said, "You can almost hear, if you listen carefully now, across the country, in living rooms and bars and wherever people watch this, folks turning to each other and saying 'Wow, why isn't she on the ticket?'"[17]

An article in the *Philadelphia Inquirer* at the same time predicted that there would be a woman on the next ticket, in either the Democrat or Republican party. Even further, the article predicted that there could be an "all female face off for the vice president's job. Elizabeth Dole for the G.O.P and Dianne Feinstein for the Democrats."[18] Even though Elizabeth consistently denied that she had any plans to run, one article described that "all the demurring in the world will not slow supporters and star-starved Republicans from dreaming up 'other Dole' scenarios for 2000."[19] One of those was Republican activist Earl Cox, who in 1996 tried to draft retired General Colin Powell for a White House run. As soon as Elizabeth stepped down as Red Cross president, Cox and other Dole supporters had begun a national movement to "Draft Dole" and held a kickoff rally in Elizabeth's hometown in late January.[20]

After Elizabeth Dole stepped down from the Red Cross, she visited Iowa and New Hampshire, which increased speculation in the press that her announcement of an exploratory bid would be imminent. "I think she is going to run, unless she finds some compelling reason not to,"[21] said Tom Daffron, a political adviser who had been tapped to coordinate Dole's campaign.

RHETORICAL STYLE

Elizabeth Dole has become an important contemporary American politician, and her well-prepared and engagingly delivered public speaking has contributed to her success. The most compelling rhetorical trait is Dole's ability to address more than one purpose in the same speech, which is known as "rhetorical multi-tasking."[22] Elizabeth Dole is able to meet the specific exigencies of her speech, as well as cast a wider net and pave the way for a new initiative. For example, in 1988 at the G.O.P. Convention, she was designated as the speaker who was to explain the "gender gap" to the audience and try to decrease the amount of female voters who were likely to vote for the Democratic opponent. The phenomenon known as the "gender gap" emerged during the Reagan administration when support for Reagan's policies was waning. In 1980, Ronald Reagan had received almost as many votes from women as he had from men; the difference was only 8 percentage points, with fewer votes being cast for him by women. Two years later, however, public opinion polls and other sources revealed that the gap between male and female supporters was widening. Elizabeth Dole addressed this problem in 1984 and again in 1988.[23] Her speech also highlighted her knowledge of workforce issues and once George H. W. Bush won, Elizabeth was tapped for the labor secretary position. In 1998, Elizabeth Dole toured the country, giving a speech titled "An America We Can Be." The speech was replete with stories of her early D.C. days and described for the audience the progress that has been made with respect to women's issues. At the same time, she was disclosing her resume to the audience, which would help her if she decided that she wanted to run for political office. When she resigned from the American Red Cross is 1999, the speech got more attention for what was only hinted at in the speech—a possible political future—instead of the explicit purpose of the speech, which was for Elizabeth to step down as president of the humanitarian organization. This ability for Elizabeth to make the most of her speeches relates to a quote attributed to her at an exhibit on American women at the Hoover Library in Stanford: "Women have had to be over achievers to succeed. We worked twice as hard as men to be considered as good."

Another notable trait of Elizabeth Dole's public speaking is the novel approach that she takes when planning her presentations. Elizabeth Dole knows that in order to capture her audience's attention, in an ever-increasingly fast paced and media saturated society, she must do something unusual that will ensure her speech looks interesting to the audience. From descending the steps at the G.O.P. Convention in 1996, to holding up props as she speaks, she has capitalized on catching the audience by surprise, and thus, holding its attention better than if she stayed still and didn't incorporate these strategies into her speeches. Elizabeth Dole commented on some of the thinking and planning that made her 1996 G.O.P. Convention speech such an attention-getting speech, and she acknowledged that her unorthodox introduction created curiosity in her audience:

> But I think when the audience saw me come down, they all got quiet. They all wondered "what is she doing?" And because of that, they were more attentive and cooperative as I walked around the audience. And the Secret Service did a wonderful job of keeping the aisles clear. That walking around really works well for me in other speeches as well. I like doing that and I frequently use that style when I speak for the American Red Cross and I speak to victims and their families. I think that it is a very effective way for me to reach the audience. The audience seems to respond so much better when I move around and I am not behind the podium with bright lights glaring at me. I now feel that the podium is a barrier between the audience and me.[24]

Elizabeth Dole is a speaker who has been able to effectively present herself in this media oriented age. Elizabeth Dole's speeches show a high degree of media savvy, which media scholar Thomas Hollihan observes is imperative for the modern politician to be successful:

> Candidates who have an attractive image, who can create memorable sound bites, and who demonstrate that they possess media savvy are likely to make the best impression on voters.[25]

For example, in her 1996 G.O.P. Convention speech, she was widely compared to talk show host Oprah Winfrey. Not only is the comparison to Oprah Winfrey apt because Elizabeth Dole moved around the audience like a hostess making eye contact with guests at her party, the comparison is a good one because, like Winfrey, Dole's speech focused on the impact that Bob Dole made in the lives of people and she had those people in the audience, ready to stand and provide proof in the form of their presence, that Bob Dole made a difference in their lives. And viewers of talk shows, such as the Oprah Winfrey Show, would have recognized this formula, (of the host and admiring audience) because it makes for good television. Dole's 1996 G.O.P. Convention speech was truly a "made for TV" speech, in that it was visual and in that it resembled a talk show, it was familiar to viewers. The engaging way that Elizabeth Dole, attractive and agile, moved about the audience, was far more entertaining and visual than it would have been had Elizabeth merely stood behind the podium and delivered her speech in the same way that the other speakers at the convention. The different method she chose called attention to herself and the purpose of her speech, which was to trumpet the benefits of a Bob Dole presidency. After the success of her 1996 speech, she repeated the style in her speeches for the American Red Cross and she would frequently stand next to a child who was effected by a natural disaster and describe the benefits that the Red Cross was able to administer.

Another hallmark of Elizabeth Dole's public speaking is her penchant for preparation. Many political careers have been hurt by poorly prepared public speaking, however, this is the opposite for Elizabeth Dole. She doesn't like to be caught unprepared for anything, and her public speaking is no exception. Her husband, by comparison, has a public speaking style that has been described as "shooting from the hip" and by his own admission, he doesn't give public speaking nearly the attention that Elizabeth does:

> She is much more disciplined [than I am] I hear a voice coming out of the bedroom and it is Elizabeth rehearsing her speech. She probably gave it twenty eight times already, but she is giving it the next day and she just wants to rehearse it twice. Now, if I've given it once, [a speech] well the old story in the Congress is that you only give a speech once, and that is when you read it for the first time. (Laughter) That's why we're not any good. You don't hear any good speeches in the senate any more, and that is because we're reading them.[26]

Elizabeth Dole's preparation has served her well. Throughout her career, she has been asked to make speeches, and it has been her anticipation of the event that has made her successful. For example, her speechwriter, Kerry Tymchuk, described a time when Elizabeth was in Poland as secretary of Labor and she knew that she would be attending dinners with dignitaries. Just in case she would be asked to give a toast, she had worked with Kerry to prepare appropriate toasts. He noted that "the male secretaries were over there stumbling through their remarks, and she has these beautiful toasts memorized. People were crying when she was finished."[27]

Although being prepared is most often considered a positive attribute, Elizabeth Dole's preparation was ridiculed when Elizabeth Dole was a presidential candidate. The *New York Times* described Elizabeth as a "controlled performer and well-known perfectionist."[28] Another article noted that "she displayed a caution with the public and the press, limited her time for casual schmoozing with both."[29] Another columnist went further, saying, "Dole was positively awful as a candidate. . . . She rarely ever gave a hint of what we expect of leaders, instead following the down-to-the-second script developed by her aides. Combined with her saccharine delivery, the script failed, if only because all who heard her could tell how exactly scripted she was."[30] Cartoonist Garry Trudeau lampooned Elizabeth Dole in his "Doonesbury" strip as a Stepford-like personality who spouts sound bites on command, never varying so much as a semicolon. Ari Fleisher, Dole's communications director, wondered why men are called "disciplined" and women are "scripted."[31]

Many of the topics of Elizabeth Dole's speeches are based on the foundation of her Methodist religion. Growing up in the Piedmont region of North Carolina, in what she described as "the buckle of the Bible Belt,"[32] she is a devout Christian, who crafts her speeches and their message in light of her own core belief system. As a presidential candidate, her religious background was evident. Similar to Abraham Lincoln, who in his inaugural address in 1861 ended his speech with "when again touched, as surely as they will be, by the better angels of our nature," when Elizabeth Dole began her exploratory bid on March 10th, she pledged to "call America to her better nature." The theme of religion was focused upon in the 2000 race by several front running candidates. Vice President Al Gore wanted to reclaim God for the Democrats, and he talked of involving faith-based groups in government and social programs. George W. Bush coined the term "compassionate conservatism" and said that Americans needed to talk again about the "values" that made them great.[33] During her exploratory bid, Elizabeth Dole reprised a speech that she gave in 1987 at the National Prayer Breakfast and spoke at the 15th Annual Philadelphia Prayer Breakfast. In the speech, Elizabeth shared with her audience her spiritual journey and describes a time in her life when she had to find a way out of the "spiritual starvation" that was caused by her hectic career. She told her audience that her "spiritual journey began many years ago in a Carolina home where Sunday was the Lord's Day, reserved for acts of mercy and necessity."[34] She drew parallels between Queen Esther's experiences and her own. She told her audience that "'dependence' is the true meaning of the story of Esther. She said that she had to learn that dependence is a good thing, that when I've used up my own resources, when I can't control things and make them come out my way, when I'm willing to trust God with the outcome, when I'm weak, then I am strong."[35]

Newsweek reported that she portrayed her possible candidacy as a witness for Christian decency. "There's yearning to make us a better nation," she said. "We need to get back to basic values: personal responsibility, honesty, integrity . . . cooperation over conflict." Leading the Red Cross, she said, she'd enabled people to share their blessings. "Aren't we blessed?" she asked.[36]

Through Elizabeth Dole's long career, humanitarian interests have been at the underpinning of all of her work. Her speeches reflect the ways that she plans to apply her faith to practical matters. Her faith has been lived through the choices she has made to serve others and spearhead causes. If she won the presidency, there is sufficient evidence to suggest that she would have continued to communicate her faith through her speeches and in her initiatives.

Elizabeth Dole likes to warm up her audiences with humorous stories or even a conversational "how are you doing?" when the situation is more casual. She does this to create rapport and goodwill with her audience. A warm and engaging person interpersonally, she attempts to create the same reciprocity of a conversation at the beginning of her speeches. She often retells stories of her Washington, D.C., career and particularly likes to stress the progress that women have made in the mostly male corridors of politics. It is also common for Elizabeth Dole to remind the audience of her experience and education. This was especially true during her exploratory bid for the presidency, when she was frequently described as a candidate who "never held elected office." For example, in the speech she gave at the United State Naval Academy in April 1999, she reminded her audience of her tenure as Red Cross president when she said, "And for eight years I was honored to join thousands of Red Cross workers and volunteers who share these values, who're making a positive difference at home and abroad. I know that many other people from humanitarian organizations— a number of you—here tonight—share that passion for service."[37] Later in the same speech she furthered her ethos with her audience when she mentioned her role as Secretary of Labor, as it pertained to the topic of the speech. She said, "As United States Secretary of Labor, I found myself in Poland in the summer of 1989, meeting with Solidarity labor leaders. It was

August and the Soviet bloc was crumbling."[38] Once she gets to the thesis of her talk, she is likely to organize her speech in a problem-solution format. The stories that she often tells in her speeches perform an important function, since they link the ideals that she believes America must return to, or the progress upon which America should continue to build upon in order to create a strong country. The storytelling device that Elizabeth Dole so often employs in her speaking is an important part of her organization, and one that deserves note. Quite often, Elizabeth Dole tells a series of stories as her entire speech. This narrative style serves to create a warm and engaging environment for the audience, since narrative style is one of the most enjoyable for an audience. Speech scholar W. Lance Bennett states that "narratives help us impose order on the flow of experience so that we can make sense of events and actions in our lives."[39] Elizabeth said that telling stories instead of using a lot of data in speeches is "one thing I've learned." She explained: "You start out thinking that they [the audience] really want to know the statistics and the policy, and a lot of times audiences are much more interested in the vignettes and the little stories that illustrate it than the hard data."[40] An example of storytelling from one of Elizabeth Dole's presidential campaign speeches is evident in this speech she gave at Melrose High School in Massachusetts. She said, "For a brief period—when I was working toward a master's degree in education and government, I had the opportunity to serve as an 11th grade history teacher. Back then in the public schools, the classroom was really a showroom—a showroom of American excellence and achievement. Needless to say, we've lost a lot of ground in the last few decades, for a variety of reasons. I spent an afternoon combing through forty years of dusty files. Lo and behold, I found the name of a surviving member of the force. Well I tracked him down in West Roxbury and recorded his memories on tape. He was such a hit with my class that they insisted he come in and tell his story in person!" She also interacted with her audience when she asked: "Would the teachers in the audience please raise your hands? I won't call on you! Now let me ask you to please stand up, so we can show our appreciation for you. Thank you. Teaching is not just a job, it is a calling, a noble endeavor. Thank you for all you do for our children." Later in the same speech she told a story about her experience at Ground Zero: "One of the most emotional experiences of my life was a visit to Ground Zero. As I walked on that now hallowed ground, through the wreckage of the World Trade Center, three of my life's most important experiences came together."[41] She then went on to tell of how the transportation and labor departments, as well as at the Red Cross were all organizations affected by the World Trade Center terrorist attacks of 2001. She was able to relate more closely to the tragedy because of her experience in those organizations. By telling those stories, she connected with the audience and established her credibility as a leader.

Dole's ability to master her material—her rhetorical memoria—is impressive. President Bill Clinton's "photographic memory" was greatly discussed when he was in office. His ability to read something once and know it was one of the hallmarks of his communication ability. Elizabeth Dole's ability for retention is similar to that of Bill Clinton's. Her ability to memorize huge passages, without forgetting anything, is one of the best speaking assets she has. Kerry Tymchuk, a speechwriter for Elizabeth Dole, commented on her talent with respect to the work he did on Elizabeth Dole's 1996 G.O.P. Convention speech. He said, "I was on the convention floor, with a script of the speech in my hand, and Mrs. Dole did not miss a word."[42] Granted, Elizabeth Dole gave a very similar version of this speech on the stump for her husband throughout the campaign year. But only those who follow her around, such as reporters, would know that she wasn't giving that speech for the first time. Elizabeth Dole's ability to deliver her speeches over and over again, while still captivating her audience, as she did in 1996, I have dubbed "well-rehearsed spontaneity." This is clearly a gift for any politician. In an interview with Geraldine Ferraro, she described Elizabeth Dole's repeat performances in a negative way. She said, "She does something that I won't do, she has a shtick that she repeats so often, you could almost hear her G.O.P. Convention speech when she spoke to the Chamber [an event they both attended]. That reminds me of something that happened on this campaign [NY senate race again Charles Schumer]. Chuck [Schumer] has a 'sub speech' and the first time you hear it, you think 'this guy is terrific,' and then when you hear it for the twenty-fifth time, you say, 'God is he able to move off that at all?' but of course, people are listening to the candidates, and most of them are not listening for the twenty-fifth time."[43] Ms. Ferraro described an important aspect of speech delivery for politicians. If they repeat a speech often, like Elizabeth Dole does, they will master the delivery and wow the crowd. If they create a new speech each time, they may not be as dynamic to the audience.

When Elizabeth Dole launched her exploratory bid for president she told her audience, "I'm not a politician, and today, that may be a plus."[44] One of the most substantive speeches of her exploratory presidential race was to Yale Medical School graduates when she held a bottle of children's aspirin in her right hand and a handgun trigger lock in her left. She said, "This will protect our children," holding up the black trigger lock. "It will also help you as future physicians, so you don't have to treat accidentally wounded children in hospital emergency rooms."[45] In the speech, Elizabeth wanted to distance herself from the other Republican candidates on the issue of gun control. She told the audience of her belief that guns should come with safety locks and that no civilian needs an assault rifle. Response to her stand on gun control was mixed, depending on the crowd. At Yale, she was warmly applauded, but in New Hampshire, where the state's motto is "live free or die" there were boos from the crowd when she made a similar speech. One audience member remarked after her speech, "I don't know what she was thinking. Half the guys [in the audience] were packing."[46] At another campaign stop in New Hampshire, Elizabeth made a stance on education. She said, "We can't run public schools by remote control from Washington," Dole said. She advocated universities strengthening the requirements for those studying to be teachers and more parent involvement in the schools.[47]

Bob Dole had been keeping a low profile in the campaign. When asked why Bob wasn't more visible, Elizabeth told the *New York Times*, "It's important that I go solo here for a while. Bob will certainly be willing to do his share of campaigning, but I'll be making the decisions."[48] Not much about her husband appeared in the press during Elizabeth's bid, until the interview Bob gave to a reporter in mid May hit the newsstand. The headline on the front page of the *New York Times* said it all: "As Political Spouse, Bob Dole Strays from Campaign Script." In the article, Bob Dole said that he wanted to give money to John McCain's campaign, especially since McCain needed the money and had been a loyal supporter to Bob when he ran again Bill Clinton in 1996. Even worse, he was not very confident about Elizabeth's exploratory bid. He said, "I'm sort of leaning that she'll do it [run for president]. . . . But she hasn't told me point blank. If there's no response out there, or if it looks impossible, this is not her whole life. If she can't raise the money, obviously it's pretty hard to be a candidate."[49]

The press reaction to Bob Dole's *New York Times* interview focused on how badly his comments may have hurt Elizabeth's chances to have a successful bid for the presidency. Journalist Gail Collins was one of the most critical of Bob Dole. She said, "If Elizabeth Dole seriously wants to be a presidential candidate, the first thing she is going to have to do is lock up her husband." She even went as far as to say that the timing of Bob Dole television commercials for Viagra, the medicine for erectile dysfunction, was planned in order for him to steal the limelight away from Elizabeth. Collins concluded, "With spouses like this, who needs opponents?"[50] But Elizabeth laughed off the issue publicly and noted that Bob was "in the woodshed" while she continued to make her exploratory bid.

Elizabeth Dole's exploratory bid got a major boost when she finished third in the Iowa Straw Poll. Two-thirds of Dole's vote in the Iowa straw poll came from women, many of whom had never been involved in politics.[51]

While Elizabeth Dole's campaign speeches were substantive and the numbers of people in her audience were large, her campaign manager, Tom Daffron, admitted in early October that Elizabeth's inability to raise enough money was a concern. He said, "It's been a hard go for us," to a reporter who claimed that the "curiosity in Dole exceeds [financial] support." In other words, there were large crowds that came to see Elizabeth Dole campaign, but everyone in the audience wasn't contributing to her campaign.[52] Columnist Ellen Goodman echoed this thinking when she said, "More voters seemed interested in her as a celebrity than as a candidate."[53] Frequently women brought their daughters to her speeches, so that young girls could see that a woman could vie for the presidency.

On October 20, 1999, with Bob Dole by her side, Elizabeth Dole abandoned her bid to be America's first woman president, saying, "The odds are overwhelming. It would be futile to continue." While her campaign raised $4.7 million, compared with then–Texas Governor George W. Bush's $57 million, she was at a tremendous financial disadvantage.[54] When she announced her withdrawal, Elizabeth Dole talked about "seeing some women sit up a little straighter because you are trying to empower them. In fact, parents would bring their daughters to see 'a woman.'"

WHY NOT MADAM PRESIDENT?

Elizabeth Dole was repeatedly described as the "first" woman to wage a serious campaign for president and some articles went so far as to say that Dole was the first *viable* female presidential candidate in American history. But a closer look at the obstacles to her presidential aspirations shows that she was neither the first or viable. *Boston Globe* columnist Ellen Goodman summed up this concentration on Dole's gender and pioneering status:

> Her opponents delivered eulogies to her gender. George W. Bush praised her as a "trailblazer" and "an inspiration to a lot of women." John McCain said "Someday a woman will be president of the United States and Elizabeth Dole will have led the way." . . . The broadcasts and newspaper stories all described her as "the only woman in the race." Even the sign in her own headquarters went from "Let's Make History" to "She Made History."[55]

About half the money Elizabeth Dole raised was from women, but it wasn't enough for her to get into the really big fund-raising that a person needs to make it. According to Marie Wilson of the White House Project, the "big payers 'didn't gather around this woman and say, you're the person we want to win with.'"[56] According to New Jersey Governor Christine Todd Whitman: "It's been one of the biggest barriers to women achieving success in public office." Pat Schroeder says that is why she had to drop out of the race in 1988, but she thinks that women are now making enough money to make donations. And that people will start donating more when they see women running credible campaigns—campaigns that have a chance of winning.[57]

A "generation gap" may have also been a culprit in Elizabeth Dole's failed presidential bid. Elizabeth's message may not have resonated with younger women. She may be able to bridge the "gender gap," but she doesn't seem able to bridge the "generation gap." She spoke to an audi-ence of young career women in Manhattan who were only lukewarm about her stories of what she went through to get where she is. She is quoted as saying: "Although I predate the [women's revolution], I was deeply involved in living it." She talked about her mother's reaction to her decision to go to law school and the story was received "tepidly." They want to hear less of her history-of-feminism and more of what she will do to make things better for them. Her campaign message was also muddled. Elizabeth equivocated somewhat when she was asked whether a woman would be able to win the presidency. On the one hand she said, "yes" absolutely and that "people are not thinking male/female or African American/Hispanic American—it's who's the best qualified." Yet she was not entirely comfortable with that, since she told a group of New York women that the women's movement doesn't exactly fit her. Quoting her: "For most women of my generation we struggled individually to find the answer to our own identities. When we women knocked on the doors of America's law schools and medical schools and business schools in the '50s and '60s, we were simply following out dreams, which seemed as natural to us as staying home and getting married was to others." R. Sean Wilentz, history professor at Princeton University, has said: "That she is a woman is a reason, not the reason to vote for her. . . . Nor is it the reason she's running. She's running because she thinks she can run the country better than the other guys can.[58]

As a presidential candidate, Elizabeth Dole faced negative press coverage that portrayed her perfectionism as a drawback. Her husband could not rise to the surrogate role as expertly as she had for him, and she was not seen as a fresh face. Furthermore, that she had never been elected to political office before running for president was, perhaps, the most obvious drawback of all. After she lost re-election to the senate in 2008, the potential for a presidential future for Dole was further detoured.

Although she was a Republican star in the 1980s and she made an attempt at the presidency in 1999, Elizabeth Dole's political career ended abruptly in 2008. Ultimately, because of her star turn in 1996 at the Republican National Convention and her effectiveness as a surrogate to her husband, her imprint on the American public may be more as that of the spouse of Bob Dole than an independent politico.

NOTES

1. Elizabeth Dole, March 10, 1999, Exploratory Committee Announcement, www
.4president.org/speeches/2000/elizabethdole2000announcement.htm (accessed
November 21, 2010).

2. Ibid.

3. Molly Meijer Wertheimer and Nichola D. Gutgold, *Elizabeth Hanford Dole,
Speaking from the Heart* (Westport: Praeger Press, 2004), p. 208.

4. Susan J. Carroll, Carol Heldman, and Stephanie Olson. "'She Brought Only
A Skirt: Gender Bias in Newspaper Coverage of Elizabeth Dole's Campaign for the
Republican Nomination," unpublished paper, White House Projects Conference,
Washington, D.C., February 20, 2000.

5. This biographical section was culled from several sources including: Robert
Dole, Elizabeth Dole, Richard Norton Smith, and Kerry Tymchuk, *Unlimited Part-
ners, Our American Story* (New York: Simon and Schuster, 1996), Richard Kozar,
Elizabeth Dole (Philadelphia: Chelsea House Publishers, 2000), and Molly Meijer
and Nichola D. Gutgold, *Elizabeth Hanford Dole; Speaking from the Heart* (Westport:
Praeger Press, 2004).

6. Molly Meijer Wertheimer and Nichola D. Gutgold, *Elizabeth Hanford Dole,
Speaking from the Heart* (Westport: Praeger Press, 2004), *Unlimited Partners*, p. 47.

7. Dole, Dole, Smith, and Tymchuk, p. 52.

8. Mary Leonard. "A Life in Politics; Liddy's Way; In Elizabeth Dole's Formative
Years, Hints of Her Drive to Challenge, Compete," *Boston Globe*, May 9, 1999, A1.

9. Ibid.

10. Ibid.

11. Kozar, *Elizabeth Dole*, p. 38.

12. Dole, Dole, Smith, and Tymchuk, *Unlimited Partners*, p. 10.

13. "Dole's Mistake: 'Godless' Ad Drove Donors, Voters to Hagan," Miami Herald. November 11, 2008, www.miamiherald.com/news/politics/AP/story/766805
.html (accessed November 22, 2010).

14. Katie Leishman, "A Very Private Person," *McCalls*, April 1988, p. 135.

15. Ellen Goodman, "A Dole on the National Ticket?" *Boston Globe*. April 5, 1988,
p. 10A.

16. Marjorie Williams, "Bob & Liddy Dole, Doing the Town; On the Run with a
Well-Oiled Political Act," *Washington Post*, August 16, 1988, p. E1.

17. Henry Louis Gates, Jr., "The Next President Dole 2000," *The New Yorker*, October 20 and 27, 1997, p. 228.

18. Dick Polman, "Female Faces in the 2000 Race?" *Philadelphia Inquirer*, April
12, 1998, p. E4.

19. Ron Fournier, "President Dole? Some see Elizabeth as a hot prospect," *The
Morning Call (Allentown, PA)*, 20 May 1998, p. A14.

20. "Elizabeth Dole Resigns Red Cross Post, May Test Presidential waters," www
.cnn.com/allpolitics/stories/1999/01/04/presodent.2000/dole/ (accessed November 20, 2010).

21. Steve Campbell, "Daffron to Run Elizabeth Dole's Exploratory Campaign,"
Portland Press Herald (Maine), March 7, 1999, p. 2C.

22. The term "rhetorical multi-tasking" was coined in my co-authored book
(with Molly Meijer Wertheimer), *Elizabeth Hanford Dole: Speaking from the Heart*
(Westport, CT: Praeger, 2004). It was first presented in a paper, "Rhetorical Multi-

tasking of Elizabeth Dole," Pennsylvania Speech Communication Annual Conference, Bloomsburg, PA, 1999.

23. Eileen Putnam, "Mrs. Dole Acknowledges Gender Gap, Asks Women to have an Open Mind," *Associated Press*, August 16, 1988.

24. Elizabeth Dole, interview with Nichola Gutgold, April 7, 1998.

25. Thomas A. Hollihan, *Uncivil Wars Political Campaigns in a Media Age* (Boston: Bedford/St. Martin, 2000), p. 39.

26. Bob Dole, interview with Nichola Gutgold and Molly Meijer Wertheimer, December 17, 2001.

27. Kerry Tymchuk, interview with Nichola Gutgold, September 11, 2000.

28. Katherine Q. Seelye, "The Dole Candidacy; The Overview," *New York Times*, October 21, 1999, p. A1.

29. Linda Feldmann, "Dole's Candidacy Had Historic Impact," *Christian Science Monitor*, October 21, 1999, p. 1.

30. Michael Kramer, "Liddy Without Tears," *Daily News* (New York) October 24, 1999, p. 47.

31. Eleanor Clift and Tom Brazaitis, *Madam President: Women Blazing the Leadership Trail* (New York: Routledge, 2003), p. 99.

32. Elizabeth Dole, interview with Molly Meijer Wertheimer and Nichola Gutgold, July 8, 2003.

33. Ann McFeatters, "Presidential Candidates Saying Something of Values; Religious References Fill States of GOP, Democratic Hopefuls," *Pittsburgh Post-Gazette*, May 30, 1999, p. A-11.

34. Molly Meijer Wertheimer and Nichola D. Gutgold, *Elizabeth Hanford Dole: Speaking from the Heart* (Westport, CT: Praeger, 2004), p. 134.

35. Ibid., p. 137.

36. Howard Fineman and Matthew Cooper, "Back in the Amen Corner," *Newsweek*, March 22, 1999, p. 33.

37. Molly Meijer Wertheimer and Nichola D. Gutgold, p. 210.

38. Ibid., p. 213.

39. W. Lance Bennett, "Storytelling in Criminal Trials: A Model of Social Judgment," *Quarterly Journal of Speech*, Vol. 64 (February 1978), pp. 1–22.

40. Elizabeth Dole, interview with Molly Meijer Wertheimer and Nichola Gutgold, July 8, 2003.

41. Molly Meijer Wertheimer and Nichola D. Gutgold, pp. 239, 241.

42. Kerry Tymchuk, 1996 G.O.P. Convention Speech, email to Nichola Gutgold, November 11, 2000.

43. Geraldine Ferraro, interview with Nichola Gutgold, October 20, 1998.

44. Mike Glover, "Dole Joins Exploratory Offering 'Better Nature,'" *Associated Press*, March 10, 1999, www.lexis.nexis.com (accessed November 10, 2010).

45. Bridgette Greenberg, "Dole Pushes Gun Control in Commencement Speech," *Standard-Speaker* (Hazleton, PA), May 25, 1999, p. 2.

46. John F. Dickerson and Nancy Gibbs, "Elizabeth Unplugged," *Time*, May 10, 1999, www.time.com (accessed 22 February 2004).

47. Amy Diaz, "Dole: Milosevic Must Be Defeated 'Absolutely,'" *The Union Leader* (Manchester, NH), May 25, 1999, p. A13.

48. Richard L. Berke, "As Political Spouse, Bob Dole Strays from Campaign Script," *New York Times*, May 17, 1999, p. A1.

49. Ibid.

50. Gail Collins, "Politics: Taking the 'Help' Out of 'Helpmate,'" *New York Times*, May 18, 1999, p. A22.

51. "A Softer Look, a Strong Appeal," *Newsweek*, August 30, 1999, p. 4.

52. Diana Jean Schemo, "Curiosity in Dole Exceeds Support," *New York Times*, October 6, 1999, p. A28.

53. Ellen Goodman, "Gender Spotlight Cuts Both Ways," *Boston Globe*, October 24, 1999, p. E7.

54. "Dole Drop Out; Her Poor Showing Wasn't Just a Money Problem," *Pittsburgh Post Gazette*," October 22, 1999, p. A22.

55. Ellen Goodman, p. E7.

56. Ibid.

57. Paul Alexander, "Vice Can be Nice," *Mirabella*, September 2000, pp. 66–69.

58. Ibid.

Former Kansas Senator Nancy Kassebaum

Dianne Feinstein and Tony Bennett ride a newly refurbished cable car in 1984

Maryland Senator Barbara Mikulski

Former North Carolina Senator Elizabeth Dole engagingly addresses her audience

Speaker of the United States House of Representatives Nancy Pelosi smiles warmly as she addresses her audience.

Maine Senator Olympia Snowe

Washington Governor Christine Gregoire

Secretary of Health and Human Services Kathleen Sebelius

Former Hawaii Governor Linda Lingle, wearing a traditional Hawaiian lei, addresses the people of Hawaii.

6

Nancy Pelosi:
Tangled-Up in Stereotypes

Nancy Pelosi is, of course, the first woman to serve as Speaker of the House. That means that she technically has come closer to the presidency than any other woman in American history, for the Speaker is second in the line of succession. Nonetheless, her name only occasionally comes up when the topic is prospective presidential candidates.[1] Perhaps, for a while, she was overshadowed by fellow San Franciscan Dianne Feinstein, who was indeed talked about as a possible president. At that point, Pelosi was still gaining power. Once she had power, perhaps she was overshadowed by Hillary Clinton, who seemed, as 2008 approached, to be *the* woman with the claim on the nomination. Serving in the House of Representatives also did not help her, for that body is usually not thought of as a presidential proving ground. However, what really hurt Pelosi is how she could not escape stereotypes that commentators—and, perhaps, some colleagues—entangled her in. As a result, she comes across as almost cartoonish when in reality she is an accomplished political leader.

LEARNING POLITICS, BALTIMORE-STYLE

Nancy Pelosi is, like Mikulski, a "Baltimore Girl." That statement may surprise those who think of her as quintessentially Californian or, more specifically, San Franciscan, but her roots are not in the West but, rather, in the Baltimore neighborhood known as "Little Italy."[2] There, she was the youngest child and only daughter of legendary Baltimore politician Thomas D'Alesandro. "Big Tommy," as he was called, served in the U.S. House of Representatives, but he became famous in Maryland politics not for his service in D.C. but for his service in his city, where he would serve as mayor. He would give up his House seat to become Mr. Mayor, and he would play that role in both the City Hall office and in the foyer and parlor of his "Little Italy" home. It was in that foyer that Nancy began her political career, taking her turn writing down the requests of those who came to the door of Mayor D'Alesandro. As some will note long after Pelosi and San Francisco become fused in political discussions, there will always be much of this old-style Baltimore politicking in her way of doing business.

Nancy's mother, Annuciato, known as "Big Nancy," wanted to go to law school. She got close, but never fulfilled her dream. She was determined that her daughter would have the opportunities that she had not. Thus, "Big Tommy" and she sent Nancy to Notre Dame Academy, where she was two years behind Mikulski. There, Nancy absorbed the school's emphasis on service, but, rather than furthering her education in Baltimore and serving the people there as Mikulski had done, Nancy went off to Trinity College in Washington, D.C. Trinity had a good academic reputation, but it also had a "finishing school" image, providing the young women who attended the social graces as well as the knowledge to succeed in life, careers, and marriage. One can imagine "Big Tommy" and "Big Nancy" wanting just this mix of education and polish for their darling only daughter.

After receiving her Trinity B.A., Nancy went to work on "The Hill." She got a job in Maryland Senator Daniel Brewster's office. She was primarily a receptionist. Brewster saw the political advantage of having a D'Alesandro in the outer office. Marylanders would not try to steamroll their way past "Big Tommy"'s daughter. Also working in Brewster's office at the time was another just out of school. He was not in the outer office, but inside as a legislative aide. His name was Stenny Hoyer.

Hoyer will, of course, play a role in Nancy Pelosi's distant future—sometimes rival; eventually the "number two" to her "number one" among House Democrats, but the man who would play a role in her immediate future was one she met in a course in African politics that she enrolled in at Georgetown University while a Trinity student. This man, Paul Pelosi, she married, and then she left Washington with him to set up housekeeping in metropolitan New York. Quickly, Nancy was pregnant with their first child, and her career in politics seemed very much on hold.

With Paul and children, she will later move to San Francisco. There, Nancy will gradually become increasingly involved in the politics that, one might say, were in her D'Alesandro blood. She will become involved not as a candidate or as a staffer but as a fund-raiser. Taking advantage of Paul's connections among more wealthy Californians, Nancy would increasingly show the social graces that she learned at Trinity by hosting events and using them to add to the Democratic Party's coffers in the state. Initially, they would be in her home, and her children would help cook the food and serve it. Then, they became larger, grander events. Her fund-raising clout would eventually earn her a succession of leadership positions on the state's Democratic Party committee.

Years passed since she left Washington, D.C., but the opportunity to return was suddenly there. Her children were almost all raised: only sixteen-year-old Alexandra was at home. A Congressional seat was available, almost for the taking. Pelosi's California political mentor, Representative Phil Burton passed away; his widow Sela, who had been appointed to take her husband's seat in Congress, fell critically ill. Sela, from her hospital bed, suggested Pelosi for the job. So, Pelosi consulted with her teenage daughter, who quickly told her mother to seize the day. So, at an age (forty-seven) later than most entering politics, Nancy Pelosi found herself a "freshman congressman" representing a fairly liberal San Francisco district.

Pelosi's political forte was fund-raising, not public speaking. As a gracious hostess, she had also acquired both a sense of style and a knack at getting supporters of progressive causes to open their checkbooks. So, given this strength, one would expect Pelosi to rise in the House of Representatives based on skills that do not always make the news. She would be behind the scenes, helping her party find money for future campaigns.[3] Yes, she would be a legislator; and, yes, she would occasionally speak; but her strength was in garnering financial support—not so much for herself, for her district was safely Democratic, but for other Democrats.

Pelosi's success—and rise to the top—may well be explained by the coincidence of her most striking strength and party leader Richard Gephart's most striking weakness. The Missouri congressman was certainly well-thought-of by his colleagues. However, he was not adept at filling the party coffers. Nancy was—he raised $2.5 million in ten years; she raised $140 million in seven—and this skill, arguably, allowed her to leap-frog others who were interested in positions in the Democratic Party's House leadership.[4] Her rise, then, was less because of her legislative work and her rhetorical skills and more because she could "schmooze" with the best of them and, thereby, raise money.

Pelosi's House career was not just "schmoozing"; there were a number of legislative triumphs she could cite as she campaigned for a leadership post. These triumphs were not headline-makers. Many of them held more meaning for her San Francisco constituents than those following the national press. So, in sum, Pelosi was a reliable liberal vote who took care of her constituents' immediate concerns and could raise money for her fellow House Democrats who were facing tough reelection campaigns as well as for Democrats out there who the Party felt could win seats away from Republicans.

RHETORICAL STYLE

As she rose in the House, Pelosi recognized that her rhetorical skills, as they were exhibited through public speaking, were a liability. She addressed this liability by seeking coaching. That coaching allowed her to acquire a style that was both more relaxed and more forceful, but she would never totally overcome tendencies that made her come across to audiences as stiff and strident. Stridency, it should be noted, as a stylistic characteristic, can often be the result of trying to be forceful without sufficient comfort. This stridency will be something Pelosi could never entirely overcome.

Pelosi's voice will increasingly emerge as both that of the liberals in the House and, then, Democrats in general. As the public and perhaps also the press heard that voice, it was sometimes the strident one—liberal views that might be voiced with a finesse by others but came across sharply from her. This tone suggested that Pelosi was an ideologue who did not know the meaning of the word "compromise." The truth was that Pelosi had her beliefs and also knew her constituents' beliefs but also was not only willing to compromise when appropriate but capable of negotiating such compromises because, one-on-one or even in small groups, the stridency vanished. This gracious, flexible—to a point—Pelosi was known to many of her colleagues on both sides of the aisle who would sing her praises. For example, Representative Tom Cole of Oklahoma, who was chairing the National Republican Congressional Committee in 2007, said that he "admire[d] her political leadership"; Representative David Dreier, who at the same time was leading California's Republican delegation in the House, said she "represented San Francisco very well" and was "a dedicated hard worker"; and Representative Dick Armey, once the Republican House majority leader, said, "I am a big fan," and that "she is an able person and serious about her work and a very pleasant person with whom to work."[5] Armey also noted, "If I had been majority leader and said, 'I like Nancy Pelosi,' I would be crucified." So, some of the flack her stridency has evoked on the part of Republicans may have more a part of the partisan politics "game" than an expression of their honest assessment of her.

The academic assessment of Pelosi's work suggests why even some Republicans expressed a degree of admiration. Ronald Peters and Cindy Rosenthal, in *Speaker Nancy Pelosi and the New American Politics* (2010), have outlined what skills were important for leaders in Congress today. They have pointed to hyper partisanship, the ability to raise money, the ability to design an expansive media landscape including the Internet, and skill communicating with a diversified electorate. Their assessment of Pelosi was that she fit this definition almost perfectly—partisan, yes, but also skilled and savvy enough to earn admiration, even from political opponents.[6] However, Pelosi's positive traits, known to academic analysts and known to members of the House from both parties, were often lost on the public, who served by mainstream media, alternative and more ideological media, and late-night comics, thought Pelosi to be as politically rigid and rhetorically stiff as her often-mocked, always smiling, botoxed face. She was *the* liberal voice, and, if you didn't like the liberal take on matters, she was someone therefore to be disliked and refuted. *Politico* commentator Glenn Thrush would term Pelosi "one of the most despised political figures in the country."[7] If she is, then she is despite political skills, skills touted by academic commentators and recognized and respected by some Republicans in Congress.

Pelosi's rhetoric did indeed have an occasionally strongly partisan quality once she became the minority leader. But one needs to understand her situation then rhetorically. She was no longer just a representative from California or a representative from California serving some role in the party leadership. Rather, she was the voice of the party, a party dominated in the House by liberal-leaning Democrats. Her persona, then, was one that required a degree of forcefulness. In addition, the usual exigence requiring her to speak was to present clearly and strongly her party's position on an issue. Again, this exigence required a degree of forcefulness.

The role of Speaker was, as she in public comments seemed to recognize, not the same as the role of party leader.[8] There was a presumption on her part that she was now leading the entire House, not just her party. Over time, however, the role of Speaker has become increasing less nonpartisan, creating, in 2007, a dual, sometimes contradictory persona and exigence. Different Democrats have enacted this persona and responded to this exigence in different ways through the years: "Tip" O'Neill's way of being Mr. Speaker was different from Carl Albert's; Republicans have enacted the role in different ways as well. Pelosi, arguably, although knowing she was "Madam Speaker" of the entire House, still was too much of the party leader. If she tipped the balance in the partisan direction, she would not be the first to do so, however.

Given Pelosi's lack of comfort in her ability as a public speaker, it is not surprising that her voice as Speaker (as well as that of leader) came across as strident. It is also not surprising that she relied heavily, throughout her House career, on issued statements as opposed to actual floor speeches. Unfortunately, a text does not allow one to overcome a strident tone if those reading the text import that tone into it. Using statements eliminates the difficulties of actually speaking, and it furthermore guarantees the precision of the message's words. However, statements are read, and they are not read neutrally. Readers read the words, hearing a voice they either embrace or reject. Pelosi then did not escape the problem of stridency by relying heavily on released statements.

Tracing her rhetorical career in the House both points to trends and highlights a consistency in tone. Early, she could be strident, but she tended to save her strongest rhetoric for the Chinese government, not the Republican opposition in Congress. In October, 1996, for example, in a released statement, she termed "the trial and sentencing" of dissident Wang Dan "a mockery of justice," and she scolded China's "authoritarian government" for "its disregard for its own Constitution and for international norms and standards."[9] A year later, in another released statement, Pelosi pointed to the Chinese "government's abuse of power and its people." Of specific concern was a policy of organ harvesting from the corpses of executed prisoners. She declared that the policy "mocks the very principles that are the bedrock of any law-abiding nation" and argued that it was "an affront to the American people and our sensibilities." Two years later (April, 1999), she is still reflecting the concerns of her many Chinese-American constituents by, in a released statement, criticizing the Clinton administration for hosting Chinese Premier Zhu Rongji despite his government's "abysmal record on human rights." She calls on Clinton to take a stronger stance, although she does point to some positive steps the president has taken. After all, Pelosi is a Democrat: she will only take criticism of a sitting Democratic president so far.

In September 1998, however, Pelosi, in a released statement, defended Clinton during the impeachment proceedings. She termed the release of Clinton's Grand Jury testimony "a blatant political move" by Republicans designed for no other purpose than "to further humiliate the President over an affair he has already admitted." She further declared that the release, "pushed through by the Republican majority of the Judiciary Committee, violates the basic principles of fairness." In her mind, the Republican leadership was intent on "consum[ing] the nation's attention with salacious allegations about the President's private life."

The impeachment proceedings, the weakening of the Democratic president, and the strengthening of the Republican opposition in Congress seem to have pushed Pelosi from strong rhetoric in service of her constituents' concerns to strong rhetoric directed against Republicans. In March 1999, for example, she attacks—again, in a released statement—the Republican-authored budget for "trading health care, education and law enforcement for tax cuts." She terms these cuts "risky" and repeatedly indicates that they benefit "the wealthy." Her rhetoric matches that used by Al Gore in the 2000 presidential race, as well as by John Kerry in 2004 and Barack Obama in 2008. Pelosi is, in other words, beginning to sound her party's keynotes. The broadening of her rhetoric coincides, not surprisingly, with her becoming part of her party's leadership in the House. One can argue cause-effect either way: her broadened rhetoric led to her being considered for election to a leadership position; her positioning herself eventually to be minority leader led her to broaden her rhetorical concerns. The truth is probably both: Pelosi was moving beyond the concerns of her San Francisco district at the same time she was looking for opportunities to serve the Democratic Party in Congress

After George W. Bush became president, she continues in this vein—challenging the Republican position on a variety of issues. When, in July 2002, the Bush administration decided to withhold $34 million in international family planning funds from a United Nations effort, Pelosi—in a released statement—accused the Bush administration of "turning back the clock on human rights for the poorest women of the world." According to Pelosi, "The poorest women on this planet [were] being held hostage to the extreme elements in the Republican Party." When, in November 2003, the Republicans in the House proposed an energy bill, Pelosi—in a speech on the floor—termed it "disgraceful," complained about how it came out of a "back-room deal" between Republicans and special-interest groups, such as "the Haliburton crowd," and pointed to the bill's "special interest giveaways" and how "big energy" will "feast on a buffet of new tax breaks."

In March 2004, Congressional Democrats released a report on the Bush administration's budget and, specifically, how it affected African Americans. In a released statement, Pelosi first noted how "Democrats are fighting every day for the issues African Americans care about." Then, she noted how the Bush budget cut programs important to this vital Democratic Party constituency while giving "additional tax cuts [to] those who need them least," how "instead of providing African Americans with an opportunity to achieve the American dream, he [Bush] is mortgaging their future on irresponsible tax cuts for those who need it least."

Her comments reflect those of the 2004 Kerry campaign. In June 2005, she continues—and, one might argue, intensifies the questioning of the Bush Iraq policy that Kerry had offered. In a speech on the House floor, Pelosi pointed to how the war in Iraq had "already consumed nearly $200 billion [and] ended the lives of over 1,700 of our troops." She called the war "a grotesque mistake" and scolded the president repeatedly for "a lack of planning." Although anti-war groups in the Democratic Party sometimes complained that Pelosi's rhetoric was not strong enough, here it seemed fairly strong. She didn't call Bush a "murderer," and she didn't declare his policy "stupid." Nonetheless, she delivered a strong indictment of the president's Iraq policy.

In July 2006—again, in a floor speech, Pelosi used the occasion of a Republican bill to protect the pledge of allegiance to assault that party on a number of counts. the Republicans have "undermined the security . . . of the middle class"; the Republicans have, at the same time they have blocked a modest increase in the federal minimum wage, given themselves in the Congress a $30,000 raise over the past nine years. The bill itself infuriated her because it was "an assault on the Constitution of the United States," by "strip[ping] the courts of their power to be a check and a balance to the other branches of government." But, more than that, the bill infuriated her as an example of what she termed "divide and distract" politics, a "freak show" orchestrated by "a bunch of thieves" to obfuscate behind patriotic rhetoric how the Bush administration and the Republican Congress "went to work on the American people," especially, "our children, our children, our children." In Pelosi's view, the people's health, education, economic security, and safety were in danger because of the Republican agenda. Those Republicans in Congress were, in her opinion, "dishonor[ing] the oath of office that we all take." One might well argue that her rhetoric was becoming inflammatory.

Her increased stridency—and her increased willingness to speak on the floor now that she was party leader—sometimes was even directed against her fellow Democrats. In April 2001, for example, she argued on the floor against a bill that, in further criminalizing violence against pregnant women, would have implicitly undercut *Roe v. Wade*. Her tone here is sarcastic. She responds to Representative Chris Smith, a Democrat from New Jersey, that, "could it be that, as a woman, I know a little bit more about this subject than maybe he does? Could it be that as a mother of five, a grandmother of four, and hopefully more grandchildren to come, that I understand how reprehensible violence against a pregnant woman is?"

After the 2006 mid-term election, Pelosi became Speaker of the House. In theory, this is a less partisan role. So, given the forcefulness and stridency that emerged in Pelosi's rhetoric after the late 1990s, one might ask, does her rhetoric change as she assumes the high office two removed from the presidency? The answer is largely no.

There were forceful words undoubtedly interpreted as having strident tones. On September 17, 2007, for example, she released a statement that scolded the Bush administration, accusing it of "the subversion of federal law enforcement for partisan purposes" and a "persistent disregard of constitutional rights." Even years into the Obama administration, Pelosi is still attacking Bush. In a statement released on September 20, 2010, she refers repeatedly to the "Bush recession." She uses this tactic to make Republicans responsible for both the recession and the failure to address it. Referring to the latter, she cites "months of Senate Republican obstruction and delay" that "have made it clear that [Congressional Republicans] will oppose all efforts to help small businesses," while "taking care of big corporations and sending American jobs overseas."

She even used her office spokespeople to voice attacks. On September 22, 2010, hitting almost all the bases, spokesman Nadeam Elshami said, "Congressional Republicans are pledging to ship jobs overseas; blow a $700 billion hole in the deficit to give tax cuts to millionaires and billionaires;

turn Social Security from a guaranteed benefit into a guaranteed gamble; once again, subject American families to the recklessness of Wall Street; and take away patients' rights. Republicans want to return to the same failed economic policies that hurt millions of American[s] and threatened our economy." The statement sounds like a campaign speech.

On some occasions, Pelosi did sound more like the Speaker who presides over all, as opposed to a party leader. However, even when she was "Madam Speaker," a partisan edge appeared. For example, on September 28, 2008, she spoke at a news conference occasioned by the defeat of the Emergency Economic Stabilization Act. In her address, she used the term "bipartisan" six times. She argued that the Democrats "delivered on our side of the bargain" and scolded the Republicans in Congress for not acting in a bipartisan manner. "Clearly," she said, "that message has not been received yet by the Republican Caucus." One might argue that her speech called for bipartisanship; however, a more accurate reading of the address is that she was using the stick of bipartisanship to beat Republicans with. A similar use would be two years later, on September 21, 2010, when she scolded Senate Republicans for "put[ting] partisan politics ahead of our troops, our security, and our values" when they blocked a motion to open debate on the Defense Authorization Bill, allegedly because it contained a repeal of "Don't Ask, Don't Tell" and enacted the Dream Act. The non-partisan position, she implied, would be to allow debate, but she rhetorically blurs the debate issue with the support for troops and the two controversial matters buried in the bill and thereby suggests that the non-partisan position would be to repeal "Don't Ask, Don't Tell" and enact the Dream Act. She is, in other words, using an accusation of nonpartisanship against the Republicans to make their objections to the controversial matters look bad.

After losing her position as Speaker and becoming majority leader once again, the forcefulness—and the stridency—continued. On April 15, 2011, she spoke on the floor, telling Republicans there that their "leadership is asking you to cast a vote today to abolish Medicare as we know it." In a series of antitheses, Pelosi tells Republicans and others what the Republican-authored budget does: this budget "ends Medicare as we know it as they give big tax breaks and subsidies, tens of billions of dollars[,] to Big Oil; this budget reduces Medicaid for our seniors in nursing homes, sending them away from nursing homes[,] while it gives tax breaks to companies that send jobs overseas; this budget hurts our children's education, in fact, it increases the cost of higher education for nearly 10 million of our young adults while it gives tax breaks to America's wealthiest families." She further notes that the Republicans have held the majority for 100 days and "not one job has been created." Instead, she said, stressing the absurdity, "We are here to abolish Medicare instead." She finally noted how Republicans have argued that the budget deficit is immoral, and she responded that,

"It's been immoral for the 8 years of the Bush Administration. I didn't hear anybody say 'boo' while we were giving tax cuts to the rich, having two wars unpaid for, and giving a prescription drug bill to the private sector."

On May 4, 2011, she spoke on the floor, accusing the Republican majority in Congress of "pursuing an extreme and divisive legislative agenda that will undermine women's health." In addition to criticizing what she termed "an unprecedented and radical assault," Pelosi also attacked the House Republicans for wanting to raise taxes on women, raise taxes on small businesses, and grant "giveaways for Big Oil."

Speaking on the floor of Congress is sometimes scripted, sometimes not. In general, Pelosi's rhetoric seems stronger—and, therefore, more likely to evoke the ire of opponents—when she is not scripted. Thus, it is not surprising that some of her most provocative comments occur in interviews. During the 2004 elections, she called DeLay "not only unethical, but delusional" and President Bush "oblivious, in denial, dangerous."[10] Interviewed by *The Hill* in June 2006, she scolded the Republican leadership in the House for not allowing any bills offered by Democrats to even be voted on.[11] Interviewed on CBS' "60 Minutes" in October 2006, she labeled her political opponents "immoral" and "corrupt."[12] In a CNN interview in July, 2008, she termed Bush "a total failure."[13] A month later, in an interview with KGO Radio talk show host, she "blasted Senator Joe Lieberman" for his negative comments on Barack Obama and she "chastised" Senator Hillary Clinton's supporters for being "less than gracious" toward the presumptive Democratic presidential nominee.[14]

The content of Pelosi's statements and addresses could be quite forceful. Sometimes, in her use of adjectives, she pushed buttons that undoubtedly prompted fury from the opposite side. Pelosi was far from the only member of the House using such language, however. Her rhetoric, largely because of verbal and non-verbal qualities associated with discomfort, had a stridency the similar rhetoric of others lacked. She could then be a rather polarizing figure despite her considerable assets as a leader. Many Republicans did speak less than kindly about her. For example, Vice President Dick Cheney scolded her for her off-the-cuff remarks on foreign policy matters, and former Speaker Newt Gingrich called for her to resign in 2009, because of what he referred to as her "contempt for the men and women who protect our nation."[15] The Drudge Report would post unflattering pictures of her; the Republican National Committee would create a website firenancypelosi.com depicting her surrounded by literal fire.[16] And Democrats as well would sometimes express their displeasure. According to New York *Daily News* writer Michael Goodwin, in 2006, as she is about to assume the Speaker's role, "some Democrats complained Pelosi was making them look extreme," and, in late 2010, after the Democrats lost the House, the number of complaining Democrats increased. Illinois Congressman Mike Quigley described her as "politically toxic" and Pennsylvania Congressman Tom Holden said, "She just drove the bus . . . off the Grand Canyon."[17] Thus, she would begin any national campaign with high negatives. This in and of itself probably disqualified her from serious presidential consideration. The party was not likely to choose as its nominee someone with such negatives. But why did such a capable politician evoke such negativity? The answer goes beyond a rhetorical style that could at times be strident.

WHY NOT MADAM PRESIDENT?

Kathleen Hall Jamieson's work in *The Double Bind* again provides a useful lens through which to view a woman politician's plight.[18] Pelosi arguably became caught in four double binds and only managed to escape one.

The one she escaped was the Womb/Brain bind. She did so by using a strategy Jamieson terms "sequencing." Pelosi had her family first; then, she sought public office. She did not, of course, go from no political involvement to seeking a Congressional seat, but the political work she did while raising her children was compatible with the homemaker image. She hosted parties; she engaged in much one-on-one fundraising; and she attended California party meetings. Only the last might, in some eyes, exceed what would be appropriate for a mother of many, but she segued into that after her children were no longer small.

However, her sequencing strategy perhaps helped trap her in another double bind, the aging/invisibility bind. Pelosi did enter politics later in life than many. Thus, by the time she achieved leadership roles in the House of Representatives, she was "old." The word "old" must be understood in a gendered way, for, in our culture, "old" is reached at an earlier age by a woman in politics than it is for a man. Recall that some, when Hillary Clinton lost the Democratic nomination in 2008, said that that run was it for her because she would be too old in 2012 or 2016. They said this even though John McCain, the Republican nominee, was older in 2008 than Clinton would have been in either 2012 or 2016. An aging man can look distinguished in our culture; an aging woman just looks old—such is the prejudice. A response to this problem for a woman may well be to turn to cosmetic surgery. We do not know if Pelosi turned to botox injections for political reasons. Nonetheless, she did, and her doing so has evoked mockery. More about that mockery later. Her strategy, then, to overcome the aging/invisibility double bind may have drawn attention to her aging.

Pelosi's turn to cosmetic surgery may, however, have had more to do with her desire to maintain a particular feminine image. In her childhood, she was dressed-up by "Big Nancy" and "Big Tommy" in nice girlish attire. After several sons, they treated little Nancy like a little princess. The finishing school atmosphere at Trinity probably reinforced this tendency to look good and look feminine. Her "work" as social hostess on behalf of California Democrats also virtually required such an appearance. Once elected, she maintained this emphasis, so much so that media commentary often noted the color of her attire—purple or lilac—and the designer—Armani—in a manner they certainly would not for males in politics and in a manner they were becoming less inclined to for other females in politics. Looking good was part of Pelosi's image, as was her smile. So, given several decades of looking feminine, Pelosi ran smack into the feminine/competent double bind.

Her response was to blend the two. Before she entered politics *per se,* she projected a self-image of spouse and mother who was a highly competent fund-raiser. The picture may have struck some as incongruous, but Pelosi seemed to be counting on her success as fund-raiser overcoming any concerns that her femininity meant, in any sense, that she was "lite." In politics, she did not deny her spouse/mother role. In fact, when she ceremonially assumed the position of Madam Speaker, she surrounded herself with the members' children and grandchildren who were in the chamber that day. She often brought her children and grandchildren into her day-to-day discussions of political matters; and she frequently talked about public policy in terms of serving our collective children. According to Marie Wilson, founder of The White House Project, her stressing her feminine side allowed some—for example, Bush and Cheney—to infantilize or minimize her. They found it strategic to undermine the blend she was mixing. Others, in stressing her den-motherish ways or suggesting that she was too led by emotions, did not find the blend compelling.[19]

Pelosi's walk through the minefield of double binds was, then, not without small explosions, but what really caused her problems was the silence/shame double bind. She was outspoken, and, as the earlier analysis of her rhetoric showed, stridently so. That stridency may have increased somewhat after she became leader because, now, she was the House Democratic Party's point person on numerous matters of policy. As noted earlier, her discomfort with speaking may have created or at least exacerbated the stridency her audiences heard. Peters and Rosenthal undertook a formal analysis, using the framework for a "feminine style" outlined in 1995 by Robson and Blankenship.[20] Peters and Rosenthal found that Pelosi "has aimed to combine femininity and force, to take advantage of her gender when it is useful, to downplay it when it might prove a liability. In effect, she has sought to reverse the double-bind, letting it work to her advantage."[21] Perhaps that blend is what an objective analysis quoting a feminine Pelosi, as well as a forceful Pelosi, shows. However, her stridency seems to have skewed the picture listeners—even readers—had of her away from a balance.

A major strategy that Pelosi used to counteract this stridency was what linguist Robin Lakoff terms "niceness," that is "expressions of interpersonal positive politeness by speakers in public roles."[22] "Niceness," increasingly expected of presidential aspirants, is not, however, "evaluated similarly for both sexes."[23] Although the gender difference is narrowing, "women are expected to be polite under more circumstances, and to more kinds of people than men," and "women's politeness is apt to be more deferential and more indirect." Only by exhibiting this "niceness" will a woman in politics be considered "competent, benevolent, and worthy of trust"—in other words, electable.[24]

In her 2005 article in the *Journal of Politeness Research*, Lakoff discusses Nancy Pelosi as Speaker of the House. The job, according to Lakoff, is one that demands "disciplining members of his own party and keeping them in line"; the job demands "severity" and "toughness." Pelosi, because of the requirement that she be "nice" in a gendered manner, had to pursue the job in a different manner. She had to "nice-ize" "a role that formerly was not seen as requiring politeness in any form and particularly not Niceness."[25] Lakoff may well have her politics wrong: the roles of whip and leader require the disciplining, tough person, not the role of Speaker, who historically has been less political than the leader. This quibble aside, Lakoff's question is still relevant: it simply applies more to the two periods when Pelosi served as leader than to the four years she served as Speaker. So, how did Pelosi do so? According to Lakoff, her many stories about her children and grandchildren played a role, as did the constant availability of chocolate—"a quintessential woman's, and womanly food"—in her office and at meetings she conducted—in "nice-izing" the job she was in.[26]

The question to ask then is did this "niceness" overcome her stridency? Parallel is the broader question—did her interpersonal skills, exhibited in mentoring and fund-raising, as well as in offering chocolate—overcome her stridency?

For some, the answer is very clearly no. After all, Pelosi is "Nazi Nancy" and the "Wicked Witch of the West" (and, less derisively, "Queen Nancy") in the words of conservative commentators. Chris Matthews can declare that she's "going to castrate Steny Hoyer," and Rush Limbaugh can suggest that her picture be hung in every cheap motel room to deflate the male libido.[27] On the other hand, those who have worked with her characterize her as gracious; she is famed not just for her fund-raising acumen but for her strong mentoring skills; and, according to Peters and Rosenthal, her style blends the feminine and the masculine. This is a blend that has worked well for others in politics. How do we get from this profile of someone highly competent to "Nazi Nancy"? The answer undoubtedly rests in a combination of what Pelosi says and how

Pelosi says it. Added to this combination of substance and style are the facts that Pelosi represents California, both "blue" and "out there" in its presumed politics, and—more narrowly—San Francisco, which is even more "blue" and "out there." The combination is just too much for any "niceness" to overcome.

But, even if conservative commentators fail to assess Pelosi fairly, do others in the populace see her as "Nazi Nancy" or in a more balanced manner as a forceful liberal politician who can hit nerves but can also charm? The answer seems to be largely no. This is very much the puzzle that the case of Nancy Pelosi poses. Anyone who serves in the House of Representatives will have difficulty seeking the presidency. It is assumed that representatives have focused too narrowly on their districts and, therefore, lack the larger view senators and governors have. True or not, this prejudice against House members does exist. So, that is a strike against Pelosi, but the second strike is the image people hold of her that, although it may not be as extreme as "Nazi Nancy," is certainly negative. She has not remained silent, and, therefore, she suffers the shame of being assailed with the "b-word."

The puzzle—that is, why she cannot escape the silence/shame double bind with even arguably "neutral" voters—may well be solved by considering media coverage of Pelosi. The traditional media has treated her fairly, although it has conveyed to readers and viewers how she is depicted by other media. Traditional media, then, has served as a perhaps unwitting conduit for coverage that does meet the standards of fairness traditional media tries to adhere to. Saying such things as "some term Pelosi" or "Pelosi is characterized by some as" technically absolves traditional media of responsibility for Pelosi's negative image; however, many readers and viewers may well not be attending to the qualifying language and just hearing that "Pelosi is" some less-than-flattering noun or adjective. Also, one should ask what traditional media cover. They cover controversy, and, in doing so, they are likely to cover Pelosi's forceful and strident side. They do not cover the mentoring conversations, the effective meetings, the successful schmoozings of either colleagues or donors, and the offering of chocolates. Traditional media did cover the rather unusual way Pelosi chose to install herself as Speaker with the children and grandchildren—hers and others'—in the forefront. That coverage, however, while softening her image and, perhaps, making her less of a b_____, may have hurt her when it came to the womb/brain and/or feminine/competent double binds. Some in the audience, then, might have responded by saying, yes, she's nicer than I thought but she's not the political leader we need either because political leaders (read: male political leaders) do not surround themselves with children in that way. She might have been accused, in some minds, of turning the floor of the U.S. House of Representatives into a daycare center.

NOTES

1. Pelosi was mentioned in 2000 as a vice-presidential candidate, evoking skepticism in print from *San Francisco Chronicle* writer March Sandalow, and *Parade* magazine did feature her a few years later as a possible first woman president. See Vincent Bzdek, *Woman of the House: The Rise of Nancy Pelosi* (New York: Palgrave Macmillan, 2008), pp. 126, 151.

2. Biographical information about Pelosi is gleaned from two primary sources: Bzdek, *Woman of the House*; and Marc Sandalow, *Madam Speaker: Nancy Pelosi's Life, Times, and Rise to Power* (New York: Modern Times, 2008).

3. Russell Berman, "'Speaker' Details Pelosi's Rise to Power," *The Hill*, May 21, 2010.

4. Bzdek, *Woman of the House*, p. 152.

5. Edward Epstein, "Stronger Than Ever After 20 Years: Pelosi Marks Milestone, Having Risen from Quiet Obscurity to Become House's Leading Voice," *San Francisco Chronicle*, June 10, 2007; Jennifer Steinhauer, "With the House in the Balance, Pelosi Serves as a Focal Point for Both Parties," *New York Times*, October 30, 2006.

6. Ronald M. Peters, Jr., and Cindy Simon Rosenthal, *Speaker Nancy Pelosi and the New American Politics* (New York: Oxford University Press, 2010).

7. Glenn Thrush, "Pelosi Laughs Off Plummeting Popularity with the Public[;] House Speaker Says Her Leadership is Effective," *Star-Ledger* (Newark), July 28, 2009.

8. Laurie Kellman, "Dems Dominant; Pelosi Promises to Govern 'from the Middle,'" *Chicago Sun-Times*, November 6, 2008.

9. Pelosi's statements and speeches are quoted from press releases and press archives at her Congressional website, http://pelosi.house.gov/news.

10. Marc Sandalow, "Election Aftermath: How Pelosi Propelled Democrats to Power; As Minority Leader, She Got Members to Stick Together, Recruited Moderates as Candidates and Raised Millions of Dollars," *San Francisco Chronicle*, November 10, 2006.

11. Josephine Hearn, "Pelosi: It's Definition Time for Democrats," *The Hill*, June 13, 2006.

12. Bob Dart, "Political Aftershock: Nancy Pelosi; The Next Speaker Wins Praise for Her Tough Pragmatism; Critics Say Her Style is Abrasive and Confrontational," *Atlanta Journal-Constitution*, November 9, 2006.

13. "Pelosi's Failure," *Washington Times*, July 21, 2008.

14. Zachary Coile, "Pelosi Chastises Lieberman for Attack on Obama," *San Francisco Chronicle*, August 14, 2008.

15. Ian Bishop, "VP Spanks Nancy for 'Behavior' Problem," *New York Post*, April 6, 2007; Carolyn Lochhead, "No Letup as Republicans Keep Blasting Pelosi for Comments; CIA Controversy," *San Francisco Chronicle*, May 22, 2009.

16. Joel Connelly, "Desperate GOP Sets Its Sights on Pelosi," *The Seattle Post-Intelligencer*, October 16, 2006; Joe Garofoli, "GOP Candidates Parlay Dislike of Pelosi into Fundraising Push," *San Francisco Chronicle*, March 27, 2010.

17. Michael Goodwin, "The Mouth That Roared Could Stymie Dems," *Daily News* (New York), May 21, 2006; Sheldon Alberts, "Polarizing Leader Seeks New

Role; U.S. Speaker Nancy Pelosi Faces Dark Days; Last-Minute Plea Falls in Deaf Democrats Ears," *Nanaimo Daily News* (Brtitish Columbia), November 13, 2010; Ben Wolfgang, "Holden Says Pelosi is Responsible for Democrats' Losses, Should Step Down as Party Leader," *Republican & Herald* (Pottsville, PA), November 6, 2010.

18. Kathleen Hall Jamieson, *Beyond the Double Bond: Women and Leadership* New (York: Oxford University Press, 1995).

19. See Bzdek, *Woman of the House,* pp. 116–118.

20. Deborah Robson and Jane Blakenship, "A 'Feminine Style' in Women's Political Discourse: An Exploratory Essay," *Communication Quarterly,* Vol. 43, No. 3 (2005) pp. 353–366.

21. Peters and Rosenthal, *Speaker Nancy Pelosi,* pp. 224–225.

22. Robin Tolmach Lakoff, "The Politics of Nice," *Journal of Politeness Research,* Vol. 1 (2005), p. 175.

23. Ibid., p. 177.

24. Ibid., p. 178.

25. Ibid., p. 180.

26. Ibid.

27. A good account of the negative commentary Pelosi has evoked is found in Peters and Rosenthal's study.

7

Olympia Snowe:
Seeking a Sensible Center

"Essential to the success and stability of any government is the equal voice and participation of women."

—Olympia J. Snowe[1]

During the early months of Wisconsin Republican Senator Joseph McCarthy's campaign to expose Communists and Soviet spies who were allegedly infiltrating the U.S. government, neither Democrats nor Republicans challenged their colleague's claims in a floor speech. On June 1, 1950, that changed when Maine's Republican Senator Margaret Chase Smith rose to speak on the Senate floor and delivered her Declaration of Conscience. Without ever naming McCarthy, she spoke of "a serious national condition that could result in national suicide and the end of everything that we Americans hold dear." She decried the lack of leadership that was turning the Senate into "a forum of hate and character assassination." She described the perspective from which she spoke: "I speak as a Republican. I speak as a woman. I speak as a United States Senator. I speak as an American."[2]

Those same words easily describe the approach Maine's second woman senator, Olympia J. Bouchles Snowe, has taken since her election to the U.S. House of Representatives in 1978. Snowe may disagree with her party's president or leadership, but she is philosophically comfortable as a Republican, just as Nancy Kassebaum was although she also frequently disagreed with leadership. Snowe does not call attention to herself as a woman candidate, but she has dedicated her career to improving women's lives. Many elements of her style fit a more feminine approach to governing. She is one of the most highly respected members of the Senate, and she puts the country's needs above party and political gamesmanship. Thus, Snowe, like

103

Smith, is known for her independence, her intelligence, and her integrity. Those qualities have brought her praise for her bipartisan approach, but they have also brought criticism from members of her own party. In many respects, her moderate positions have made it impossible for her to rise to a position on a national ticket.

A LIFE OF TRAGEDY AND TRIUMPH

Olympia Bouchles was born February 21, 1947, in Maine's capital of Augusta to a Greek immigrant father and a first-generation mother with roots in Sparta.[3] By the time she was ten she had lost both parents—her mother to breast cancer and her father from a heart attack. She was sent to live with an aunt and uncle and their five children in Auburn, Maine, and her brother was sent to live with other relatives. A year later her uncle also died. After her mother's death, her father had sent her to a Greek Orthodox girls' boarding school in Garrison, New York, which she continued to attend for five years after her relatives' guardianship commenced. She traveled by train to visit her family, first her father and brother and then her aunt and cousins, often having to change trains at Grand Central station where she once had to spend the night sleeping on a bench. She considered her early life experiences to be instrumental in creating her independent spirit as much as being from independent spirited Maine. Her sophomore year, she returned home to attend high school. She graduated from the University of Maine in Orono in 1969 with a major in political science. After graduation she married Peter Snowe, a friend of one of her cousin's who shared her interest in politics.

Both Snowes began their political careers soon after their marriage. Olympia was elected to the local Board of Voter Registration and then went to work on the staff of freshman Congressman William Cohen who later served in the Senate and as President Clinton's Secretary of Defense. Peter Snowe was elected to the Maine House of Representatives in 1972, but shortly after taking office in 1973 was killed in a car accident. Olympia Snowe ran for his seat in a special election and succeeded her husband just as Margaret Chase Smith had replaced her husband in Congress after his death. Snowe served in the Maine House until 1977 and then entered the Maine Senate for two years until she won the seat previously held by Congressman Cohen who was elected to the Senate in 1978. It was the same year that Geraldine Ferraro was elected to Congress from Queens. Snowe became the youngest Republican woman at thirty-one and the first Greek-American woman elected to Congress. In 1994 she was elected to the U.S. Senate succeeding Democrat Majority Leader George Mitchell who retired. That election gave her the distinction of being the first woman in the United States to be elected to both houses of her state legislature and to both houses of Congress.

Senator Snowe has enjoyed great popularity, easily winning most of her election contests and experiencing approval ratings as high as 79 percent in 2006.[4] She won her first House race over her Democrat challenger by 10 points. In her first reelection bid in 1980 she won by the astounding margin of 57 points. Of her six remaining House races the last two were close with winning margins of only three and seven percentage points. However, she quickly rebounded and won her first Senate race in 1994—a year that saw sweeping Republican victories—by a margin of 60–36 percent, defeating the other member of the House from Maine, Tom Andrews. She was reelected with 69 percent of the vote in 2000. In 2006, a year in which Democrats regained control of the both houses, she defeated Jean Hay Bright, an author and organic farmer, 74–20. This was the election that put the first woman, Nancy Pelosi, into the Speaker's seat in the House.

During Snowe's tenure, the number of women in the Senate has grown to 17 percent. Research shows that "women act as vigorous advocates for women's interests. . . . Women perceive themselves as representatives of women and women's interests. They have introduced more initiatives concerning women, children, and families to the legislative agenda."[5] Snowe has certainly made a difference on women's issues even with smaller numbers of women in Congress than currently serve. She was an integral part of the bipartisan Congressional Caucus for Women's Issues and served as co-chair with Patricia Schroeder. The Caucus advocated for the Family and Medical Leave Act and the Civil Rights Act of 1991 that protects women from employment discrimination. Snowe was instrumental in calling out the National Institutes of Health (NIH) for concentrating research on major diseases on male subjects to the point of not including women in clinical trials related to heart health. The Caucus's work, with Snowe as a leader, helped to establish the Office of Women's Health at the NIH. "The Caucus introduced the Women's Health Equity Act (WHEA), an omnibus package of 22 bills in the areas of research, services, and prevention" for a wide variety of women's health issues.[6] In introducing another important piece of legislation, the Economic Equity Act of 1987, Snowe explained the complexity of women's issues in that they involve not just women: "Balancing the competing interests, the demands and needs of working families is the center of the lives of millions of American women and, to an unprecedented extent, the lives of their husbands, employers and children."[7]

While serving in the House for sixteen years, Snowe was one of only two members of the Maine delegation. From 1983–1987 the other was John McKernan, Jr., an attorney and Republican activist, who went on to become Maine's governor from 1987 to 1995. McKernan was instrumental in convincing Snowe to run for Congress in 1978 even though "she says the working paper he drew up, elaborating on the hardships and obstacles of a congressional campaign, nearly caused her to abandon the idea."[8] In what was described as "possibly . . . the most poorly kept secret east of the Piscataqua,"[9] the two dated for ten years. On February 24, 1989, Governor John McKernan and Representative Olympia Snowe were married. She became the only state first lady to serve simultaneously in Congress. Snowe admitted that the loss of her first husband "prolonged the courtship" with McKernan. She explained the journey she made from a young widow to confident Congresswoman and new wife:

> I don't believe I could have jumped into another marriage until I was absolutely certain of where I was going in life. I knew I had to develop my own sense of professionalism and be comfortable with what I was doing first. You have to have your own identity. It's important for women. I think it's important not only for their own self-fulfillment, but also for their own future security.[10]

While some Democrats hoped that the political marriage might lead to a retirement,[11] the political power couple maintained their separate careers while simultaneously serving the people of Maine. The only time when one career potentially affected the other was when McKernan was wrapping up a second term, which saw his popularity drop, and Snowe was running for a first term in the Senate. Voters were encouraged to send a message about McKernan by not voting for Snowe, but most "voters were clearly capable of distinguishing her record and her skills from those of her very public husband."[12]

Less than two years after their marriage, McKernan and Snowe suffered another tragedy when McKernan's twenty-year-old son, Peter, collapsed after a run and died several days later. Snowe told an interviewer that "his is the one death that still haunts her."[13] Snowe believes that the tragedies she suffered in her life provide her with the empathy she needs to represent her constituents. She explained:

> I understand when people are suffering. My family—we didn't have a lot. And, you know, terrible things happened. You just have to pick yourself up and say, "Now what do I do?" And hopefully there are people there to help you through, one way or another. . . . In some ways, I look at my job as making it work for people. That's what I do.[14]

Toni Bernay, a psychologist who studied women leaders, described how Snowe's past influenced her as a legislator: "She swore that no other little girl should have to go through this. She wanted to work for better health care. That became her leitmotif. . . . Women are passionate about causes and decide to run for office so they can effect change."[15] Whether it was in the Maine legislature or both houses of the U.S. Congress, Olympia Snowe has been tireless in finding ways to "make it work" not only for women, but for her Maine constituents and her fellow Americans. Her rhetoric reflects her compassion and passion as well as her attention to the underlying facts that motivate her positions and implications of policy making.

A MODERATE VOICE

In a 2004 interview on National Public Radio Democrat Senator Kent Conrad of North Dakota and Olympia Snowe discussed the difficulty of being in the political middle of their respective parties. Snowe explained the situation as one in which "the sensible Senate has eroded over the last 10 years with the loss of consensus-forging leaders." She explained that there was a need to create a coalition with "the willingness to search for that common ground, because ultimately, I happen to believe that that is the blueprint by which we can extricate ourselves from this confrontational morass that has characterized the operations of the United States Senate, particularly in recent years."[16] An examination of speeches made during legislative debate or hearings, epideictic speeches on a variety of topics, and interviews provides insight into Olympia Snowe's independent character and values as well as her rhetorical style. Snowe has an easy delivery technique that is more conversational than formal with a noticeable Maine accent in her voice and lively facial expressions. Her style suits her message of connecting issues directly to constituents and presenting facts in a reasoned, organized manner. Her Congressional speeches employ few rhetorical flourishes choosing rather to emphasize statistics, examples, and unanswered questions in her straightforward statements. Her ceremonial speeches reveal her compassionate and humble side.

Having spent over half of her life in legislative bodies, Snowe thinks and speaks like a legislator first and foremost. The majority of her formal rhetoric is related to legislation. Her official Senate website has a YouTube link with multiple examples of her committee and floor speeches.[17] Regardless of the topic, Snowe's speeches have several common characteristics. First is an explication of her philosophy about good government and the most effective legislative process. Snowe's rhetoric is replete with examples of a desire for the "sensible center,"[18] which has as its hallmarks consensus building, collaboration, and common ground. Language about responsibility and doing something "right" is common. Second is her adherence to her philosophy about "doing it right" through use of facts and analysis based on the policy's soundness. She is essentially a "policy wonk" who engages in the research and knows the questions to ask about what isn't there as well as what is. Last is her attention to both her Maine constituents and the larger public interest as exemplified by her use of references to constituents and to what Americans think about an issue. She described her decision-making process when examining a piece of legislation, and implicit in the statement is her emphasis on bipartisanship, and doing what is right:

> I believed it was important to evaluate the facts, look at the issue, and determine whether or not this was the most effective solution to the problem at hand, irrespective of whether it was a Republican, Democratic, conservative, or liberal idea. The question was "Is it a good idea?"[19]

In an interview at a 2010 forum sponsored by *Fortune* recognizing powerful women, Snowe further elucidated her belief about the basic tenets of public service and their relationship to good government. In response to a question about what she meant by the phrase "process dictates product," she explained in terms that again emphasized the art of compromise, review, and government over politics:

> First of all, determining the facts. Not using three talking points. It's so customary in Washington these days to get three, four talking points. Talking points don't make the legislation. And I think we've lost the art of legislating. That means getting the facts, drafting the legislation, drafting the provisions, actually reading those provisions, understanding the effects and implications. . . . We aren't doing our homework. . . . Public service is about solving problems. That's what it's all about. And that's my definition of public service. If that is my objective to see there's a problem, how can we solve it? And I approach every problem with the mindset I plan to solve it. And nothing is insurmountable if there is the political will to do it. . . . We haven't done our jobs well in Washington. . . . [We've lost] the sensible center. It's where most Americans are. It has dissipated in the political process. If we lose that, that's not good for Maine and it's not good for America. . . . It's all about campaigning. It's never about governing. . . . People just aren't listening anymore to one another. They are listening to those with whom they agree. They aren't listening to those with whom they disagree. And that's fundamentally wrong.[20]

In late 2009 Congress was again tackling health care reform. Snowe was a member of the "group of six" that worked to build compromise. She was the only Republican to vote the Senate bill out of committee but later voted against the final version because of changes that were made without the thorough review of economic impact that she called for. After the committee vote in October 2009, Chris Matthews interviewed Snowe on MSNBC's *Hardball* about her role and the prospect of passage. Snowe outlined what would have to happen to gain bipartisan support and ease the minds of citizens in both Maine and throughout the rest of the country:

> We have to work in a methodical, practical way not with arbitrary deadlines in sorting through these issues. As you know this is highly complex. It is costly.

Given the context of the times in which we find ourselves people are apprehensive and concerned about whether Congress will give it the right amount of attention and forethought to do it right . . . and that we don't create unintended and perverse consequences.[21]

In her speeches and statements regarding the health care debate, Snowe made it clear that Congress had not exerted what she considered to be appropriate due diligence. In November 2009 Snowe spoke out on the floor and urged Congress to have all of the facts before moving forward. She described the effort as "one of the most complex and intricate undertakings the Congress has ever confronted" and urged an "effective, common-sense and bi-partisan" approach to crafting the legislation. She accused Democrats of an "artificially generated haste" intended "to ram it and jam it" through the process without having complete information on important economic aspects" of reform initiatives.[22] In December she issued a statement with specific details to underscore her objections to a hasty vote. In the statement she demonstrated her propensity for research and arguments well supported by data, her ability to ask tough questions, and her belief that public servants have a responsibility to do their work in a way that is thorough and accountable to the American people. The following excerpt from that statement is consistent with her philosophical statements about public servants and her belief that good legislation is well-researched legislation:

Furthermore, we still don't have answers to some of the most fundamental questions that people will be asking at their kitchen tables. These are the critical questions relevant to peoples' daily lives, such as, what does this mean for me? How much will my health insurance plan cost? How much will my deductible or my co-pay be? How much am I going to have to pay out of pocket? Not one single member in Congress—Republican or Democrat—can answer those questions, and that is why I wrote to the Congressional Budget Office on December 3rd requesting a complete analysis of these and other key issues as it is imperative that we have those answers before proceeding.

Ultimately, there is absolutely no reason to be hurtling headlong to a Christmas deadline on monumental legislation affecting every American, when it doesn't even fully go into effect until 2014. When 51 percent of the American people in a recent survey have said they do not approve of what we are doing, they understand what Congress does not—and that is, that time is not our enemy, it is our friend. Therefore, we must take a time out from this legislative game of "beat the clock," reconvene in January—instead of taking a three week recess—and spend the time necessary to get this right. Legislation affecting more than 300 million Americans deserves better than midnight votes on a bill that cannot be further amended and that no one has had the opportunity to fully consider—and the Senate must step up to its responsibility as the world's greatest deliberative body on behalf of the American people.[23]

A cross-section of statements Snowe has made over her thirty-two-year history in Congress illustrates that the diligent approach she took on health care reform was not unique. She does her homework and she analyzes the situation in order to prevent unintended and perverse consequences. She lives her definition of what public service should be by holding hearings that bring the facts to light. She includes statistics and other data that apply to both Maine and the country. She holds her Congressional colleagues to a high standard of governing. One example comes from a 1999 town meeting on the status of the VA Hospital in Togus, Maine. She once again demanded answers before action: "Even with the increase [in funding], important questions remain about funding, referrals to Boston, understaffing, access, and a range of other issues. . . . Changes must be carefully scrutinized and understood by veterans, and the VA must be held accountable." She went on to outline actions that needed to be taken before decisions about the hospital's status within the system was decided and she expressed her commitment to her responsibility as Maine's senator, using characteristic language calling for collaboration: "The obligation I feel to Maine veterans is enormous, and it is an obligation that I strive to fulfill every day in the U.S. Senate. I hope that the VA will begin to work with us to rebuild the trust in the VA that has been lost."[24]

A second example relates to job creation as a way to help the country rebound from the prolonged recession that started in 2008. Snowe issued statements in May 2011 in response to the Small Business Regulatory Freedom Act and in September 2011 to President Obama's speech to a joint session of Congress on jobs. In the first, Snowe's Republican philosophy of reducing regulation as a key to job growth was the focus. Her statement again reflects her desire for careful study and it emphasizes bipartisan collaboration—a hallmark of her approach. In this excerpt, she also relies on what she learned from talking to constituents. In the *Fortune* interview, Snowe explained that she returns to Maine nearly every weekend and listens to what concerns her constituents. She claimed that by doing so, she didn't need to conduct polls. The talks she has on Main Street become an important part of her arguments:

> Regulations require regular review. When I talk with business owners in Maine and elsewhere, the single most cited barrier to job growth is the uncertainty about federal regulations. The cost of ensuring compliance with the evermore complex web of mandates and regulations is choking employers' ability to innovate and create jobs. . . . Our amendment incorporates ideas supported by Republicans and Democrats, and will achieve our shared goal of reducing the regulatory burden faced by job creators.[25]

Four months later in her response to the president's address, she repeated the theme about regulation and included statistics to bolster arguments growing from the anecdotal evidence she received in Maine:

At the root of this crisis is the stark lack of a climate conducive to job creation. In Maine, I have convened business roundtables, met with small business owners, held Main Street tours and talked with people from all walks of life. Without exception, potential job creators are yearning for predictability, consistency and permanence in the policies emanating from government. . . . Small businesses, simply by the nature of their size, currently face an annual regulatory cost of $10,585 per employee and shoulder a regulatory compliance cost more than 30 percent higher than larger firms. Leveling that field for small business could save an average $32,000 for a 10-person firm which is enough to hire one additional person. Across our economy, that would open opportunities for millions of people.[26]

Other legislation produced similar arguments. Her attention to detail was evident in February 2010 when she urged Health and Human Services Secretary Kathleen Sebelius "to reexamine the formula that is being used to distribute emergency funding from the Low-Income Home Energy Assistant Program (LIHEAP)." Snowe's reasons were based on a careful study of methodology, which she believed contradicted the program's intent:

I am deeply troubled by the methodology used to determine the release of emergency funds for this program. This year alone, we have seen a radical difference in the amount of funding that was distributed to certain states and this was based on logic that demonstrates a lack of understanding of the intent of the LIHEAP program.[27]

While these examples illustrate a highly reasoned and technical approach to constructing her arguments, Snowe's rhetoric is not completely devoid of emotional language or literary devices such as metaphor or alliteration. In a *Wall Street Journal* opinion article that she co-authored with Senator Jim DeMint, she argued for a balanced budget amendment. In addition to the typical statistical evidence, the article also expounded on the values the two senators upheld to guide decision making:

As senators and representatives, we take an oath to uphold the Constitution. By amending the Constitution, Congress will be forever bound to match our nation's expenditures with our revenues. Toothless resolutions and statutory speed bumps have proven easy to evade or ignore. Indeed, the reason many lawmakers don't want a balanced budget amendment is the exact reason why we need it: It would permanently end the types of legislative trickery that have now brought our country to the fiscal brink. . . . A constitutional amendment to balance the budget is imperative if we are to provide continuity of fiscal responsibility, and ensure that we never return to the recklessness of the past and present. It's time Congress passed the amendment and gave the states—and "We the People" their say.[28]

Snowe's epideictic speaking is far less extensive than her deliberative. However, a few examples indicate that the type of language she used in the

Wall Street Journal piece works its way into more formal ceremonial speaking. At a reception following her swearing-in for a third term in the Senate, she relied on alliteration once again to articulate her governing philosophy. She said, "There is strength in compromise, courage in conciliation, and honor in consensus."[29] In a tribute on the first anniversary of 9-11, she employed antithesis and irony throughout, with statements such as: "We're moved to grieve for what and who we lost, while we embrace all that we have retained as a nation, the hearts of Americans and freedom-loving people across the globe are beckoned at once by sorrow and resolve—and we should heed the call of both," and "In a horrific irony, the forces of darkness has their way on an especially bright and beautiful morning."[30]

Snowe also calls on American icons to reinforce her government philosophy. In a response to President Clinton's radio address in 2000, she invoked the memory of Dr. Martin Luther King as she looked forward to a new millennium—one which she described as characterized by opportunity and optimism—to call for collaboration:

> On this weekend when we celebrate the life of Martin Luther King, Jr., we are reminded that our nation is at its strongest when we work past our differences, when we move forward together, united in our vision, and inspired by a shared desire to create a better, more advanced world for the next generation.[31]

Similarly, in her September 11 remembrance, she reminded us of Abraham Lincoln's words at Gettysburg: "It is for us the living . . . to be dedicated here to the unfinished work which they who fought here have thus far so nobly advanced. It is . . . for us to be here dedicated to the great task remaining before us." She then used those words to remind Americans that such is the American spirit: "That is our call yet again today, as we defend freedom from the blunt and bloody instruments of terror and fear. That is the destiny to which we must rise. And let there be no mistake—we are equal to the challenge."[32]

When taken as a whole, Olympia Snowe's rhetoric is a combination of intelligent analysis tempered with a compassionate understanding that laws affect people and a philosophical premise that good government is good politics. One last example illustrates how she takes any opportunity to espouse her philosophy and apply her brand of logic. In her speech accepting the Alice (Paul) Award on September 21, 2011, Senator Olympia Snowe paid tribute to Alice Paul and leading suffrage advocates Elizabeth Cady Stanton, Susan B. Anthony, and Lucretia Mott by explaining how the statue commissioned by Paul and the National Women's Party of the three heroines had languished for seventy-five years in the Capitol basement before its installation in 1997. She recounted objections that it weighed too much, that it was unattractive, would cost too much to move. . . . So I said that it begs the question of how all of the other statues, male statues I might add, ended up in the rotunda. [But] it wasn't about the weight of a statue; it was about the weight of an argument and the worthiness of a cause because it does matter what adorns the rotunda. It's the epicenter of democracy.[33]

Olympia Snowe's roots are at the epicenter of democracy and perhaps it is her Greek heritage that causes her to care so much about deliberation and a public voice in her decision making.

WHY NOT MADAM PRESIDENT?

A review of Olympia Snowe's credentials presents a picture of experience, competence, and distinctions that should catapult a senator into national prominence and consideration for a spot on a presidential ticket. In 2006 *Time Magazine* named Senator Snowe one of the top U.S. senators. The list included headliners Ted Kennedy, John McCain, Arlen Specter, and Richard Lugar. Snowe was the only woman from among the sixteen serving in the Senate who was selected.[34] In recognizing her as "The Provider," *Time* described her this way:

Because of her centrist views and eagerness to get beyond partisan point scoring, Maine Republican Olympia Snowe is in the center of every policy debate in Washington. Last year she was one of 14 Senators who reached a compromise on President Bush's judicial nominees that prevented a Senate meltdown between the two parties. More recently, she helped craft an agreement to increase congressional oversight of the Administration's no-warrant surveillance program, helping ease tensions between the Senate and the White House.[35]

The same year that *Time* recognized her, the White House Project listed her as one of "8 in 08." Snowe, fellow Maine Senator Susan Collins, and Senate colleagues Hillary Clinton and Kay Bailey Hutchison, along with Atlanta Mayor Shirley Franklin, Secretary of State Condoleezza Rice, and Governors Janet Napolitano and Kathleen Sebelius rounded out the list.[36] In 1988 she appeared along with Kassebaum on a long speculative list of potential vice presidential running mates for Vice President George Bush; however, her name was not the source of much speculation. *Congressional Quarterly* "cited her for her centrist leadership" in 1999.[37] During her time in the House, she "co-chaired the Congressional Caucus on Women's Issues for 10 years and provided leadership in establishing the Office of Women's Health at the National Institutes of Health." In 2005 *Forbes* listed her as the fifty-fourth most powerful woman in the world largely because of the weight of her vote on several key issues and her position on the Senate Finance Committee "with jurisdiction over two-thirds of the entire federal budget."[38]

Snowe's committee assignments and responsibilities gave her the necessary background on key issues to hold her own on any national political stage. Her House assignments included Budget, Foreign Affairs, and Subcommittees on International Operations and Human Services. In addition to her Senate seat on Finance, she also served on or currently serves on the Armed Services Committee, Committee on Small Business & Entrepreneurship, the Subcommittee on Health Care, the Select Committee on Intelligence, and the Committee on Commerce, Science & Transportation. In 2003 when the Republicans recaptured the Senate majority she became chair of the Committee on Small Business and Entrepreneurship and chair of the Subcommittee on Sea Power.

She is best known, however, not for her formal roles but for her bipartisanship. She co-chairs with Democrat Senator Mary Landrieu a consensus-building group called the Common Ground Coalition. During her House tenure she was known as a "Gypsy Moth"—one of the Northeastern Republicans who teamed with Southern Democrat "Boll Weevils," to forge bipartisan consensus. In 2005 she was part of a group in the Senate known as the "Gang of 14" that "defused a confrontation between Senate Democrats (who were filibustering several judicial nominees) and the Senate Republican leadership (who wanted to use the nominations as a flashpoint to eliminate filibusters on nominees through the so-called nuclear option)."[39]

Such a record should demonstrate a person's electability when combined with the high popularity ratings Snowe has with both independents and Democrats in her home state. However, Snowe's party tends to select more conservative candidates for president, and Snowe's independence, liberal voting record on issues such as abortion, and breaks with her party's presidents and party leaders, have resulted in her never being a serious candidate for either position on a Republican ticket. Snowe "voted with the American Conservative Union only 28 percent of the time in 2007; no other Republican in the U.S. Senate more often voted in opposition to the positions favored by these conservative groups."[40] Conservative groups frequently label her a RINO—Republican in Name Only. Snowe defends her positions by arguing that she reflects her constituency and as a "lifelong Republican" other members of her party "could probably borrow more from me in that sense, in terms of being in touch with your constituents."[41]

After her original support of "Obamacare" and the rise of the conservative Republican "Tea Party," Snowe's popularity began to decline among Maine Republicans. In September 2010, 63 percent of Maine Republicans were ready to replace her—up slightly from 59 percent after her committee vote on health care the previous year. Maine's Republican party is dominated by conservatives who make up 70 percent of the party's voters.[42] A poll in March 2011 showed that Snowe would have a difficult time winning a Republican primary if it were held then but if she ran as an independent, she would win a fourth term:

> Yesterday we showed that Olympia Snowe would have a very difficult time winning the Republican nomination for another term in the Senate from Maine. Our general election numbers in the state show that there is one easy way she could return to the body in 2013 though—running as an independent. In four match ups we tested that included Snowe as an independent along with a Democrat (we looked at Rosa Scarcelli and Emily Cain) and a Republican (we looked at Scott D'Amboise and Andrew Ian Dodge) she gets anywhere from 54–57% of the vote, finishing in first place with Democrats, Republicans, and independents alike. Despite her mediocre numbers within her own party, Snowe's overall approval rating of 60% to 32% disapproval makes her one of the most popular Senators in the country. That's because her numbers with Democrats (67% approval) and independents (63% approval) far outrun her standing with Republicans (just 49% approval).[43]

In addition to problems with the conservative base of the party, Snowe is also experiencing attacks on her husband's credibility. While there were virtually no problems with their joint political careers, like other women politicians (Geraldine Ferraro and Diane Feinstein), Snowe has found that her husband's business affairs are fair game. A potential Republican primary challenger called on Snowe to resign as a result of a lawsuit filed against the for-profit college for which her husband serves as chair of the board. Snowe called the attacks a "smear campaign" and "libelous."[44]

As this is written, the election is over a year away and that is multiple political lifetimes. What lies in the future for Senator Snowe is the talk of pundits and politicos from both parties, but Snowe continues to do what she has always done. She returns to Maine, she talks to people, she decries Congress's all-time low public approval ratings saying, "I'm embarrassed by all of us."[45] And she continues to espouse her philosophy of governance. At the Alice awards ceremony on September 21, 2011, Senator Snowe praised her Senate colleague Dianne Feinstein and her former House colleague Lindy Boggs—both Democrats. She closed her remarks with the following:

> You can only solve problems by talking to people with whom you disagree to get anything done, and we have to relearn the legislative process here in the United States government. That's my commitment. That was the spirit that I brought to my early years serving in the House of Representatives and doing what I thought was important on behalf of women's issues but also was important for this country. The obstacles before this great nation of ours are not insurmountable if we refuse to be intractable. And I think we should jettison the red and the blue states and unite under the red, white, and blue.

Olympia Snowe will never hold the title of Madame President or Vice President, but in the big picture, that may not be as important as the what she has brought to the Congress of the United States that resulted in advances for women, putting members of both parties on notice to remember why they are there, and brokering deals that moved the process along. While Olympia Snowe occasionally despairs of the lack of the "sensible center," she remains firmly in that spot and as long as she is in the Senate, she will continue to make democracy work as it should.

NOTES

1. "Snowe Leads Senate Women in Renewed Call for Women's Rights," Press Release, March 28, 2011, http://snowe.senate.gov/public/index.cfm/2011/3/snowe-leads-senate-women-in-renewed-call-for-women-s-rights (accessed September 20, 2011).

2. Margaret Chase Smith, *Declaration of Conscience* (Garden City, NY: Doubleday & Company, 1972), p. 13.

3. Biographical information on Olympia Snowe is taken from Martha Sherrill, "Olympia Snowe: Listening is Everything," *Kennebec Journal*, May 8, 2011, www.kjonline.com/news/olympia-snowe-listening-is-everything_2011-05-08.html (accessed August 15, 2011); "United States Senator Olympia Snowe Biography," http://snowe.senate.gov/public/index.cfm/biography (accessed August 15, 2011); "Senator Snowe at Fortune's Most Powerful Women Forum," October 21, 2010, www.senate.gov/cgi-bin/exitmsg?url=http://www.youtube.com/watch?v=0Q1DxY_ecbg (accessed September 2, 2011); and "Olympia Snowe," *Wikipedia*, http://en.wikipedia.org/wiki/Olympia_Snowe (accessed August 15, 2011).

4. Olympia Snowe videos, www.videosurf.com/olympia-snowe-126743 (accessed September 1, 2011).

5. Julie Dolan, Melissa Deckman, and Michele L. Swers, *Women and Politics: Paths to Power and Political Influence*, 2nd ed. (Boston: Longman, 2011), p. 240.

6. Patricia Schroeder and Olympia J. Snowe, "The Co-Chairs' Report: The Congressional Caucus for Women's Issues in the 102nd Congress," in Paul Ries and Anne J. Stone (eds.), *The American Woman 1992–93: A StatusReport* (New York: W.W. Norton & Company, 1992), p. 442.

7. "Women's Rights Bills Offered," *Chicago Sun-Times*, June 4, 1987, www.highbeam.com/doc/1P2-3829141.html (accessed September 20, 2011).

8. Ellen J. Bartlett, "A Marriage Made in the House," *Boston Globe*, February 23, 1989, www.highbeam.com/doc/1P2-8109451.html (accessed September 20, 2011).

9. Ibid.

10. Ibid.

11. Ibid.

12. Linda Witt, Karen M. Paget, and Glenna Matthews, *Running as a Woman: Gender and Power in American Politics* (New York: Free Press, 1994), p. 296.

13. Ibid.

14. Martha Sherrill, "Olympia Snowe: Listening is Everything."

15. Paula Voell, "Making Girls into Leaders: Authors Look at the Backgrounds of Powerful Political Women," *Buffalo News*, May 15, 1992, www.highbeam.com/doc/1P2-22403010.html (accessed September 20, 2011).

16. Steve Inskeep, "Interview: Olympia Snowe and Kent Conrad Talk About Being Moderates," *NPR Morning Edition*, November 26, 2004, www.highbeam.com/doc/1P1-102858846.html (accessed September 1, 2011).

17. http://snowe.senate.gov/public/index.cfm/videoclips.

18. Ron Schechter, "How Do You Succeed as a Maverick in Your Own Party?" *Yankee*, March/April 2007, p. 102.

19. Ron Schechter, "How Do You Succeed as a Maverick in Your Own Party?" p. 102.

20. "Senator Snowe at Fortune's Most Powerful Women Forum."

21. Chris Matthews, "Olympia Snowe—The Only Republican to Vote Obamacare out of Committee," YouTube, www.youtube.com/watch?v=NhimkgtSr5c (accessed September 19, 2011).

22. "Olympia Snowe Is Right," *Wall Street Journal*, December 10, 2009, http://online.wsj.com/article/SB10001424052748704007804574573841915542278.html (accessed September 1, 2011).

23. Olympia Snowe, "Political Positions of Olympia Snowe: Health Care, December 2009," *The Political Guide*, www.thepoliticalguide.com/rep_bios.php?rep_id=68597412&category=views&id=20100528161059 (accessed September 1, 2011).

24. Capitol Hill Press Releases, "Statement of U.S. Senator Olympia J. Snowe on Maintaining Services at the Togus VA Hospital," *Capitol Hill Press Releases*, October 27, 1999, www.highbeam.com/doc/1P1-29422525.html (accessed September 20, 2011).

25. "It's the Economy (and the Four R's)—Senator Olympia Snowe," *States News Service*, May 3, 2011, www.highbeam.com/doc/1G1-255262498.html (accessed September 2, 2011).

26. "Sen. Snowe Reaction to POTUS Jobs Speech," *States News Service*, September 8, 2011, www.highbeam.com/doc/1G1-266511208.html (accessed September 20, 2011).

27. "Snowe Blasts Administration for Cutting Critical Funds for LIHEAP Program," *States News Service*, www.highbeam.com/doc/1G1-218160767.html (accessed September 2, 2011).

28. Olympia Snowe and Jim DeMint, "The Only Reform That Will Restrain Spending," *Wall Street Journal* (Eastern edition), July 7, 2011, www2.lib.ku.edu:2048/login?url-http://proquest.umi.com/pqdweb?did=2392464421&Fmt=3&clientld=42567&RQT=309&VName=PQD (accessed September 10, 2011).

29. "Sen. Snowe Sworn in for Third Term in U.S. Senate," *US Fed News Service*, January 5, 2007, www.highbeam.com/doc/1P3-1190236491.html (accessed September 20, 2011).

30. "Statement of U.S. Senator Olympia J. Snowe Commemorating the Anniversary of September 11th," *Capitol Hill Press Releases*, wwww.highbeam.com/doc/1P1-67371278.html (accessed September 20, 2011).

31. Olympia Snowe, "Senator Olympia Snowe Delivers Republican Response to the President's Radio Address," *Washington Transcript Service*, January 15, 2000, www.highbeam.com/doc/1P1-29451753.html (accessed September 20, 2011).

32. "Statement of U.S. Senator Olympia J. Snowe Commemorating the Anniversary of September 11th."

33. "Snowe Honored for Breaking Gender Barriers," September 21, 2011, http://snowe.senate.gov/public/ (accessed September 23, 2011).

34. www.time.com/time/magazine/article/0,9171,1184052-7,00.html.

35. Perry Bacon, Jr. "America's 10 Best Senators," *Time*, April 24, 2006, www.time.com/time/magazine/article/0,9171,1184052,00 (accessed September 19, 2011). html#ixzz1Ye7xYNVt.

36. The White House Project, http://198.65.255.167/v2/9for08/pollbios.html (accessed November 11, 2010).

37. "United States Senator Olympia Snowe Biography."

38. Ibid.

39. "Olympia Snowe," *Wikipedia*.

40. Susan J. Carroll, "Voting Choices," in Susan J. Carroll and Richard L. Fox (eds.), *Gender and Elections: Shaping the Future of American Politics*, 2nd ed. (New York: Cambridge University Press, 2010), p. 131.

41. Stephanie Condon, "Does Olympia Snowe Still Fit in the GOP?" *CBS News*, November 4, 2009, www.cbsnews.com/2102-503544_162-5523604.html?tag=contentMain;contentBody (accessed September 22, 2011).

42. Public Policy Polling, "63% Say Trade Out Snowe," September 13, 2010, www.publicpolicypolling.blogspot.com/2010/09/63-say-trade-out-snowe.html (accessed September 23, 2011).

43. Public Policy Polling, "Snowe a Shoo-In Either as Republican or Independent," March 9, 2011,www.publicpolicypolling.com/main/olympia-snowe/ (accessed September 23, 2011).

44. Jonathan Riskind, "Snowe Calls Rival's Charges False and 'Libelous' Smears: GOP Challenger Questions Her Husband's Business Practices," *Portland Press Herald*, May 11, 2011, www.highbeam.com/doc/1P1-192536328.html (accessed September 20, 2011).

45. "Olympia Snowe on Debt Ceiling Debate: I've Never Seen a Worse Congress," *Huff Post Politics*, August 10, 2011, www.huffingtonpost.com/2011/08/10/olympia-snowe-debt-ceiling-deal_n_923348.html (accessed September 23, 2011).

8

Christine Gregoire:
A Competent Communicator

On November 4, 2008, a triumphant Christine Gregoire stepped up to the microphone flanked by her adoring family. With uncharacteristic enthusiasm and no-holds-barred joy she declared: "So! Just so you know, the race has been called by CBS, NBC, ABC and yes . . . (huge applause, cheers, and whistling) . . . my friends, America is back; we are proud; we have a new president: Barack Obama! I can't wait: January 20th history in the making, inaugurating Barack Obama!"[1]

After sharing her unbridled enthusiasm for the new president-elect, Governor Gregoire proceeded to the main purpose of the speech: to declare victory in her race for governor that would give her a second term to serve the people of Washington. Narrowly elected by less than 133 votes[2] out of 2.9 million cast in 2004, her 2008 victory must have felt especially sweet. Elected by the people of Washington by a decisive margin in her re-election effort was a clear signal that Washingtonians were pleased with her leadership. When she took office as governor in 2005 she had to overcome the disputed gubernatorial race and a two-year deficit of $1.8 billion. But those challenges were likely far from her mind when she approached the podium on election night 2008, a two-term governor obviously thrilled with herself and the outcome of Washington state's election, as well as the new opportunities for the country that electing Barack Obama as president would bring. Unabashedly she asked: "Can you imagine what Patty Murray, Maria Cantwell, and the rest of our delegation can do with that party in the White House?"[3]

In 2005 Washington State became the first state in the nation's history with an all-female trio in top elected positions. Her pride was palpable when she said: "I feel as though I must be one of the most blessed people in the entire world."[4] This speech was one of her most impassioned and jubilant in her tenure as governor, but Gregoire is not often joyful or passionate in her speeches, a liability to any politico in pursuit of a higher office, and specifically the presidency. Most of her public utterances are marked with a direct and serious tone with steady delivery and confident, focused messages. Gregoire offers no apology for her tendency to be more precise than pithy. Instead she explains: "I am a focused individual. People confuse my focus as being overly serious. I think it is one of the great challenges women politicians face. If you are too friendly, you are not tough enough and if you are serious, you are not the kind of person they can warm to."[5] Christine Gregoire's speech style is a reflection of her training as a lawyer, and many of her speeches focus on the topics of consensus building, teamwork, work ethic, family and making tough choices. When she introduces herself to her audience, she more often calls herself "Chris Gregoire" but sometimes uses the more formal "Christine."

This chapter will examine several pivotal speeches in the career of Governor Christine Gregoire, including her two inaugural addresses, the Democratic Radio Address given shortly after her first inauguration in 2005, her "State of the State" address in January, 2006, a speech she gave at the signing of Civil Rights Legislation in 2006, a speech at a race for breast cancer survivors—a topic of significance to Gregoire because of her own bout with breast cancer—and a Prayer Breakfast Speech in 2009.[6]

Sheri Keith notes, "Not only does the speaker's background matter in determining a speaking style, but also the issue(s) being addressed"[7] and Gregoire's lawyerly training is almost always evident, even in celebratory moments when precision should rightly give way to whimsy. Gregoire is a competent communicator who appears always to be an in control and focused administrator, more than a politician. Inaugurations are jubilant, and she allows for that briefly in introductions, but she wastes no time zeroing in on the economic woes of the times in which she was elected, both in her first term, and the economic recession that deepened during her second term. This analysis argues that while Gregoire has ability to lead she lacks the required magnetism, inspiration, and referent power that could take her beyond the state level of government.

BACKGROUND

Born Christine O'Grady, she was raised in Auburn, Washington, by her mother, who worked as a cook and supported the family. She rode horses, picked blueberries, and learned the value of hard work and a good education. After graduating from Auburn High School, she entered the University of Washington. She graduated with a teaching certificate and Bachelor of

Arts degrees in speech and sociology. As a speech major, she had many courses related to public speaking. She commented, "I like public speaking. It gives me a chance to be passionate about issues I care about. I get energized from it."[8] She was inspired to follow a career in law and public service by John F. Kennedy who was an inspirational leader of her generation. Christine Gregoire also graduated from the University of Washington and Gonzaga University Law School. She married Mike Gregoire, who worked as a health care investigator for the state of Washington and they have two daughters, Courtney and Michelle.

"She never missed a high-school soccer game and spent Sundays in the kitchen, cooking five meals to store in the freezer so the family could eat together during the week," said Courtney, twenty-eight.[9] Both daughters also credit their father who "spent countless hours carting them from soccer practice to piano lessons, from ballet to church groups."[10] She served as the director of the Washington Department of Ecology from 1988 until 1992, when she was first elected attorney general. She was re-elected twice. While serving as director in the department of ecology, she negotiated a tri-party agreement in 1989 with the Environmental Protection Agency and the Department of Energy to clean up waste at the Hanford Nuclear Reservation. It was during this time that Christine Gregoire's star began to rise and she gained recognition as an astute negotiator and leader. As attorney general she sued several times to try to get a more adequate cleanup progress. She was also heavily involved in the lawsuit against the tobacco industry in the 1990s and won the state a $4.5 billion share of the settlement, including a $500 million bonus for her lead role. Her assault against the tobacco industry earned her the nickname "tiger lady." Michael Moore, attorney general of Mississippi, explained: "In the talks with tobacco executives she'd go in there and really bite their heads off when she had to. We wouldn't have been able to do it to do it without her."[11] She was critical, however, when a large part of Washington State's share of the money went into the general budget and was not specifically earmarked for tobacco-related issues.

Gregoire faced controversy when in 2000 her office failed to file documents on time in an appeal of a record $17.8 million personal-injury verdict against Washington State. An independent investigation forced state attorney Janet Capps to resign. Capps later sued the state for wrongful termination. Documents from the independent investigation show that Gregoire's deputies attempted to influence the report on whom was responsible for the missed deadline. This event is considered the low point in Gregoire's career and her biggest political liability.[12] As governor, Gregoire signed a measure making Washington the second state, after California, to grant paid leave to workers after the birth of a child. She has also signed bills expanding gay rights and championed education and gambling reforms. She was viewed as a possible candidate to replace Justice David H. Souter, who announced his retirement from the Supreme Court in early 2009. President Obama eventually selected Sonia Sotomayor. In May 2010, the *Seattle Times* reported that Gov. Chris Gregoire was on the White House list to replace Elena Kagan as the solicitor general.[13]

RHETORICAL STYLE

Her no-nonsense rhetorical style may have aided her election since in 2004, the economy was a major factor for the voters of Washington. "Gregoire is defined as the candidate who will fix the economy," said Thomas Riehle, president of Ipsos-Public Affairs. He noted that "when you look at people who say the economy is worse, 72 percent are voting for Gregoire. That's almost monolithic."[14] She led Dino Rossi, a real estate executive and former state senator, 49 percent to 43 percent in many polls and was appealing to voters negatively affected by the economy. Gregoire promised that she would invest $1 million from the $1 billion from the tobacco settlement and private investment in research and infrastructure to create businesses and jobs in science companies.[15] Her rugged determination, hard work, and stamina would serve her particularly well right after the votes were cast for governor in 2004. Rossi led after the initial ballot count and the first recount. Despite calls by some Republicans to concede, Gregoire stood firm, at one point referring to Rossi's forty-two-vote margin as a "tie."[16] After a hand recount Gregoire won, but her somber speaking style, even upon her ultimate victory, reminded the audience of the long campaign, and the two grueling recounts.

In her first inaugural address she spent little time reveling in her victory and instead laid out plans for providing health insurance to all children in the state, improving education, and fixing transportation bottlenecks that plagued the Puget Sound region. That Gregoire had barely won, that her own health woes were fresh in her mind, and the crippling state economy were all reasons to keep her optimism at bay. She presented herself as pragmatically as possible when she reflected on the impressive legacy that includes technological innovation and excellent schools and businesses. She then incorporated a scheme of anaphora with the next set of utterances. Anaphora is a scheme or repetition in which successive sentences begin with or incorporate the same language. She soberly noted that while much is there to be thankful for, there is significant work to be done in Washington State. Her use of repetition in these phrases added urgency to her assertions. She said:

When citizens don't have confidence their tax dollars are being used efficiently and effectively, we have work to do.

When we lose 20 percent of our manufacturing jobs in five years, we have work to do. When half a million people have no health insurance, we have work to do.

When children start kindergarten already behind because they didn't get early education, we have work to do.

When a third of our high school students don't finish high school on time, we have work to do.

And when Hood Canal, Puget Sound, Lake Roosevelt, and the Spokane River are polluted, we have work to do.[17]

She asked the state to put aside partisan discord to accomplish change and improve the state. This theme of uniting to overcome discord in the state of Washington would be a theme often repeated in her speeches. In her first inauguration, she asked for citizens to "go beyond party labels" to "build the strength of the center." She said: "Our divisions are not nearly as deep as others may think or write. All of us basically want the same things." She even formed a task force to investigate the election system in an effort to put to rest the accusation that her election was a fraud and to ensure that all votes would be counted right the first time in the future. In her usual pragmatic sense she reminded the audience that "we must not promise more than we can deliver" though she set out an ambitious agenda that included job creation and business growth, improving education and health care, environmental protection and addressing veterans' issues. She concluded with a well-known Ghandi quote. She said: "As Ghandi so famously said, we must all "be the change we want to see in the world." And added: "If we want unity, we must all be unifiers. If we want accountability, each of us must be accountable for all we do. It is up to us to live up to the legacy that was left for us, and to leave a legacy that is worthy of our children and of future generations. We, my friends, can do this. And let us start today."[18]

The first inaugural address by Gregoire was given at an unprecedented moment in the state's history. The razor-thin margin with which she was elected and the souring economy forced Gregoire to call for an even greater collaborative effort than she might have if circumstances were different. In a radio address, delivered on January 22, 2005, she wastes no time getting to the point of her statement after congratulating President Bush on his inauguration and introducing herself. She utilizes a hub and spoke pattern, starting with the general theme of partnerships and collaborations and spreading out with "spokes" that are her reasons offered for creating partnerships. She states:

Like other governors, we face tough challenges here in Washington State— challenges that often frequently require a partnership with the federal government. But too often, the states feel the federal partnership is more promise than reality.[19]

The spokes in her speech include the need for more resources for law enforcement, highways and other transportation infrastructures, job creation, and better health care. She sums up her request with a direct plea:

I urge President Bush to use his new term to open the doors to the states and form lasting partnerships which will help us make our people safer, bolster our economy, and improve the future for all our children. I'm Governor Christine Gregoire from the State of Washington. Thank you for listening.[20]

Clearly, Gregoire was thrilled to have been elected, but the razor-thin margin left many wondering about her and whether or not she was legitimately elected. This would be a major political liability. Reflecting back on her campaign style in the 2004 race, Gregoire said, "I don't think in the end voters ever really got to know Chris Gregoire." "People want to know that they can have a governor who is good on policy and is competent. But they also want to know that they can have a governor that they can relate to. I'm a mom. I'm a spouse. I'm a breast-cancer survivor. I came from very humble beginnings. I'm the first in my family to have gone to college. And I'll bet most people don't know much of any of that today."[21]

She describes the delicate balance of a woman politician when she tells of the most challenging types of speeches she gives are those paying tribute to fallen soldiers. She said, "I struggle mightily when I have to speak at a funeral or a series of memorials. On the one hand, my heart goes out to them, there is always the concern: 'am I being too emotional?'"[22] That balance of strength and emotion are evident in this speech she gave for a fallen firefighter. She concluded her brief remarks with "but here's something very rare, and something we can always say about Dan. . . . He was a protector . . . . of his family and friends . . . and of anybody and everybody he came across. That was Dan's calling in life and that is Dan's legacy."[23] On January 10, 2006, she delivered a "State of the State" address titled "Building on Success" that offered evidence of the state's achievements by signaling out specific stories. She asked her audience to "consider Megan and Martin Clubb, owners and operators of L'Ecole Number 41 Winery in the Walla Walla Valley" and "Tatyana Fedorchuk, a 39-year-old mother of five and immigrant from Ukraine. She is building a new life by taking English classes and earning nursing assistant credentials at Everett Community College." She noted the success of "Barbara and Steve LeVette who live on Hood Canal. Concerned about failing septic systems fouling Hood Canal, they rallied their homeowners association to develop an innovative treatment plan through a public-private partnership."[24] Despite her effort to connect closely with her audience by pointing to specific success stories, her delivery fell short of warm and engaging.

In another speech on January 13, 2006, Governor Gregoire participated in a ceremony of the signing of Civil Rights legislation. She argued against discrimination noting succinctly: discrimination "knows no political party." She began her remarks: "In 1977, a group of thoughtful citizens took the first steps toward adding 'sexual orientation' to the state's law against discrimination. We owe these citizens a tremendous amount of gratitude because it was their first steps that brought us to where we are today . . . my signing of the Civil Rights Bill into law. Twenty-nine years: I can't think of any piece of legislation that has taken so long to work its way through the legislature. It makes this day especially historic. Today's victory is all about stopping discrimination. Some will try to cloud the issue, but the issue is clear: When is it okay to discriminate?"[25]

On June 21, 2008, Governor Gregoire made a brief speech at a race to raise money for breast cancer research. This cause is one that Gregoire personally identifies with, having survived breast cancer. It was the second year that the governor attended the event and spoke. She emphatically said, "This event is so much more than just working for a cure for breast cancer. It's also a time to celebrate the courage and determination of breast cancer survivors . . . our mothers and grandmothers . . . our daughters and nieces . . . our friends, and the woman down the street. God bless and keep you all."[26] She resists recounting her own survival of breast cancer and instead notes her continued support for health care initiatives aimed at breast cancer awareness. She pragmatically urges all those in attendance to "ask the women in your family: 'are you checking?'[27] Rarely does she offer a narrative that could engage the listener. She is more likely to describe situations without putting a human face on them. In her second inaugural address on January 14, 2009, she described the "layer of misery"[28] Mother Nature laid on Washington State during a recent flood. And a "storm" that "rolled over the nation's incredibly mismanaged mortgage and credit markets." In this speech, Gregoire foregrounds the difficult economic conditions and calls them the "most difficult and tying times maybe since the Great Depression."[29]

The most emotional moments of her speech come when she describes her daughters and husband, "First Mike," as her "best friends." She often connects her work as a governor to the goals that she has held dear as a mother. In her second inaugural address, she said, "With me today is my family. . . . My family is here not only to share this important day with me, but to remind us of just what we have at stake this legislative session—and it's the well being of all Washington families." She speaks often of her family both on the dais and in interviews. She said, "Above all, my success stems from the blessing of my great family. My husband, Mike, who has never been jealous, and two wonderful daughters."[30] The themes focused upon in this very serious inauguration address are "courage and generosity." Resolutely she said: "Our work is to help our families and businesses survive at a time when they are forced to juggle bills and cut back spending . . . when too many stores, restaurants and car dealerships are struggling for customers . . . and last month, when 75 percent more Washington workers filed for unemployment benefits than a year ago."[31] In this speech she fails to name names, so often a popular trope in speaking, and one that enlivens examples. This second inaugural is much more urgent and negative in tone than her first one. The state's economic woes increased and the country's economic condition also worsened, which is no doubt the cause of Gregoire's more direct and urgent call for collaborative efforts from all of Washington's citizens. Though her speeches are well written and sometimes even sentimental, her pragmatic, unsmiling delivery fails to offer audiences a completely moving experience.

WHY NOT MADAM PRESIDENT?

Christine Gregoire's greatest rhetorical strength is the clarity with which she communicates. She lays out her thoughts with precision, and though well conceived, her speeches often lack the personality and character that attract voters. She is more an administrator than political personality, and that is her biggest liability as a motivational rhetor who must inspire legions of followers to be successful on the national stage. The ability to communicate orally is crucial to successful politicians and while Gregoire is capable, she lacks the charm and inspiration of a truly charismatic politician. It would not be surprising for Gregoire's policy speeches to lack imagery or warmth, but even the most ceremonial speeches, particularly those given to honor breast cancer survivors and even the most jubilant of moments, such as her second inaugural address, lack the powerful emotion such events offer trigger. Her speech more often is marked by objectivity and pragmatism, than inspiration and platitudes.

In November 2007 Governor Gregoire graced the cover of *Governing* magazine honored by the insiders' national publication as one of the nation's top public officials. The only governor on the list of nine officials, she was cited for her work on government accountability and her "negotiator-in-chief" style of dealing with tough problems. The magazine calls her a "deft and inclusive dealmaker" and says Gregoire runs one of the most open state governments in the country.[32] This adulation for Governor Gregoire focused on her tough, decisive leadership. A couple of years later, speculation abounded in the press when she cancelled a speech. She explained her cancelled speech: "In August, I had the honor of participating in the farewell ceremony for the Washington Army National Guard troops in Yakima as they left to serve Operation Iraqi Freedom. I promised I would visit them."[33] In a conference call from Baghdad Gregoire told reporters that she had only just learned of the speculation her absence prompted, and that she ran for re-election last year because she wanted to be governor: "I made it clear early on I would not accept an appointment."[34] There was no mention of being flattered to have been thought of as Obama administration potential, instead simply a terse response almost chastising the press for the inquiry. Her straightforward approach was front and center in 2010 when, as chair of the National Governor's Association, she told the large new class of twenty-nine newly elected governors that the vicious campaigns are over and voters want bipartisan solutions to the major problems facing every state. She said: "We are at a historic time in our country. We put the elephants and donkeys aside and we're prepared to govern."[35] In addition to her direct and non-flourishing way of speaking, Gregoire's enduring image problem derives from the squeaky-close 2004 election against Rossi. Many voters believe the race was unfairly awarded to her, and her public image suffered from multiple press conferences by Republicans charging that she is an illegitimate governor. Gregoire, who is often described in the press as "intense," describes herself as a "recovering lawyer" and is a fact-laden speaker. Her reserve and frankness are apparent in even ceremonial speeches that would lend themselves to a less strict and formal presentation. That she is a proud and patriotic public servant is without question, but the impression on the audience is usually more mundane than impassioned. Despite her major in speech communication in college and her awareness of the tricky rhetorical tightrope politicians face trying at once to be serious as well as likeable, her no-nonsense business approach may suggest that personal style could be the main reason why Christine Gregoire never became a national political figure. A unique sense of mission and purpose often mark the oration of an impassioned speaker who is determined to take up a cause. In contrast, Christine Gregoire's speech, though earnest and pertaining to important, often patriotic and noble causes, often lacks the sense of excitement and wonder that are usually part of the sense in an audience that history is being made. The "charisma gap" that has been described by some journalists[36] when referring to Gregoire is not lost on her. She said, "I've faced that problem as other women politicians do. It started when I ran for attorney general. I won three times and proved I was tough enough. As governor, I'm accused of being 'too tough.' It is one of the unique obstacles that face women leaders."[37] Recognizing the gravity of her style, she remarked, "Now, I have been accused at times of being serious person and being tough, as if there was something bad about that. In fact, I can be serious. And I can be tough. But you know we are in difficult times and I think that's the kind of leadership we need. I'm a fighter."[38]

To launch a national campaign of the magnitude needed to win the nomination for president would require of Gregoire a more inspirational communication style focused on positive outcomes. This vexing rhetorical problem also faced Bob Dole, a male presidential candidate, who fought against a persistent image as dour and somber. It may be an even bigger problem for women politicians, who have to prove they are tough, especially in times of economic turmoil and war, and also show that they are likable, fun, and tender, too. Faced with severe economic troubles in Washington, Christine Gregoire is a speaker who is most often resolute, measured, and precise in her execution. An exacting, no-nonsense, analytical approach comes more naturally to her and has likely served her well as governor. Her somber approach, however, may have limited her potential to reach a national audience, one that would want to probe more deeply into her emotive side and one that would require her to show a personality that would remind voters more of themselves and the hope of a positive tomorrow than a tough taskmaster facing stark realities.

NOTES

1. Tom LeGro, "Washington Governor Wins Re-Election," *PBS Newshour*, November 5, 2008, www.pbs.org/newshour/vote2008/reportersblog/2008/11/washington_gov_gregoire_wins_r.html (accessed June 15, 2011).

2. Several sources cite the final vote cast differently. The reports range from 129–133 votes. For example, http://topics.nytimes.com/topics/reference/timestopics/people/g/christine_o_gregoire/index.html (accessed June 22, 2010) notes 133 votes and several other sources cite 129 votes, for example, http://seattletimes.nwsource.com/html/localnews/2002284078_felons22m.html (accessed June 23, 2010).

3. Governer Christine Gregoire website, www.governer.wa.gov/speeches/default.asp (accessed June 17, 2010).

4. Ibid.

5. Phone interview with Governor Christine Gregoire, July 20, 2010.

6. Speeches obtained from two sources: *Vital Speeches of the Day* and Governor Gregoire's official website: www.governor.wa.gov/speeches/default.asp (accessed June 17, 2010), and Christine Gregoire, "Working Together on All Levels of Government," *Vital Speeches of the Day*, February 1, 2005: ABI/INFORM Global, ProQuest (accessed May 20, 2010).

7. Sheree Keith, "Women Who Spoke for Themselves, Working Women, Suffrage, and the Construction of Women's Rhetorical Style," in Janis L. Edwards (ed.), *Gender and Political Communication in America* (Lanham, MD: Rowman and Littlefield, 2009), p. 33.

8. Phone interview with Governor Christine Gregoire, July 20, 2010.

9. Andrew Garber, "Christine Gregoire: Smart, Intense and Struggling to Woo Voters," *Seattle Times*, October 10, 2008, http://seattletimes.nwsource.com/html/localnews/2008246892_gregoireprofile10m.html (accessed November 16, 2010).

10. Governor Christine Gregoire website, www.governor.wa.gov/about/mike/default.asp (accessed July 19, 2010).

11. Betty Holcomb, "The Tobacco slayer," *Good Housekeeping*, July 1, 1999: General Interest Module, ProQuest (accessed June 25, 2011).

12. This biographical information was culled from several sources, including "Project Vote Smart," www.votesmart.org/bio.php?can_id=15489; the official

website of Governor Gregoire, www.governor.wa.gov/about/; and "Times Topics," http://topics.nytimes.com/topics/reference/timestopics/people/g/christine_o_gregoire/index.html (all accessed June 22, 2010).

13. Andrew Garber and Kyung M. Song, "Gov. Chris Gregoire Is on the White House List to Replace Elena Kagan as the Solicitor General," *Seattle Times*, May 12, 2010, http://seattletimes.nwsource.com/html/localnews/2011848748_gregoire13m.html (accessed June 22, 2010).

14. Marcelene Edwards, "Economy's the No. 1 Issue with Voters in Tacoma, Wash., Region," *Knight Ridder Tribune Business News*, September 26, 2004, ABI/INFORM Dateline, ProQuest (accessed June 22, 2010).

15. Ibid.

16. Emory Thomas, Jr., "2004 NEWSMAKERS: The Fighters—Christine Gregoire," *Puget Sound Business Journal*, December 24, 2004, ABI/INFORM Dateline, ProQuest (June 21, 2010).

17. 2005 inaugural address, from the Christine Gregoire website, http://governor.wa.gov/speeches/speech-view.asp?SpeechSeq=213 (accessed July 21, 2010).

18. Ibid.

19. Radio Address, January 22, 2005, from the Christine Gregoire Web Site, http://governor.wa.gov/speeches/speech-view.asp?SpeechSeq=213 (accessed July 21, 2010).

20. Ibid.

21. David Postman, "Gregoire Skips the Coffee Klatch on Way to Announcing Re-election," *Seattle Times*, April 7, 2008, http://blog.seattletimes.nwsource.com/davidpostman/2008/04/gregoire_skips_the_coffee_klatch_on_way_to_announcing_reelection.html#start_comments (accessed July 2, 2010).

22. Phone interview with Governor Christine Gregoire, July 20, 2010.

23. "Gov Addresses the Memorial Service of Chief Dan Packer's," August 7, 2008, www.governor.wa.gov/speeches/speech-view.asp?SpeechSeq=162 (accessed July 20, 2010).

24. State of the State address, 2006, from the Christine Gregoire website, http://governor.wa.gov/speeches/speech-view.asp?SpeechSeq=213 (accessed July 21, 2010).

25. Civil rights legislation speech, 2006, from the Christine Gregoire website, http://governor.wa.gov/speeches/speech-view.asp?SpeechSeq=213 (accessed July 21, 2010).

26. Breast cancer awareness speech, June 21, 2008, from the Christine Gregoire website, http://governor.wa.gov/speeches/speech-view.asp?SpeechSeq=213 (accessed July 21, 2010).

27. Ibid.

28. 2009 inaugural address, from the Christine Gregoire website, http://governor.wa.gov/speeches/speech-view.asp?SpeechSeq=213 (accessed July 21, 2010).

29. Ibid.

30. Phone interview with Governor Christine Gregoire, July 20, 2010.

31. 2009 inaugural address, from the Christine Gregoire website, http://governor.wa.gov/speeches/speech-view.asp?SpeechSeq=213 (accessed July 21, 2010).

32. "Magazine Ranks Gregoire in Top 9," *Seattle Times*, November 2, 2007, http://seattletimes.nwsource.com/html/politics/2003989178_gregoire02m.html (accessed July 1, 2010).

33. Andrew Garber, "Mystery Solved: Gov. Gregoire Visiting Troops in Iraq," *McClatchy—Tribune Business News*, January 6, 2009, ABI/INFORM Dateline, ProQuest (accessed November 16, 2010).

34. Ibid.

35. "Washington Gov. Christine Gregoire Tells Peers: Job Is Changing," AP, November 20, 2010, www.oregonlive.com/politics/index.ssf/2010/11/washington_gov_christine_grego.html (accessed November 22, 2010).

36. Brian Miller, "The Last-Ditch, Top-Secret Campaign-Makeover Memo," *Seattle Weekly*, October 22, 2008, www.seattleweekly.com/2008-10-22/news/gregoire-gone-wild/ (accessed November 15, 2010).

37. Phone interview with Governor Christine Gregoire, July 20, 2010.

38. Colin Fogarty, "Another Final Debate in Washington's Race For Governor," *Oregon Public Broadcasting News*, October 16, 2008, http://news.opb.org/article/3298-another-final-debate-washingtons-race-governor/ (accessed March 23, 2011).

9

Kathleen Gilligan Sebelius: Realizing America's Promise

"I see young women particularly who are way too hard on themselves in terms of thinking they are not up to the job, whether it's an entry-level political position, or a corporate job, or the willingness to apply for a job."

—Kathleen Sebelius[1]

On August 26, 2008, Kansas governor and convention co-chair Kathleen Gilligan Sebelius stepped onto the stage at the Democratic National Convention in Denver to address the delegates and the viewing audience. The opportunity to be the second Democrat woman on a national ticket had passed. Her political future beyond her governorship was uncertain, but her commitment to helping Barack Obama make history was as firm as it had been in January when she announced her endorsement. Although Sebelius is a staunch advocate for electing and placing more women into public office, she didn't endorse the woman who could have shattered the last glass ceiling. Her speech at the convention fell on the same night as Hillary Clinton's—a night that had as its theme "Renewing America's Promise." While Clinton and her supporters did not realize their American dream, Sebelius also stood as a symbol of how far women have come in American politics and what dreams remained to be realized.

As Sebelius told her story, the interconnectedness of American political families surfaced. Another Kansas woman politician profiled in this book, Nancy Landon Kassebaum, once met William Howard Taft and his family when they visited her father, Governor Alfred Mossman Landon. Sebelius's family, the Gilligans, also had connections to Taft. Sebelius, a native of Ohio, opened her speech with her Taft connection:

I'm a descendent of Irish immigrants. My great-grandmother worked as a maid in the home of William Howard Taft, before he became president. Decades later, the grandson of the president and my father, the grandson of the maid, served back-to-back to represent the same district in Congress. Now, that is the American dream. It's my story, and it's the story of millions of others.[2]

In telling her story, Sebelius compared her family's realization of America's promise to Obama's humble beginnings and Kansas heritage. Sebelius's own history as a legislator, insurance commissioner, governor, and U.S. Secretary of Health and Human Services is one of supporting policies that make it possible for her constituents to realize their own ambitions.

A REPEATED THEME, BUT ALSO A FIRST

The Gilligan family's ascension over three generations from humble immigrant roots to a prospective vice presidential bid is a story that is repeated in various forms throughout the country in political circles as well as in boardrooms, higher education institutions, courthouses, and many other venues.[3] Another story that is repeated in American politics and within the pages of this book is the influence of family. Many American political family dynasties exist: Kennedy, Bush, Taft, Rockefeller, Dodd, and Landon, to name a few. While father-to-son passage of a political mantle is more common, this book features three women—Nancy D'Alesandro Pelosi, Nancy Landon Kassebaum, and Kathleen Gilligan Sebelius—who carried on their fathers' political legacy. In Sebelius's case, she and her father were the first father-daughter combination to hold governorships. Her father, John J. "Jack" Gilligan, was Ohio's governor from 1971 to 1975 while Sebelius was attending college at Trinity Washington University in the District of Columbia. Jack Gilligan served on the local board of education and city council in their hometown of Cincinnati before being elected to a single term in the U.S. House of Representatives. Gilligan's campaigns were a family affair, and Kathleen Sebelius often recounted in speeches that she thought all children spent their weekends putting out yard signs and going door-to-door with campaign materials. Political socialization at an early age and family attitudes about gender roles are cited in studies of women's political activity and ambition to be major factors in the decision to run for office.[4] Women from political families are more likely to view politics as a noble profession and involvement with campaigns reduces their fears of entering into a world dominated by men. In Sebelius's case, "Her parents prepared their children for schoolyard antagonism by helping them understand the reasons for their father's votes, which Sebelius said taught her at an early age to defend a political position."[5]

Along with having a father as a role model, Sebelius also holds the distinction of being the daughter-in-law of another congressman, Republican Keith Sebelius, who represented Kansas from 1969–1981. He followed Bob Dole as the representative from the first district in western Kansas. "Her close relationship with her father-in-law also helped her understand the point of view from across the aisle."[6] Her husband, Gary, is a federal magistrate judge. The couple met in Washington, D.C., while he was a law student at Georgetown and she was working at the Center for Correctional Justice. They were married in the Ohio governor's mansion on December 24, 1974. They have two sons, Edward ("Ned") and John. In her endorsement speech of Obama on Kansas Day, January 29, 2008, in Obama's mother's hometown of El Dorado, Kansas, Sebelius credited her two sons with convincing her to back Obama. Ned supported Obama because of his policy positions, but younger son, John, explained, "Anybody who could get Michelle Obama to marry him has to have something going for him."[7] Ned, who worked on John Kerry's 2004 presidential campaign, married Lisa Anderson Rockefeller, a descendent of William Rockefeller, John D. Rockefeller's father. Thus, the political bloodlines run deep and broad in the Gilligan-Sebelius families.

Sebelius moved to Topeka, Kansas in 1974 with her husband who practiced law. Prior to her first run for office, Sebelius worked as a special assistant to the Kansas secretary of corrections for three years and as the executive director and lobbyist for the Kansas Trial Lawyers Association for eight. While working, she also earned a master's degree in public administration from the University of Kansas and started her family.

In many ways, Sebelius exemplified a new breed of political women who were able to achieve a work/politics/life balance. Unlike Nancy Kassebaum—who took on more traditional roles and put off running until her children were raised—and other women of that generation, Sebelius launched into politics with young children. As late as 2003, research showed that this was exceptional since family structure still impeded women's decisions to run: "Women . . . who have traditional family structures, or hold traditional attitudes about gender roles . . . were 27% less likely than men to consider running for office" and, in general, family responsibilities influenced women's political career decisions more than men's.[8] In an interview with her alma mater in Washington, D.C., she explained how she made it work:

> We've really tried hard to balance family issues and political issues. . . . I have always wanted to be at home and be available to the kids, and I've been very lucky to have had jobs where I could work on issues that I thought were important and yet not have to give up time with the kids and family. Both Gary and I felt that it was very important that their lives were as normal as possible, that they participate only when they wanted to, and that this was my job, not their job.[9]

In 1986 she left her job to run for the state legislature in a Topeka House district that was favorable to Democrats. She considered her decision to leave a position that "required much travel" a "pro-family choice because she could spend more time with her children who were both under five when she was elected to the legislature."[10] Several years ago one of the author's was preparing to emcee a reverse news conference fundraiser for a women's organization at which Sebelius, who was insurance commissioner, and two other people in the news would grill the media. Sebelius's aide provided some insights into Sebelius's personality when asked for anecdotes to use in an introduction along with the usual biographical fare. The aide immediately responded that Sebelius was a mother first and told about her being called out of a staff meeting because John had left an important textbook at home. Sebelius went home, retrieved the book, delivered it to him at school, and returned to her staff meeting.

From 1987 to 1995 Sebelius served in the legislature. In 1994 she decided to challenge a "good ol' boys club" in the state insurance commissioner's office. The office was one that had virtually been handed down from one commissioner to his second in command since 1946 largely because Democrats rarely won statewide down ballot races. In fact, no Democrat or woman had ever held the office. The cozy arrangement and close ties with the insurance industry resulted in a scandal that created an opening for Sebelius. The incumbent, Ron Todd, was deputy to twenty-year-veteran Fletcher Bell. Bell retired in 1990 but not before collecting $95,000 in workers' compensation for hurting his back while reaching for a briefcase in his car. His designated heir, the incumbent Ron Todd, retired and then returned to work prior to announcing his run for Bell's seat in 1990. This enabled him to collect state retirement and a salary. Taking advantage of the scandal in her advertising, a popular name in western Kansas, and her network from days with the trial lawyers, Sebelius waged a successful campaign that stressed her refusal to accept funds from the industry she would regulate. She stressed the need to represent the public interest. After taking office in January 1995, she kept her word by blocking a merger of Blue Cross-Blue Shield with Indiana-based Anthem, Inc., because her research indicated it would raise costs for Kansans. She easily won reelection and set her sights on higher office. She was named one of *Governing Magazine's* Public Officials of the Year in 2001.

In 2002 there was an open seat for governor and Sebelius defeated Tim Shallenburger, a conservative Republican legislator, by 8 percentage points—53 percent to 45 percent. While Kansas is a bright-red state and has been Republican since its entry into the Union in 1861 as a free state, Democrats are successful in winning the governorship. Between 1957 and 2003 when Sebelius took office, Democrats held the seat for twenty-four years—over half the period. One of the Democrats was the State's first woman governor, Joan Finney, who was elected in 1990. One reason Democrats often win the governorship is that contentious Republican primaries, similar to the one in 2002, split the moderate vote and produce a candidate who is more conservative than most Kansas Republicans. Democrats in Kansas are known for being fiscal conservatives and social moderates; thus, they are able to secure votes from both independents and moderate Republicans. Sebelius also broadened her appeal to Republicans by adding a Wichita Republican businessman, John Moore, to her ticket as lieutenant governor. He switched his party registration a few days before being announced as her running mate. She promised to cut unnecessary state spending by doing a top-to-bottom review of state spending and bolster support for education.

During her first term, Sebelius cut government spending, dealt with a major budget deficit, which was reduced without raising taxes, and worked with the legislature to resolve an education-funding crisis caused by a state Supreme Court decision. The constitution required "adequate" funding for K-12 education. Studies done by independent consultants concluded that the mandate was not being met, but the Republican-controlled legislature resisted Sebelius's recommendation for increased property, sales, and income taxes to make up the difference. At the end of the regular legislative session, the issue remained unresolved and a rare special session was called. A compromise was finally reached with only the first year's funding identified.

In 2006, Sebelius easily won reelection over state senator Jim Barnett by more than twice her 2002 margin—57.8 percent to 40.5 percent. Once again, she convinced a notable Republican to switch parties and join her on the ticket. Her running mate, Mark Parkinson, was a former member of the Kansas House and Senate and past chair of the Kansas Republican Party. As a moderate, he saw himself more closely aligned with Sebelius than with the conservative wing of the Republican Party that was gaining strength in the legislature. During Sebelius's tenure several members of the legislature and an attorney general candidate also switched parties.

Sebelius was elected chair of the Democratic Governors Association in 2006 and garnered national attention as a result. After Obama's win in 2008, she was mentioned as a possible cabinet member but said she wasn't interested. She was originally not offered a position, but when President Obama's first choice for Secretary of Health and Human Services, Tom Daschle, had to withdraw, Obama tapped Sebelius due to her experience as insurance commissioner and her record on health care issues. She was accompanied to the nomination announcement by two prominent Kansas Republicans—former senator and presidential nominee Bob Dole and his replacement in the Senate, Pat Roberts. She took office on April 28, 2009. In 2009 she made the *Forbes* list of most powerful women in the world, entering at fifty-seventh. She moved up to twenty-third in 2010 and thirteenth in 2011.

BREAKING THROUGH THE BARRIERS TO ELECTING WOMEN: A RHETORIC OF COMPETENCE AND COOPERATION

Before Kathleen Sebelius ran for governor in 2002, she attended what she referred to as "Girl Governors Camp." She explained that about the time she was considering a run for governor, the White House Project reviewed its research on women running for office and determined that some of the attitudinal barriers related to women's elections at an executive level couldn't be overcome until there were women winning governorships. She explained:

> There was this whole series of women who had tried to run for governor and weren't successful. The decision was that they should redirect energies to also electing women governors because the thinking was if you couldn't be elected or seen as the CEO of your state, then you weren't going to turn the dial and elect women CEO of the country.[11]

They brought the potential candidates together a couple of times along with staff members and they

> talked about everything from media coverage to looking at the data to talking to women who had run. The godmother of the group was Ann Richards who had won and then was beaten for reelection. . . . A whole series of incredible women had been elected in their states to other offices but somehow did not make the final hurdle as governor. So I worked with them and the data was enormously powerful about what people were looking for, what were the barriers. Some of it is not necessarily cutting edge but things like the delicate balance women have to have between being tough enough to cut the deal and being experienced enough and not being influenced by special interests. Very different expectations than they were expecting of men and different kinds of strategic plans. And all of these are true whether it's at a statehouse level or for the highest office in the land.[12]

Sebelius implemented the lessons from "camp" and from work done by the Barbara Lee Family Foundation,[13] which provided practical, research-based advice for running and governing. Her rhetoric as a candidate and governor was well constructed to overcome as many barriers as possible and to capitalize on positive traits that were projected to women candidates such as being more ethical, caring more for constituents, and bringing more people to the table. An analysis of Sebelius's public statements to the media, campaign advertising, and her speeches as governor—particularly her seven State of the State addresses—demonstrate her ability to present herself as a competent CEO who could handle the national stage.

Sebelius's leadership style and rhetoric from the time she became insurance commissioner until she left the governorship was characterized by descriptions given of her during her campaign for a second term as governor:

> [She] has crafted a determined, pragmatic persona that makes Kansans comfortable. . . . Hers is an administration of caution. Most public moments are carefully scripted. She rarely steps beyond her message. She will repeat her points time and again and avoid wading into waters where she's not prepared to comment.[14]

University of Kansas political science professor Burdett Loomis, who took a leave from his academic career and worked briefly in Sebelius's administration, said that Sebelius is "well-known in the office for collecting scads of data and using them. . . . Sebelius will chew on it meticulously before deciding how to use it." A second political science professor, Bob Beatty of Washburn University in Topeka, Kansas, described her as being "careful to perfect an image of a person who is looking out for the whole state. She has avoided wedge issues."[15]

While serving as insurance commissioner, she denied the takeover of Blue Cross and Blue Shield by Anthem, Inc. A court upheld her decision. In discussing the decision with the media she emphasized her concern for consumers and her bipartisanship—themes that took her into office—and her use of information to make a decision:

> Of the probably 1,200 Kansans who came to the public meetings, only two stood up and said they were in favor. . . . These are average Kansans, Republicans and Democrats. It's a very broad cross-section of Kansas. . . . The evidence I relied on indicated that the consumers that would be hurt the most (by the takeover) would be small business owners. . . . I see (the decision) as very pro-business.[16]

Sebelius realized that regardless of what you say or do, most of the public views a candidate or officeholder through media eyes. She discovered early on that the information given at "camp" about how the media reports on women was all too true. She recounted an incident in her first campaign for governor that demonstrates how she was able to neutralize media activity that could cut into perceptions of her being on an even playing field with men:

> They talked a lot at camp about dealing with the press and that the press may tend to diminish the role of women or characterize you in a different light and it was so important to challenge those assumptions and call whoever wrote the article so it won't happen again. . . . What happened to me at the first debate I had . . . [which was a combined Republican and Democrat primary debate

with] five Republican males and me [was something] I'll never forget. John Hanna wrote the article and each of them was described by what job title they had and a little bit about them. I was the insurance commissioner, he may have mentioned that, but he also described the green sandals that I had on and that I had nail polish on my toes. And he says this in the article, literally! My press secretary, who had gone through some of this training, called him and said, "Shame on you, John. You have a 12-year-old daughter. I cannot believe this is the way you described the woman in this race. Read what you've written about Kathleen." To his great credit he apologized and he never wrote that kind of story ever again. It pointed out to me how accurate they [the White House Project staff] were. You really have to call the media out. Stop It! And at least some of the time it might be effective.[17]

As governor, she demonstrated her mastery of using the media to reinforce her message even before she took office. She had promised "a top to bottom review" of state expenditures to cut the budget. Eight days after her election she announced a team of public and private sector volunteers "she dubbed Kansas BEST," short for Budget Efficiency Savings Teams" to do the review. She "acknowledged critics who see her effort as a 'PR gimmick,' but said it's a serious move to reconfigure the state government as a more efficient service provider."[18] Such language enhanced Sebelius's image as fiscally conservative. Research shared with Sebelius at her training sessions indicated many voters have questioned women's ability to handle economic issues. However, she had cut expenses in the insurance commissioner's office and saw that experience as providing the credibility she needed in her run for governor. She commented that the office "turned out to be a very good place to be. It helped me develop financial credentials. The other piece is that it allowed me to be a consumer champion, a great asset when I ran for governor."[19]

The use of special committees to protect Kansans and address a variety of other issues and jobs initiatives became a common practice in the Sebelius administration. They not only provided her with minds to tap outside of government bureaucracy, but the formation provided an opportunity to showcase her inclusiveness and her values. Late in her first term, for example, she announced the "Interagency Council on Abuse, Neglect, and Exploitation to find weaknesses in current safeguards for vulnerable Kansans and recommend steps to strengthen the state's protection of these residents." In making the announcement, she explained, "The primary mission of any government is to protect its citizens. That's a job I take seriously, particularly when those citizens have special needs."[20]

The themes she promoted in Kansas followed her to the national stage. When she was preparing to give the response to President Bush's last State of the Union address, she previewed her approach by saying,

So, there is a lot of evidence that there is really a new American majority coming together: people who don't see themselves, necessarily, as partisans, but see themselves as citizens. I'm going to talk a little tonight about that hopefulness of the American people and their willingness, really to step up and face the serious challenges that we have.[21]

The carefully controlled message was also evident in Sebelius's campaign advertising. In 2002, she emphasized her commitment to open government, hard work, and serving the people of Kansas by reminding them of the changes she made in the insurance commissioner's office. In one ad, she referred to her predecessors' scandals in the office and using a stereotypically feminine context, she literally cleaned up the office. She pulled down the heavy curtains and let sunlight in to emphasize transparency and then put on rubber gloves and said, "Let's get to work," as the voiceover enumerated her list of accomplishments including not taking money from the industry she regulated.

Other ads in 2002 had a "feminine" emphasis with the subject of education, which was discussed more in women candidates' advertising between 1990 and 2002 than in males'.[22] In one ad the voiceover enumerated her objectives and then her voice concluded with "as Governor, I'll always put our children and schools first."[23] By 2006 she had a record and had helped the state through a difficult school finance crisis. She emphasized not only her commitment to education, but also her ability to get bipartisan support to resolve the crisis:

> One ad, titled "Together," transitions from Sebelius standing in front of a parodied scene of actors posing as Kansas state legislators throwing paper at one another to a classroom with children quietly studying. Sebelius narrates most of the ad, stating: "Yup, this is how things use to be. Politicians in Topeka fighting and foot-dragging over the future of our schools, when this is where their focus should have been all along. . . . All it took was leadership to bring people together and put our kids and schools ahead of anything else."[24]

The word "together" was one that appeared in both her advertising and in all of her speeches to the legislature. She described her inaugural address as expressing "optimism about the state's future despite serious financial problems and will set the tone for the new administration. . . . What's so critical . . . . is that the citizens of this state understand as fully as possible where we are, what the game plan is (and) my optimism that we really can work through this together."[25] Just as Linda Lingle called on her adopted state's unique heritage and leaders, Kathleen Sebelius paid homage to her adopted state's pioneering spirit and motto—Ad Astra Per Aspera—To the Stars through Difficulties—which was born from its pre-statehood Bleeding Kansas days, to remind Kansans that never giving up was part of their DNA. Her optimism was as common as her calls for unity. She said in her first inaugural address:

> The pioneers were the ultimate optimists—leaving the comfort and safety of the territory they knew for the promise of a better future for themselves and their families in the land to be discovered. That same sense of optimism and dedication to a better future will help us find a path through difficult times.[26]

And in her first State of the State address the next day she expressed her optimistic belief that Kansans hadn't changed since their pioneering days:

> In both those times [Civil War and the Great Depression], Kansans faced problems far more difficult and fundamental than those we face today. They faced those problems together, as a People. They conquered those problems together, as a People. They embodied our state motto—*Ad Astra Per Aspera*—*To the Stars Through Difficulties*. Tonight I call on the legislature to bring that same pioneer spirit to the difficult task we face this year.

In the course of delivering seven State of the State addresses, Sebelius maintained the themes of her first inaugural address. The terms "come together," "common good," "cooperation," "work with me," "we should all," and "our work," were found in some combination in every speech. As a Democrat governor with a majority Republican legislature, it was the only approach that would work. She clearly established her view of government in her 2003 address, and that view was consistent with prevailing political moods: "The purpose of government is to protect and serve the people, support our communities, and build the economy. I am dedicated to reorganizing and streamlining state government."[27] She also had to acknowledge the major problems facing the state—problems which only grew as the entire nation's economy began to suffer during her final two years in office.

In each successive year as she called on the legislature to cooperate with her, she also reminded them of what they had accomplished when they did work together. Interspersed with her call to action through cooperation was the traditional litany of programs she was proposing. In 2004 she said, "A year ago, the situation was bleak, but responding to my call, you rolled up your sleeves and went to work with me to solve the unprecedented financial problems we faced." A year later, she complimented their work: "Over the past two years, working together, we have met the essential challenges of balancing the state's budget and enhancing its fiscal health, all without raising taxes." At the start of her second term in 2007, she called on the state's heritage and values again in seeking cooperation: "To build a brighter future, we must continue to advance the two values that have guided our state from its founding: an unwavering belief in the power of individual freedom, and an equally strong commitment to the common good." She then set out to change the perception of problems to one of opportunities. In her last two years in office she stressed initiatives that would create jobs: "We are called on by the future to act now to meet the challenge, and to take advantage of the amazing opportunity Kansas has to become a leader in the production of renewable energy."

As the economic situation in the nation worsened in 2008, she again exhibited a belief in the legislature's and Kansan's resiliency to overcome:

> There are serious challenges facing our state and our nation. As Kansans, we are well-suited to face these challenges and capitalize on the opportunities. We start with some tremendous advantages: a resilient spirit; a strong work ethic; a shared belief in the power of education; a diverse and growing economy; and citizens in every corner of our state who believe in something greater than themselves.

The same themes were struck in her final message to the legislature on January 12, 2009, three months before she resigned to become President Obama's Secretary of Health and Human Services. She called for unity with phrases such as "to put people before partisanship," "heavy burdens can be lifted when all of our hands lift together," and "to find common ground and to work for the common good." Her optimism that investments in higher education, cancer research, and alternative energy could create jobs was highlighted with "I have confidence in our capacity to meet our challenges. . . . Along with the challenges, there are opportunities we cannot afford to ignore," "with all of us working together, we can and will seize this opportunity," and "we have the ability by working together to correctly identify assets, mobilize efforts, unify our resolve, and get the job done for Kansas today and tomorrow." Summarizing her themes and using an alliterative style, she concluded her last major address to the legislature and people of Kansas with these words:

> Ours state's motto is as true today as it was in 1861. We will overcome our difficulties; we will reach the stars yet again. There will be a better day. The U.S. and the Kansas economies will rebound, and we'll return to positive growth. We will create jobs. And the opportunities Kansans have enjoyed for generations will not go away. This time of shared struggle will result in shared solutions and a stronger Kansas.

There was nothing flashy about Kathleen Sebelius's rhetoric. It was, however, clear in its intent to unify and to serve. She capitalized on a set of values that Kansans identify as their own—common sense, fiscal conservatism, hard work, and optimism regardless of what befalls them. She was attuned to the challenges women face and also saw them as opportunities to blend a feminine style to make tough decisions. As a result of her successes as a Democrat in a red state, it was not surprising that she would become the source of speculation about aspirations for higher office.

WHY NOT MADAM PRESIDENT?

Hardly two years after her first inauguration, Kathleen Sebelius found herself part of the vice presidential speculation for Senator John Kerry's 2004 presidential bid. At the annual Kansas Democratic Party gathering in Topeka in March, General Wesley Clark was the dinner speaker. Clark had made a bid for the nomination and was asked if he was being considered for the second slot on the ticket. He responded, "I think you should be asking your governor that." Sebelius "had been asked Friday afternoon about lingering suspicions she was angling to join Kerry on the presidential ticket" and had "shrug[ged] off the issue" as Clark did.[28]

An Associated Press story in early April listed Sebelius along with John Edwards and Republican William Cohen, the former Maine senator and Clinton defense secretary, as possible Kerry running mates. They described Sebelius as "a heartland governor" who would add "gender balance to the list . . . . and could offer Kerry a bridge to groups like the Democratic Leadership Council."[29] The following month, women's groups were reported as having "suggested a host of female leaders, including [Arizona Governor Janet] Napolitano and Governor Kathleen Sebelius of Kansas."[30] In June, with the media searching for any hints possible, news stories tied both Sebelius and Iowa governor Tom Vilsack to "the list." Both governors happened to be in Washington lobbying Congress on health care reform the same day Kerry was meeting with advisors in his Capitol Hill office to discuss the vice presidential search. Sebelius's response to the way the media connected the dots was "It's all a little odd."[31] Sebelius had denied interest in the vice presidency from the outset of the speculative talk, saying she was committed to completing her four-year term.

The Kansas media expressed skepticism at the vice presidential buzz. Her hometown newspaper stated, "No question about it, her name keeps popping up." However, the gist of the article was analysis by two local political scientists who gave little credence to the speculation. Burdett Loomis at the University of Kansas, considered her inclusion as "highly symbolic," saying, "Every list of possible running mates needs a woman on it, regardless of whether they are serious candidates for the job."[32] Rumors were stoked more in June when "one reporter opined on the Don Imus radio show—a popular forum for the political cognoscenti—that she was among three finalists to be U.S. Sen. John Kerry's running mate this fall."[33] Two reporters, one from the *Kansas City Star* in neighboring Missouri, noted that it was "time for a reality check: First off the governor said Thursday through a spokeswoman that she was not interested. Thanks, but no thanks."[34] They went on to analyze the major reasons why Sebelius was not ready for a national ticket:

> Sebelius, elected in 2002 after serving two terms as the Kansas insurance com-
> missioner, has no experience in international affairs, which are expected to be
> a key issue. It is doubtful she would get Kansas—with just six electoral votes—
> into Kerry's column: Kansas last voted Democrat in a presidential election in
> the Lyndon Johnson landslide of 1964. Heck, she might even turn off western
> Missouri voters who hold anything Jayhawk in low regard.[35]

The story also discounted any advantage her Ohio roots might bring, calling that connection "a stretch" given her father lost reelection after "pushing through Ohio's first state income tax—hardly a legacy to run on. And anyway, it's been a long, long time since Kathleen Gilligan left Cincinnati." Like other stories, they did argue, "What Sebelius does bring to the table is her gender, which could help Kerry maximize the gender gap Democrats enjoy among women voters, and the fact that she is a competent Democratic governor in generally Republican territory."[36]

The analysis proved correct as Kerry chose his Senate colleague and primary opponent, John Edwards. In an interview with Sebelius about her experiences in 2004, she responded to the question, "Were you on the radar screen for Kerry in 2004?" "If I was, I had no idea that that was the case. I knew Kerry a bit, but no."[37] Thus, her comment about the whole discussion being "odd," was truly an honest reaction.

The attention garnered from the Kerry speculation plus her achievements as a governor—something the White House Project acknowledged as important to show CEO potential—caused Sebelius to garner considerable national attention between 2004 and 2008. As a result of her successes in cutting state spending, balancing the budget and maintaining support for public education, *Time* named her one of four "rising stars from the heartland" in 2004 and cited her as one of the country's five best governors in 2005. Two years later *Newsweek* declared that she was "one to watch" as having presidential potential.[38] In 2006 she was in a tie for the twelfth most popular governor based on polling data. She was selected to head the Democratic Governors Association (DGA) in 2006 and in February as she neared the start of a reelection run, the White House Project named her one of its "8 in '08" as a possible presidential contender along with senators Hillary Clinton, Olympia Snowe, Susan Collins, and Kay Bailey Hutchison, Atlanta Mayor Shirley Franklin, Secretary of State Condoleezza Rice, and fellow governor Janet Napolitano.[39] Her national star was clearly on the rise.

She began appearing in national media coverage of major issues affecting the states. In 2005 she appeared on National Public Radio's "Talk of the Nation" with Republican Ohio Governor Bob Taft, great-grandson of

President Taft.[40] Sebelius discussed Medicaid costs and overall health care issues, job creation, business development, and education—all issues of importance nationally as well as in the state. The national attention caused her opponent in the 2006 governor's race to question whether she would serve out a second term. It was a question the answer to which did not matter to Kansans who reelected her.

In her capacity as DGA chair, Sebelius appeared on C-SPAN's "Washington Journal" in February, 2007. She discussed a wide range of issues from "war [and its impact on the Kansas National Guard and domestic readiness], wind energy, college tuition, rock music, and her own political future."[41] The national stage, however, was fraught with potential risks. When a tornado destroyed the Kansas town of Greensburg in May 2007, Sebelius "tried walking the fine line . . . between criticizing the president over the war in Iraq and appropriately representing her state's interests" when she "made no secret of her belief that the severe depletion of National Guard forces and equipment due to their deployment to Iraq and Afghanistan was taking a toll on Kansas's ability to respond to the crisis."[42] The topic was discussed previously in the February C-SPAN interview, but this time her comments produced a response from the White House, which blamed Sebelius for "a sluggish response." She backed off her attacks in what was interpreted as a realization that Federal purse strings to states were controlled by Republicans.[43] The article referenced her potential place on a 2008 ticket as did one several weeks later in coverage of her speech at a White House Project gathering in Atlanta where she was asked about Supreme Court decisions and the National Guard situation.[44]

By fall 2007, none other than James Carville was touting her as a potential vice-presidential candidate—even if it meant a two-woman ticket—with Hillary Clinton. Carville acknowledged that she was "a dark horse," but he liked her "75 percent approval rating, her father, John Gilligan, was the former Governor of Ohio. . . . [She] gets stuff done, successful in a red state."[45] In response to Carville's support, the *Topeka Capital-Journal* editorialized that the chances were "slim" of a Clinton-Sebelius ticket, but it "makes sense for the Democrats. She's proven she can raise money. She's shown she can draw support from moderate Republicans. She's worked effectively with GOP legislators."[46] The opinion writer then went on to discuss a potential drawback that would surface frequently in the next year: "She's not particularly charismatic, but who cares? If an electrifying personality is a requirement for the job, explain how Al Gore and Dan Quayle held it for a combined 12 years."[47]

While she wasn't known to be a dynamic speaker, as noted previously, she was selected to give the Democrat's response to President Bush's final State of the Union address. The choice was made by Senate Majority Leader Harry Reid and Speaker of the House Nancy Pelosi. There was some speculation that the Sebelius choice was a "not so subtle clue about her [Pelosi's] preference for Obama" especially since the response came "the night before Sebelius announced she, too, was endorsing Obama."[48] Regardless of the motive, Reid and Pelosi extolled her leadership and bipartisanship skills. They described her as "a forward-thinking, solutions-oriented Democratic leader. Her record of accomplishment in Kansas is evidence of what can be achieved when leaders reach across the aisle on behalf of all Americans."[49] During the same week that her selection to give the response was announced, Sebelius and Alaska Governor Sarah Palin were profiled in a *Vogue* article on women governors titled "Altered States." Sebelius appeared in an Oscar de la Renta gown. The article focused on her popularity in a traditionally Republican state and her legislative successes.[50] The next month Oprah Winfrey's *O* magazine also had a feature on Sebelius.

Governors from both parties were pushing for one of their club to be on the ticket because they could "provide management experience lacking at the top of each ticket. . . . They can also claim they are Washington outsiders at a time when the public is craving change and when both nominees are, by their occupations, Washington insiders."[51] By May, the *Washington Post* gave Sebelius their top spot out of all those on the speculative lists because of

> her ability to further bolster Obama's strengths while not exacerbating his weaknesses. Sebelius would affirm Obama's core message of change and would give Obama's run even more historic weight. Sebelius's electoral success in traditionally Republican Kansas would also echo Obama's pledge to change the electoral map in the fall.[52]

Throughout the summer, the intensity of the search and attention grew. This time Sebelius was, indeed, vetted for the position.[53] She was one of the top four contenders along with Delaware Senator Joe Biden, Virginia Governor Tim Kaine (who was originally from Kansas and whose grandparents shared the same hometown as Obama's), and Indiana Senator and former Governor Evan Bayh. The Associated Press assessed her qualities compared to the other three as being

> the least-known contender among those Obama is believed to be considering. And her presence on the ticket still might not be enough to win over her solidly Republican state and its six electoral votes. Also die-hard Clinton supporters might react negatively to Obama's decision to put a woman on the ticket other than Clinton.[54]

The Clinton issue was mentioned by others. *Newsweek's* Jonathan Alter noted that "bypassing Hillary to pick another woman might be seen as insulting, at least at first, by voters who think Hillary earned it."[55] The *New York Times* opined that

> If he does not choose Mrs. Clinton, several Democrats said, it would be difficult for him to name any woman—like Gov. Kathleen Sebelius of Kansas, someone for whom he has had warm words. Both Clinton and Obama advisers said such a move could create a backlash among women who supported Mrs. Clinton.[56]

In her book, *Big Girls Don't Cry: The Election That Changed Everything for American Women*, Rebecca Traister suggested that the Clinton bypass issue would have created a major rift among some Clinton supporters:

> Rumors swirled that Obama might pick another woman for the ticket, a choice that would suggest he understood the importance of having female executive leadership. Names began to float; Kansas Governor Kathleen Sebelius seemed the most serious possibility. The vocal PUMAs [Party Unity My Ass] were not just unimpressed by this; they were steamed. . . . Even some of the more reasonable Hillary loyalists were dismayed by the more systemic problem that this imagined plan laid bare: the paucity of women in government left a pitiful few to choose from, and the names being bandied about seemed pallid substitutes for the steam engine Clinton had become.[57]

While many saw Sebelius as a long-shot for other reasons, primarily a lack of foreign policy experience,[58] others saw her as Obama's choice because he would be comfortable with her.[59] Sebelius acknowledged in an interview that she and Obama had a comfortable working relationship that began when they met at the 2004 DNC convention where he hit the national stage with his keynote address. The Kansas connection was a starting point, and "he joked at the time that I could be his governor and he could be my senator" since Republicans held those positions in their respective states. Sebelius campaigned for Obama and had occasional phone conversations with him but seldom saw him during the campaign.[60] In an interview with a Missouri Fox affiliate Obama "was effusive—to put it mildly—in his praise for Sebelius. 'I love Kathleen Sebelius. . . . I think she is as talented a public official as there is right now. Integrity. Competence. She can work with people in all walks of life.'[61] All of that, however, was not enough in the end to overcome the need for a running mate with more foreign policy experience.

Sebelius explained the entire process she went through as "surreal," and "flattering," and in the end she agreed with the choice of Senator Joe Biden:

> There was a point in time when he called and said are you willing to be vetted as a possible candidate for vice president. It really was not something that I ever expected.

Frankly I think he made the absolutely correct and very good choice about the incredible skills and background Joe [Biden] had. And looking at where the candidate was going to be perceived to have weaknesses . . . there was clearly a need to have someone who had more experience than he had in his time in the Senate. Although he had clearly done some things on nuclear proliferation issues, and that [having someone with experience] became a very important piece of the puzzle. It was a very interesting several months journey but one that ended exactly where it should have.[62]

Kathleen Sebelius did come very close to following in Geraldine Ferraro's footsteps on a national Democrat ticket. She was a legitimate and serious finalist to be Barack Obama's running mate and she proved the White House Project and the Barbara Lee Foundation to be correct in what it will take to get a woman to the top. In many ways, Sebelius is the poster-woman for how to break the last glass ceiling. She has the CEO experience, she has the financial competence from both her insurance commissioner's and governor's roles, she is bipartisan, she has attracted men and women voters, she can raise money, she balances masculine and feminine traits—she can be tough but not threatening—and she had and continues to have a national stage. While she didn't have direct foreign policy experience, her role as commander-in-chief of the National Guard troops took her to the war zone and caused her to see the relationship between foreign and domestic policies. She was more experienced politically than men who were on tickets such as John Edwards, Dan Quayle, or even George W. Bush. However, just as many qualified men are passed over because the choice of a running mate is a complicated multi-dimensional decision, so it is with women. If Obama's foreign policy resumé had been longer, Sebelius would not have had to add to anything (and Jimmy Carter, Ronald Reagan, Bill Clinton, and George W. Bush had no such experience when they ran at the top of the ticket). If she could have delivered six more electoral votes in what could have been a close election, the geographical balance issue would have gone away. If, as some news reports indicated, it was going to be difficult for Obama to name a woman either because of the Clinton factor or because it might be "too much of a good thing" to have potentially the first African-American president and first woman vice president, then maybe there was no way around the timing issue.[63] In other words there are many "ifs" to consider with any vice presidential selection, and with a woman some are highlighted more than with men.

When Sebelius was asked how women can overcome the biggest attitudinal barrier and experience deal breaker—no foreign policy expertise in this volatile and unpredictable environment of terrorism and political uprisings—she presented an optimistic viewpoint. As she did in her speeches as governor, she saw opportunities where there were obvious challenges. Just as Sebelius surrounded herself with competent advisors and did her homework before making decisions, she believes that anyone who does that, regardless of experience in foreign policy, can overcome the deficit. She pointed to Obama as an example: "I think if you look at what President Obama was able to do with filling out the ticket and having a lot of advisors, a lot of supporters, mastering a lot of information . . . and then complementing his strengths with Joe Biden's" the obstacles are diminished. Sebelius pointed out that male governors have gotten past the foreign policy issue, but there is

no question that 9-11 does change people's perception of the world. [However,] I'm not sure that there is any one person or one set of experiences that helps master this very complicated and volatile part of the world. So I have every confidence that women are as capable as are their male counterparts in mastering the material and getting the best possible advisors and having the ability to convince the American public not only that this is something you take very seriously but you're capable of making tough calls and tough decisions and know the terrain as well as anyone else. It's ironic [but with] the uncertainty, the volatility, the unpredictability of this changing world. . . . I'm not sure there is anybody who can say [what to do] with certainty and confidence regardless of what they have been doing, absent 15 years on the foreign relations committee and a thousand trips overseas even with that they may not have all the mastery of what they need. . . . Mastering the world of the past is not necessarily managing the world of the future. That may help women in some ways.[64]

Kathleen Sebelius concluded her speech at the Democratic National Convention with another optimistic message: "We will create opportunities that once again will make this country a place where the children of maids and the children of presidents share a common destiny. And that's the kind of change America needs." Sebelius is a product and an agent of change as are the other women profiled in this book. At this point, her political future beyond the Obama administration is still uncertain. But in many ways, her experiences starting with her first run for office and her insights into the challenges women face will take future women candidates not just one step closer to realizing the ultimate dream of "anyone can grow up to be president," but all the way to the White House door.

NOTES

1. Madeleine M. Kunin, *Pearls, Politics, & Power: How Women Can Win and Lead* (White River Junction, VT: Chelsea Green, 2008), p. 147.
2. Kathleen Sebelius, "Democratic Convention Speech Text," in *Huffington Post*, August 26, 2008, http://www.huffingtonpost.com/2008/08/26/kathleen-sebelius-democra_n_121636.html (accessed November 2010).

3. All general biographical information about Kathleen Gilligan Sebelius is extracted from three sources: U.S. Department of Health & Human Services website, www.hhs.gov/secretary/about/biography/index.html; Ballotpedia, http://ballotpedia.org/wiki/index.php/Kathleen_Sebelius; and Wikipedia, http://en.wikipedia.org/q/index.php?title=Kathleen_Sebelius&printable=yes; http://marriage.about.com/od/politics/p/ksebelius.htm.

4. Edmond Costantini. "Political Women and Political Ambition: Closing the Gender Gap" in Karen O'Connor, Sarah E. Brewer, and Michael Philip Fisher (eds.), *Gendering American Politics: Perspectives from the Literature*, (New York: Pearson Education, 2006), pp. 79–85; Richard L. Fox and Jennifer L. Lawless, "Family Structure, Sex-Role Socialization, and the Decision to Run for Office," in Karen O'Connor, Sarah E. Brewer, and Michael Philip Fisher (eds.), *Gendering American Politics*, pp. 87–96; Kay Lehman Schlozman, Nancy Burns, and Sidney Verba, "Gender and the Pathways to Participation: The Role of Resources," in Karen O'Connor, Sarah E. Brewer, and Michael Philip Fisher (eds.), *Gendering American Politics*, pp. 87–95.

5. Lisa Wangsness, "Obama Finds Kindred Soul at Helm in Kansas: Sebelius Rise in VP Derby," *Boston Globe*, July 14, 2008, www.highbeam.com/doc/1P2-1685480.html (accessed August 31, 2011).

6. Wangsness, "Obama Finds Kindred Soul."

7. Kathleen Sebelius, Barack Obama Endorsement Speech, January 29, 2008, YouTube, www.youtube.com/watch?v=1nHp90Z2NJk (accessed November 11, 2010).

8. Fox and Lawless. "Family Structure," pp. 89, 91.

9. Elizabeth Palmer, "Profile: Kathleen Sebelius," TrinityDC.edu, in http://marriage.about.com/od/politics/p/ksebelius.htm.

10. Kunin, *Pearls, Politics, & Power*, p. 25

11. Kathleen Sebelius, interview with Diana B. Carlin, June 17, 2011.

12. Ibid.

13. See the Barbara Lee Family Foundation, *Keys to the Governor's Office, Unlock the Door: The Guide for Women Running for Governor*, (Cambridge, MA: The Barbara Lee Family Foundation, 2001); the Barbara Lee Family Foundation, *Speaking with Authority: From Economic Security to National Security*, (Cambridge, MA: The Barbara Lee Family Foundation, 2002); the Barbara Lee Family Foundation, *Cracking the Code: Political Intelligence for Women Running for Governor*, (Cambridge, MA: The Barbara Lee Family Foundation, 2004); the Barbara Lee Family Foundation, *Positioning Women to Win: New Strategies For Turning Gender Stereotypes into Competitive Advantages*, (Cambridge, MA: The Barbara Lee Family Foundation, 2007).

14. Chris Moon, "Sebelius Crafts Pragmatic Persona," *Topeka Capital-Journal*, October 15, 2006, http://www.highbeam.com/doc/1P2-7373856.html (accessed September 1, 2011).

15. Moon, "Sebelius Crafts Pragmatic Persona."

16. "Sebelius Gets Rave Reviews," *Topeka Capital-Journal*, February 14, 2002, http://www.highbeam.com/doc/1P2-7306493.html (accessed September 1, 2011).

17. Kathleen Sebelius, interview with Diana B. Carlin.

18. "Kansas Governor-Elect Puts State Audit Plan in Motion," *The Wichita Eagle*, Knight Ridder/Tribune Business News, November 14, 2002, http://www.highbeam.com/doc/1G1-95099010.html (accessed August 31, 2011).

19. Kunin, *Pearls, Politics, and Power*, p. 142.

20. "Governor Sebelius Appoints Individuals to Protect Vulnerable Kansans," US Fed News Service, July 25, 2006, http://www.highbeam.com/doc/1P3-1083374041. html (accessed August 31, 2011).

21. Political Transcript Wire, "Rep. Nancy Pelosi, Sen. Harry Reid and Gov. Kathleen Sebelius Hold a News Teleconference," January 28, 2008, http://www .highbeam.com/doc/1P3-1419719851.html (accessed September 1, 2011).

22. Dianne Bystrom, "Advertising, Web Sites, and Media Coverage: Gender and Communication Along the Campaign Trail," in Susan J. Carroll and Richard L. Fox (eds.), *Gender and Elections: Shaping the Future of American Politics*, (New York: Cambridge University Press, 2006), p. 177.

23. Ibid.

24. Ibid, p. 250.

25. John Hanna, Associated Press, "Sebelius: Speech Will Embrace Wide Audience," January 13, 2003, http://cjonline.com/stories/011303/leg_speech.shtml (accessed September 13, 2011).

26. Jim McLean and Chris Grunz, "'That Same Sense of Optimism and Dedication to a Better Future Will Help Us Find a Path through Difficult Times': A New Day for Kansas Sebelius Pledges Positivity, Persistence in Economic Plight," *Topeka Capital-Journal*, January 14, 2003, www.highbeam.com/doc/1P2-7319429.html (accessed August 31, 2011).

27. Kathleen Sebelius, State of the State Address, 2003. All of her addresses are found at www.kansas.gov/government/legislative/journals/.

28. Ric Anderson, "Economy, War Called Key Issues," *Topeka Capital*-Journal, March 6, 2004, www.highbeam.com/doc/1P2-7336940.html (accessed September 1, 2011).

29. Associated Press, "Kerry Taking Time to Make Selection, Vice President Pick May Not Be Done by Convention," April 5, 2004, www.highbeam.com/doc/1P2-9912667.html (accessed August 31, 2011).

30. Glen Johnson, *Boston Globe*, Knight Ridder/Tribune Business News, "Kerry Has Time on His Side in Vice-President Selection," May 2, 2004, www.highbeam .com/doc/1G1-116127227.html.

31. Ron Fournier, Associated Press, "Rockefeller's Name Arises as VP Possibility for Kerry, Jay Won't Say Whether He's Been Contacted for Post," *Charleston Gazette*, June 17, 2004, www.highbeam.com/doc/1P2-13856383.html (accessed September 1, 2011).

32. Chris Moon, "But One Kansas Professor Says She Could Be Viable in 2008," *Topeka Capital-Journal*, April 16, 2004, www.highbeam.com/doc/1P2-7339622.html/ print (accessed August 31, 2011).

33. Matt Stearns and Steve Kraske, "Kansas Governor an Unlikely Pick for Kerry Running Mate," Knight Ridder/Tribune News Service, http://2www.highbeam.com/ doc/1G1-118399076.html/print (accessed August 31, 2011).

34. Ibid.

35. Ibid.

36. Ibid.

37. Kathleen Sebelius, interview with Diana B. Carlin.

38. John Hanna, Associated Press, "Gilligan's Daughter a Rising Star: Governor Sebelius Has Roots Here," *Cincinnati Post*, January 30, 2007, www.highbeam.com/doc/1G1-158628560.html (accessed August 31, 2011).

39. The White House Project, http://198.65.255.167/v2/9for08/pollbios.html (accessed November 11, 2010).

40. Neal Conan, host, "Rising Cost of Medicaid," NPR Talk of the Nation, March 14, 2005, www.highbeam.com/doc/1P1-106361907.html (accessed August 31, 2011).

41. Tim Carpenter, "Sebelius Interviewed on C-SPAN," *Topeka Capital-Journal*, February 26, 2007, www.highbeam.com/doc/1)2-5811100.html (accessed August 31, 2011).

42. Julie Carr Smyth, Associated Press, "Dem Governors Walk Fine Line: Criticism of Iraq War Can Backfire for States," May 14, 2007, www.highbeam.com/doc/1G1-163397773.html (accessed August 31, 2011).

43. Carr Smyth, "Dem Governors Walk Fine Line"

44. "Matters with Kansas: Of High Courts, Tornadoes, and Abandoned Backhoes in Iraq," *Atlanta Journal-Constitution*, June 29, 2007, www.thewhitehouseproject.org/newsroom/inthenews/2007/june/20070629-TheAtlantaJournal-Constitution.php (accessed September 2, 2011).

45. James Carlson, "Carville Quick to Offer a Veep," *Topeka Capital-Journal*, October 25, 2007, www.highbeam.com/doc/1P2-9679489.html (accessed August 31, 2011).

46. "Gender Blind?" *Topeka Capital-Journal*, October 25, 2007, www.highbeam.com/doc/1P2-9679479.html (accessed August 31, 2011).

47. Ibid.

48. Anne E. Kornblut, *Notes from the Cracked Ceiling: Hillary Clinton, Sarah Palin, and What it Will Take for a Woman to Win*, (New York: Crown, 2009), pp. 188–89.

49. Sam Hananel, AP Online, "Sebelius to Respond to Bush Address," January 15, 2008, www.highbeam.com/doc/1A1-D8U6JUA80.html (accessed August 31, 2011).

50. Kirbee Yost, "Sebelius Featured in Vogue," cjonline.com, January 18, 2008, http://cjonline.com/stories/011809/sta_237706277.shtml (accessed September 2, 2011).

51. AP Worldstream , "Governors Seem a Ready Pool of Would-Be Vice Presidential Candidates," February 24, 2008, www.highbeam.com/doc/1A1-D8V0B9G03.html (accessed August 31, 2011).

52. Chris Cillizza and Shailagh Murray, "So, Candidates, Who's It Going to Be?," *Washington Post*, May 11, 2008, www.highbeam.com/doc/1P2-16409999.html (accessed September 1, 2011).

53. Kathleen Sebelius interview, with Diana B. Carlin; and Mary Clarkin, "Pick of Palin Was Rushed, Sebelius Says: By Contrast, Her 'Vetting' as a VP Prospect Was Intense, Gov Remarks During Hutch Stop," *Hutchinson News*, September 11, 2008, www.highbeam.com/doc/1G1-184740868.html (accessed August 31, 2008).

54. AP Worldstream, "Vice President Lists Have Positives and Negatives," August 19, 2008, www.highbeam.com/doc/1A1-D92LJQT05.html (accessed August 31, 2011).

55. Jonathan Alter, "The Great Mentioner at Work," *Newsweek*, June 16, 2008, , www.highbeam.com/doc/1G1-179877314.html (accessed August 31, 2011).

56. Adam Nagourney and Patrick Healy, "Political Memo: Closed Mouths, but Open Tryouts to Make the Team, *The New York Times*, July 20, 2008, http://query

.nytimes.com/gst/fullpage.html?res=9F05EFD8123DF933A15754C0A96E9C8B63&scp=1&sq=&st=nyt&pagewanted=1 (accessed September 1, 2008).

57. Rebecca Traister, *Big Girls Don't Cry: The Election that Changed Everything for American Women*, (New York: Free Press, 2010), p. 210.

58. AP Worldstream, "Obama Vice president Announcement Expected Soon," August 19, 2008, www.highbeam.com/doc/1A1-D92L96A80.html (accessed August 31, 2011); *Columbia Daily Tribune* (MO), "VP Pick Could Make or Break a Campaign," August 3, 2008, www.highbeam.com/doc/1P2-16958287.html (accessed September 1, 2011); Sophie Gilbert, "Will Kathleen Sebelius Alienate Hillary Supporters," *The Moderate Voice*, June 16, 2008, www.highbeam.com/doc/1G1-217986161.html (accessed August 31, 2008).

59. "Special Report with Brit Hume," Fox News, July 29, 2008, www.highbeam.com/doc/1P1-154688000.html (accessed September 1, 2011); James Carlson, "Is It Sebelius? Stay Tuned," *Topeka Capital-Journal*, August 20, 2008, www.highbeam.com/doc/1P2-17045851.html (accessed August 31, 2011); Jonathan Alter, "The Great Mentioner At Work."

60. Kathleen Sebelius, interview with Diana B. Carlin.

61. Andrew Romano, "The Obama Veepwatch, Vol. 5: Kathleen Sebelius," *Newsweek*, July 2, 2008, http://www.thedailybeast.com/newsweek/blogs/stumper/2008/07/02/the-obama-veepwatch-vol-5-kathleen-sebelius.html (accessed September 2, 2011).

62. Kathleen Sebelius, interview with Diana B. Carlin.

63. "Lexington: Cobbling Together a Dream Ticket," *The Economist* (US), July 19, 2008, www.highbeam.com/doc/1G1-204198910.html (accessed September 1, 2011).

64. Kathleen Sebelius, interview with Diana B. Carlin.

10

Linda Lingle:
Forgotten Politico in Paradise

When Governor Linda Lingle strode toward the podium at the meeting of the Republican National Committee in Honolulu in January 2010, she appeared to be a politico in her prime: confident, accomplished, and well-spoken. She said: "You can count on the Democratic majority in the House being toast this fall" to the boisterous applause of her supportive audience. About the gathering in Honolulu, the *New York Times* noted: "At a moment of what appears to be great if unexpected opportunity, the Republican Party continues to struggle with disputes over ideology and tactics, as well as what party leaders say is an absence of strong figures to lead it back to power, from the party chairman to prospective presidential candidates."[1]

The host of the event, Governor Linda Lingle, is a two-term governor who had been in office three times as long as then–Alaskan governor Sarah Palin when Senator McCain invited Palin to be his running mate. When Joe Lieberman, who was largely rumored to be John McCain's pick for vice president, was told that McCain had chosen Palin, he "mixed her up momentarily with Linda Lingle, the Jewish Republican governor of Hawaii."[2] Not surprising, since Lingle would strike many as a good choice, since she has more experience than many men who have run for president and many women elected politicians in the United States today.

Lingle, unlike many women in politics, did not enter into politics because it was the family business. Instead, she entered politics with the idealistic promise to her constituents of "change," and she successfully convinced voters to weigh issues and not party affiliation when she made her pitch to the Hawaiian people as a gubernatorial candidate. According to the *Honolulu Star-Bulletin*, "If John McCain was looking for a Republican woman governor and former small-town mayor from an isolated state to become his surprise running mate, he had more than one choice. Why not Hawaii Gov. Linda Lingle?"³

Like former Alaska Governor Sarah Palin, Lingle is her state's first female governor who upset established politicians. In her rise from mayor of Maui County to the state's highest office, Lingle also claimed statewide popularity after she won every county. Indeed, Lingle is one of Hawaii's most potent politicians and a woman leader with impressive credentials.

In the 1998 primary election, she faced a challenge from the late former Honolulu mayor Frank Fasi. In the primary, Linda Lingle so overpowered Fasi that she took more votes in the G.O.P. than former Governor Ben Cayetano had in his primary. In 2006, she closed out her victorious campaign for reelection with a record-setting $6.7 million raised in contributions and interest on her campaign funds.⁴

Moreover, she was not the first woman to be a major political figure in Hawaii, making it that much easier for the public and the press to embrace her bid. The absence of a legacy,⁵ which may be the most daunting obstacle facing women presidential candidates would be less of an obstacle for Lingle, given that Patsy Mink served in the U.S. House of Representatives for a total of twelve terms, representing Hawaii's first and second congressional districts. In addition, Mink sought the presidential nomination of the Democratic Party in the 1972 election, where she stood in the Oregon primary as an anti-war candidate. Kristina Horn Sheeler described the phenomenon as that of a "pioneer." The drawback to the prestige of being a pioneer, Horn Sheeler points out, is that "their pioneering achievements can easily be chalked up to the status as symbolic rather than serious leader."⁶

While Lingle might have been publicly reluctant to mention Patsy Mink as a source of inspiration because Mink was a Democrat, she warmly paid homage to Queen Liliuokalani, who ruled Hawaii from 1891–1893 and who, Lingle said, "gave us a model for leadership that is needed in today's Hawaii, and, indeed, in today's world."⁷ Queen Liliuokalani was the last reigning monarch of the Hawaiian islands. She felt her mission was to preserve the islands for their native residents. In 1898, Hawaii was annexed to the United States and Queen Liliuokalani was forced to give up her throne.⁸

That a strong woman leader was not anathema in Hawaii was important to the success of Governor Lingle's persona as a robust, substantive, and non-symbolic leader. Yet, despite all of Linda Lingle's executive experience, inspiration, the credibility from Queen Liliuokalani and Patsy Mink, and her leadership within the Republican Party, Lingle has not been mentioned in the press as a possible presidential contender. Lingle's lack of feminine markers and her almost-invisibility to the press have kept her from national politics.

BACKGROUND

Born Linda Cutter on June 4, 1953, in St. Louis, Missouri, she was the second of three children. While she was in junior high school, her family moved to southern California and her parents divorced in 1965, soon after the move, and for a time she lived with her grandparents.[9] She graduated cum laude from California State University at Northridge with a degree in journalism. While still in college, she married her first husband, Charles Lingle. In college, she was editor of the alumni newsletter and the journalism department newspaper. Upon graduation, she divorced her husband and moved to Hawaii to follow her father, a pharmacist, who moved to Hawaii to join his brother in a car dealership.[10] It didn't take long for Lingle to make long-lasting friendships and to find work in Hawaii. She rented a small apartment above a garage that belonged to a Filipino family with three children. She respected the culture and traditions of her landlords and grew close to them. The daughter, who was ten years old when Lingle began renting her modest living quarters from the family, would one day work as an assistant in the future governor's office. That she would make lasting ties and connect with the people of Hawaii are indeed hallmarks of Lingle's success.

Lingle, in her twenties and armed with her degree and writing and editing experience, soon found a job as the public information officer for the Hawaii Teamsters and Hotel Workers Union in Honolulu, where she edited a monthly newspaper for the union's members. Tapping into her family's entrepreneurial spirit, she founded the *Moloka'i Free Press*, a community newspaper serving the 6,000 residents of the Island of Moloka'i. As the paper's publisher, editor, reporter, photographer, and typesetter, she reported on community events and covered local government. This unique vantage point gave her an opportunity to meet many people and to gain an understanding of the area from the perspective of a journalist.

As a new governor, she would reflect back on her work in journalism to suggest that it would impact her attitude toward governing. She said, "I have a strong background as a journalist. Journalists have a right to this information. The whole idea is openness; opening the government up . . . I want a government that all people feel they have access to."[11] Her rhetoric reflects her journalism background in its open, straightforward, fact-driven, no-nonsense approach that consistently reminds listeners that she is problem solving and building a future for Hawaii that goes beyond the stereotypical perception of the state as a tourism mecca replete with flower leis and umbrella-topped drinks.

In 1980, Linda Lingle closed the newspaper she founded and commenced her political career when she became a member of the Maui

County Council. She was not motivated to enter politics because of any family background in it. She says, "I didn't really know any politicians. My family's attitude was negative toward politicians."[12] Her background as a journalist increased her interest in the democratic process. She saw first-hand how government had the power to change lives for the better, and she wanted to be in a position to make a difference.

To win her post to County Council, Lingle conducted a grassroots campaign against a well-funded challenger. She served five two-year terms on the council—three terms representing Moloka'i and two terms as an at-large member. In her first campaign, Linda Lingle called for change in Maui politics, a theme that has carried her throughout her political career. What is needed, the twenty-seven-year-old Moloka'i resident said, then, is a "new, higher level of local leadership." She won, Lingle explains, because she was able to persuade voters to disregard party. "I had to convince Democrats I was better than the other guy. Some wouldn't consider voting for a woman, particularly a haole."[13] "Haole" is a word commonly used to refer to white people in Hawaii. It is this achievement, to be elected to lead as a "haole," that is most remarkable of the ability of Linda Lingle to connect with her audience and to earn their trust when she was clearly the "other" in the race—a double minority, both a woman and a Caucasian.

She reflected on how she immersed herself into the Hawaiian culture and grew to understand, respect, and relate to the many different cultures within Hawaii. "When I speak to an audience, I try to think of where they are and how they would best understand my message. I respect the different ways, for example, Filipino and Japanese audiences may interpret my remarks. No two audiences are the same. While the meaning of the message may be the same, how I shape the message, knowing the experiences of the audience is key to making the speech successful. I value the opportunity to speak. I know what a privilege it is to be able to express yourself and have your message heard."[14]

Her major accomplishment was creating a Moloka'i Planning Commission so that the people of Moloka'i had a means to discuss and decide zoning and planning issues that affected them. She served on the Maui County Council for ten years before her upset election as mayor of Maui County in 1990 and she was re-elected four years later. She served the maximum two consecutive four-year terms by defeating the most prominent Democrats in the county, a former mayor and a forty-year veteran of the county council. She was the youngest, the first woman, and the only non-Maui-born person ever elected to the office. As mayor, she drew mostly praise in the press. One writer noted, "Not everyone is enamored of Linda Lingle's style of politics, but most Maui County voters seem to be."[15]

First running for governor in 1998, Linda Lingle came within a percentage point of victory. Incumbent Governor Benjamin Cayetano trailed in the media polls heading into the November election, but on the evening of the election, Cayetano and Lingle were separated by a single percentage point, forcing a recount. Lingle was defeated in the closest election in Hawaii history. The *New York Times* noted that "a struggling economy that was being dragged down by the crisis in Asia nearly allowed her to succeed."[16]

Becoming governor would not elude Ms. Lingle; she won the governorship in 2002. Reflecting back on her ability to be elected in a state with a 1 percent Jewish population, she told Phil Blazer of Jewish TV: "Well it is interesting; I think it is a combination of the people of Hawaii and their openness and also my upbringing and my respect for other people."[17] She also credits the climate of corruption for her success. She said: "I ran at the right time. There was a corruption scandal in Hawaii at the time. Hawaii is a Democratic state, so the Democrats were the ones linked to the corruption. I am a reformer and a fiscal conservative."[18]

Linda Lingle's opportunity for success came when Honolulu Mayor Jeremy Harris, whose campaign was under investigation for fundraising abuse, suddenly ended his frontrunning bid for the Democratic nomination for governor. In addition, two Democrats on the Honolulu City Council earlier were charged with theft and other crimes. That same year other Democrats came under scrutiny over alleged kickbacks. It was a particularly good time for Linda Lingle to launch her campaign and to promise voters that she would end corruption and offer Hawaiians a new beginning.

RHETORICAL STYLE

With the Kahuku High School Band on hand for the grand inaugural festivities, Linda Lingle took office as governor of Hawaii on December 2, 2002. She was committed to bringing about a "New Beginning" for the state by making state government more transparent, responsive, and accountable. When she became governor, she was the first Republican to govern Hawaii in more than forty years and also the first former mayor, first woman, first neighbor island resident, and first person of Jewish ancestry to hold the position. Other women governors in 2002 included Democrats Jeanne Shaheen, New Hampshire, and Ruth Ann Minner, Delaware, and Republicans Jane Dee Hull, Arizona, Nancy P. Hollister, Ohio, Kathleen Sebalius, Kansas, Jane Swift, Massachusetts, and Judy Martz, Montana. Asked to describe what her new state government will be like, Lingle said, "It will be pro-business. It will be more open than any other state government, and it will draw from both senior civil service executives and those without any government experience."[19]

The day of her inauguration, the *Honolulu Star-Bulletin* reported that "starting today, state bureaucrats can expect to find a boss who says 'no' to trip and equipment requests; parents of public school students can expect to be firmly lectured on responsibility and local businesses will find a new buddy on the state Capitol's top floor."[20] She won re-election for a second four-year term in November 2006 by the largest margin of victory in any gubernatorial race in state history.

The following artifacts are included in this analysis: the 2002 inaugural address, the 2006 inaugural address, 2008 Republican National Convention speech, State of the State addresses in both 2009 and 2010, and press clippings from major U.S. papers as well as *Honolulu Star Bulletin, Honolulu Star Advertiser*, and Associated Press, Hawaii.

As a two-time mayor of Maui, Linda Lingle won the Republican nomination for governor by a wide margin and faced Governor Benjamin J. Cayetano, a Democrat, in the general election on November 3, 2002. She hoped to claim victory in this overwhelmingly Democratic state by garnering crossover votes and said she would need to hold that support if she hoped to defeat Mr. Cayetano. Her recognition that it would be a challenge for a Republican to win was evident in this campaign statement: "I know that many of you have never voted for a Republican before, or worked on a campaign for a Republican. This election is not about Republicans and Democrats. It's about the future of our state." To the surprise of many, a month later, before crowds estimated at 6,000, and beside her beaming father, Richard Cutter, and her hand placed on the Hebrew-English Tanakh, Republican Linda Lingle was sworn in on December 2, 2002, as the sixth elected governor of Hawaii. In her speech, she declared that Hawaii is now "open for business."[21] She began her speech with gratitude to her family, friends, and dignitaries and also to those at work. Swelling with pride, confidence, and warmth she wanted to remember "the state's dedicated public school teachers and their students who are busy teaching and learning in classrooms across the state. Their efforts give meaning to the challenges that lie ahead."[22]

She began her governorship by making the claim that she would improve education in Hawaii, but education became one of the most criticized areas under her watch as governor.

In 2009, faced with a budget crises, the state enacted "Furlough Fridays" in the public schools, which resulted in shutting the Hawaii public schools seventeen Fridays in 2009 and twenty-four Fridays in 2010. The state's decision to reduce the school year by 10 percent made Hawaii the state in the country with the lowest number of instructional days. In her speech on this topic, Lingle laid out her agenda succinctly, cognizant of how the press might report it. She wove the three goals for her administration into her speech.

Following the speech "rule of three," Lingle's goals included: 1) restore integrity to government, 2) expand and diversify the economy, and 3) improve public education. Optimistically, she stressed the importance of not letting party affiliation stand in the way of progress. And inclusively she said:

> A good idea is a good idea, regardless of whose it might be. I look forward to sharing credit with you for the many good things that we can accomplish together for all the people of Hawaii.[23]

She ended her speech with the Hawaiian: "Mahalo, malama pono, and aloha," which means: "thanks, take care, and good-bye." Her ability to show respect for and in turn to gain the respect of the citizens of Hawaii is evident in both the warm reception she received upon becoming governor, and the positive press reports of her inauguration. This speech shows that she understood what the people of Hawaii would value in their government. The *Honolulu Star-Bulletin* reported crowds of up to 6,000 and an ebullient atmosphere. The audience was positively motivated and clearly energized to hear the words of their new governor. The first inaugural address set the tone for the themes that would emerge throughout her governorship.

Lingle speaks clearly and optimistically. She speaks in a no-nonsense, matter-of-fact style that is upbeat, but never relies on hyperbole. Her speech is unpedantic. She often evokes the language of native Hawaiians in an effort to stir those natives and also to pay homage to the rich traditions of her uniquely tropical state. Though she framed her remarks in the context of a "new beginning," the reference to Queen Liliuokalani clearly indicates her desire to preserve the traditions of Hawaii as well. Preserving the traditions of Hawaii (while at the same time innovating and creating a new economic base besides tourism) is a theme repeated often in her speeches. She notes that "because I lived in Molaka'i when I came to Hawaii I got to know the culture very well. There are only 6,000 people there. I learned early on what people valued and I was able to bring that to my work as a politician."[24]

The mood of Americans was tempered by a sagging economy, high unemployment, and the ongoing war in Iraq. Election losses around the country had sapped Republican enthusiasm for trying to finish spending measures in Congress, but the tone of Governor Linda Lingle's second inaugural address—and the ringing endorsement of her leadership in her second election victory—was nothing short of serene. Other women governors in 2006 included Democrats Ruth Ann Minner, Delaware; Janet Napolitano, Arizona; Jennifer Granholm, Michigan; Kathleen Sebelius, Kansas; Kathleen Blanco, Louisiana; and Christine Gregoire, Washington. Her Republican colleagues were M. Jodi Rell of Connecticut and the newly elected Sarah Palin of Alaska.

On December 4, 2006, when she stepped up to the dais, she acknowledged the rich beauty and natural resources of the Aloha state, and expressed "gratitude for this honor you have given me, and for making me part of your 'ohana.'"[25] She recalled her first glimpse of her new home more than thirty years before: "It was the exact scene that Keola and Kapono Beamer sang of in Honolulu City Lights. That first impression was laced with the gentle fragrance of plumeria lei that seemed to envelop the airport in those days. I got my first daylight view the next morning glancing out from an Ala Wai high rise. Those early first impressions were like most first impressions-not the whole picture"[26]

In the introduction of a speech written entirely by the governor,[27] she painted a nice picture, and the main focus in her speech was on human resources. She said: "We will never catch today's global economic waves by developing land. Instead we need to begin focusing on human development—the kind of development that recognizes our future economic success depends upon innovation and new ideas, of which there is an unlimited supply."[28] Her commitment to the unique culture of Hawaii is evident in her promise to "put into words what I believe Hawaii's destiny is in this world."[29] In a problem-solution format she set forth a challenge: "I believe we are meant to serve as a one-of-a-kind, American-Pacific-Asian model that shows others how an ever-changing and diverse society can succeed in the global economy while honoring its multi-ethnic heritage. Is it really possible to paddle at the speed necessary to catch global economic waves without losing the essence of who we are? I believe it is possible, and I believe it is imperative. The magnitude and speed of change and innovation in the world today is so great, that if we fail to move forward, by definition, we will be going backwards."[30]

Once again Lingle calls attention to the unique nature of her state: one that is rich with tradition, tourism, and a diverse population. She is determined to position the state not only as a tourist destination but as a global powerhouse. Her optimism shines through as she directs her audience to consider a new, more global mindset for the state, and she tries to counter the potential opposition to her vision of the future apart from land development by acknowledging that it exists: "Because we have based our economy on land development for so long, because even average citizens see buying and selling real estate as the only path to financial security, and because we have somehow survived the bitter public debates over land development projects, the natural inclination for many is to keep doing what we have been doing. But this would be a very unwise path for us to follow."[31] She backs up her claim with this evidence for her position:

> We will never catch today's global economic waves by developing land. Instead we need to begin focusing on human development—the kind of development

that recognizes our future economic success depends upon innovation and new ideas, of which there is an unlimited supply. I'm talking about the kind of new ideas that change lives and can change the world—new ways of creating energy, new ways of reducing pollution, new ways of growing food, new ways of creating clean drinking water, new ways of identifying and curing diseases, new ways of viewing the solar system, new ways of preserving and utilizing our ocean resources.[32]

Her rhetoric needed to convince Hawaiians that they cannot rely on tourism to keep the state competitive in the country. She uses the metaphor of waves, conjuring up the image that Hawaii brings to mind for most people: the refreshing ocean waves crashing up and down. It is apparent that from her first inaugural address to this one, Linda Lingle has grown as a speaker and in her confidence as a politician who can direct the citizens of Hawaii by telling them what they must do to stay competitive. She said, "I found writing this speech easy because I had such a command of what I am doing as governor."[33] Her loving and stern mandate for her state in this concluding passage sums up her vision for Hawaii much the same way that a parent would tell a teen child on the crossroads of adulthood what they must do: "And by working together and making good decisions, both kinds of waves will bring us to a shore we love and appreciate."[34] She ends with her usual, "Mahalo."

On September 3, 2008, Linda Lingle was the first Hawaii governor ever to speak at the Republican National Convention. Instead of speaking about the Republican Party in general, she used her time at the podium to tell the audience about another Republican woman governor, one far less experienced than she, but one that soon would overshadow the entire Republican Party. Both Palin and Lingle angled first for careers in journalism before turning to politics. They both gained political experience through the ranks of municipal government and became the first women governors of their outlying states: Linda Lingle in Hawaii, the fiftieth state, and Sarah Palin in Alaska, the forty-ninth state.

Linda Lingle athletically advanced to the podium with an energetic pace, smiling and looking relaxed. When she began to speak, she explained that she thought it was important for her to tell the audience about Sarah Palin since not many Americans, even Republicans, knew about Palin. Lingle gave an extended narrative speech about the life of Sarah Palin. In her typical straightforward, business-like approach, she got right to the subject of her speech without flowery language or excessive emotion. Smiling confidently, she said:

Good evening, and aloha. It's my honor to speak with you tonight about Senator McCain's outstanding choice of Alaska Governor Sarah Palin as our party's Vice Presidential nominee. As a fellow Republican governor, I have had the chance to get to know Governor Sarah Palin. She is a terrific individual, and an outstanding governor. Sarah is a person with proven leadership skills, and strong moral character. Because most Americans are just being introduced to Sarah Palin, I think it's important to share with you a little bit about her great personal story.[35]

The first part of Lingle's speech is biographical. She tells the story of Palin from her birth to her rise to the governorship. "Her family moved to Alaska . . . in high school, as captain, she led her basketball team to victory in the state championship. . . . She was crowned Miss Wasilla, and finished second in the Miss Alaska pageant, . . . She married her high school sweetheart, Todd . . . they have five children." The enthusiastic Republican audience cheered to hear that Sarah was on that basketball team and a former beauty queen. More information about Palin paints her as a Superwoman of sorts: Lingle's evidence to support her statement that Palin is qualified included that Palin gave a blockbuster impromptu speech and gave birth in the same day, prompting Lingle to ask: "Did I mention she was tough?" Lingle then adopts the refutational pattern when she counters the criticism that Palin had begun to receive as John McCain's choice as his running mate. As another Republican woman who began her career as a mayor, she identified with the criticism leveled at Palin for her lack of experience:

> I find it reminiscent when I hear Democratic Party leaders and their surrogates question Sarah's experience. They used that same tactic against me when I ran for governor. They said that being the mayor of Maui was insufficient experience to be the governor. Being a mayor, whether in Hawaii or Alaska, or anywhere else, is outstanding preparation for higher office, and the people of Alaska or Hawaii will tell you: Sarah and I are doing just fine.
>
> I find it especially amusing that the other party says Governor Palin lacks experience when their own candidates for President and Vice President have no executive experience. Zero. Zero. Neither Senator Obama nor Senator Biden have ever managed a multibillion-dollar budget, or been a chief executive of any city, or state, of any size, or of anything for that matter. The audience retorted: "Zero! Zero! Zero!"[36]

She reiterated her belief that a governorship is the best platform to the presidency, not only for women candidates, but for men. In a personal interview, she said: "Senators don't run anything. They don't have to worry about the garbage being picked up or the school system. Governors, whether from a small or big state, have the same set of responsibilities as the president does."[37]

She spoke slowly and clearly throughout her brief speech in support of Palin. After she refuted the charges from Democrats and the media that Palin lacks experience, Lingle offered a brief description of what makes Alaskans unique and how Palin would bring that individualism to her role as vice president. Vignettes of the Alaskan wilderness were displayed on the large monitors in the convention hall. She described Palin as an "outsider" and a "reformer" who is "truly authentic" and a "fiscal hawk" that could help fix a "broken Washington." She sarcastically noted that Alaska has the "same number of electoral votes as Delaware" (Democratic vice presidential nominee Joe Biden's home state). Lingle drew much applause when she noted that Palin has great appeal to women. Like her inaugural addresses, this partisan speech in support of Palin was enthusiastic, yet straight forward, and direct. This speech was a supportive speech for Sarah Palin as the choice of vice president. Once again Lingle relied on deductive reasoning and evidence based on her own experience to back up her claim that Palin is a good choice.

In 2009 Lingle gave a State of the State speech that may have been her most challenging annual address to the people of Hawaii. Her eighth one, the state of Hawaii was beset by deeper economic woes than ever before, and the embarrassing statistic that Hawaii schools have the lowest number of instructional days in the state was also a difficult issue facing the governor. In her usual no-nonsense way, she began: "It is a great privilege and a humbling experience to come before you each year to share my thoughts about where our state stands, and where we are headed." Interjecting a self-deprecating note, she said: "In this sense, it is a fairly typical speech."[38] She then heightened interest and curiosity in what she needed to say, noting that "this has not been a typical year. We are facing a time like no other in our state's history."[39] She quoted Winston Churchill: "I'm an optimist by nature . . . and as Winston Churchill said, 'An optimist sees the opportunity in every difficulty.'"[40] She organized her speech in a problem-solution format. After acknowledging progress made in several areas, she presented the major problem facing her state, the economic woes:

> Today's struggling economy has created a deep hole in our budget that we need to dig out of this session. The Council on Revenues has never in its history lowered its projections by so much in such a short period of time. Over the past eight months, the Council has reduced its general fund revenue projection by $1.4 billion. This downward projection reflects an unprecedented decline in tourism, construction, business activity, and consumer demand brought about by national and international events beyond our control.[41]

She offered her solution to work together, and she employed a repetition pattern to reinforce that the unpopular and hard decisions are not something she wants to do: *"Not because we want to, but because we can't afford business as usual."*[42] As she moved to discuss the energy initiative, Lingle again employed a repetition method with the phrase: *"They have a right."*[43] When Governor Lingle traveled around the state to give speeches to group of 50 to 150 in size, she often appears less formal than when giving a State of the State address or an inaugural address.[44]

Her speeches illustrate her ability to embrace the Hawaiian culture with traditional Hawaiian phrases and a knowledge of Hawaiian history. Her style of speech suggests a tendency toward pragmatic action rather than eloquence. She lays out her arguments succinctly and logically. Frequently her rhetoric succeeds in pointing out the success of her administration. Although she took a public speaking course in college, she credits the popular public speaking training course, Toastmasters, with giving her the most useful public speaking training. She says: "It was essential to my success in politics. I participated in Toastmasters for two years and it taught me that good public speaking rises from clear thinking."[45]

WHY NOT MADAM PRESIDENT?

Notwithstanding an "Anti Linda-Lingle" Facebook page that, as of March 2010, had 116 members and several articles written against Lingle, primarily for her decision to have "Furlough Fridays" in Hawaii, press about her time as governor has been mostly positive. Nationally, Linda Lingle isn't nearly as well known as other governors. It could be, as she said, "because the media is there [on the east coast] and I'm here."[46] While that is true, the same could be said for Alaska's Sarah Palin who burst onto the political scene from Alaska, a state that is remote and also, like Hawaii, not part of the contiguous forty-eight states. It certainly wasn't a place that media frequently visited or wrote about previous to Palin's selection by McCain. What is the major difference is family background, photogenic qualities and a narrative that would pair well with McCain's maverick reputation. An unmarried Jewish woman in her fifties could not sell as well as Palin's pretty motherhood package. (Lingle was married, divorced twice, and has no children.)

In July 2010 when she vetoed House Bill 488 that would have allowed single sex marriages, the blogosphere erupted with angry responses from people who said that they would never travel to Hawaii. Though it is difficult to apply standard methods of analysis to the virtual world of blogging, the power of the blogosphere to impact political races cannot be denied. As Michael Keren notes, "Today the blogger is seen as a public intellectual"[47] and the impact on their postings is wide-ranging.

Several responses questioned Lingle's own sexual orientation, and several respondents suggested that even if she is not gay, she "looks gay" and that is reason enough for her political star to rise no further than the state level. These kind of blog posts were present for years; for example, in 2008 the blogger "The Art of the Possible" asked: "But why didn't McCain choose Lingle for VP? She was married and divorced twice, and has no children. Is all of that enough reason not to pick someone for VP? She was chairperson of the 2004 RNC in New York City, where she helped the NYPD go around and arrest thousands of civilians—no small effort. She's been on TV. She's articulate. She trumpets the party line. She's the perfect fit, right? Well, there's this one other thing. Linda Lingle looks . . . gay. Was that enough to crush her chances of running for VP for the Republican party?"[48]

No question, Linda Lingle has been a likeable politician who gained the respect of the many varied cultures despite her haole status. She believes that being likeable is an imperative for successful politicians. When asked to hula dance or model in a civic group's fashion show she is likely to say "yes" if, for no other reason than to show that she is a good sport. But perhaps that spirit of sportsmanship does not extend to a willingness to campaign for national office. She said, "I enjoy campaigning for other Republicans, but I do not wish for the complete lack of privacy that being president requires."[49] While she had no familial role models to shape her career path, she credits her grandmother, equipped only with an eighth-grade education, with some of the best wisdom she ever received. She recalls her grandmother as never complaining about anything, and always seeing the best in other people. As governor, Linda Lingle has tried to bring that simple, open-hearted optimism to her rhetoric and her governing, being especially sensitive to the heritage of her audience and honoring traditional customs of Hawaii. In 2010 Democrat and former congressman Neil Abercrombie became the new governor of Hawaii and there is reason to believe Linda Lingle's political future is not over. Described as a "top-tier" recruit,[50] she is considering a run for the U.S. Senate in 2012. She said, "I will likely take a look at the 2012 Senate race here in Hawaii. You know that is when the seat comes up. Sen. Daniel Akaka [a Democrat] would have to run again in 2012. . . . So I will take a serious look at that office at that time, and depending on where the public is and what they feel about me at the time. It is something that would interest me,"[51] she said. So although Linda Lingle may have not reached the national stage as a running mate or a presidential candidate, and she may lack feminine markers many women candidates have relied upon, such as a traditionally feminine photogenic quality and motherhood, she is indeed a politico in her prime, with a record of electability and popularity, at least in Hawaii, where she has embraced the multi-ethnic population and they have embraced her.

NOTES

1. Adam Nagourney, "GOP Hits Its Stride but Faces a Rift over Ideology,"*New York Times*, January 30, 2010, p. A1.
2. John Heilemann and Mark Halperin, *Game Change* (New York: Harper Collins, 2010), p. 401.
3. "Lingle Was Not an Option," *Honolulu Star-Bulletin*, August 30, 2008, p. A1.

4. Richard Borreca, "We likely haven't seen the Last of Linda Lingle," *Star Advertiser*, October 22, 2010. www.staradvertiser.com/columnists/onpolitics/20101022_We_likely_havent_seen_the_last_of_Linda_Lingle.html (accessed November 14, 2010).

5. Nichola D. Gutgold, *Paving the Way for Madam President* (Lanham, MD: Lexington Books, 2006), p. 11.

6. Kristina Horn Sheeler, "Marginalizing Metaphors of the Feminine," in Brenda DeVore Marshall and Molly A. Mayhead (eds.), *Navigating the Boundaries: The Rhetoric of Women Governors* (Westport, CT: Praeger, 2000), p. 17–18.

7. Linda Lingle, 2002 inaugural address; http://archives.starbulletin.com/1998/10/22/news/stor2.html (accessed March 4, 2010).

8. "Queen Lydia Liliuokalani," www.uic.edu/depts/owa/history/liliuokalani.html (accessed November 16, 2010).

9. Robert D. Johnston, "Linda Lingle" *Jewish Women: A Comprehensive Historical Encyclopedia.* http://jwa.org/encyclopedia/article/lingle-linda.

10. Ibid.

11. Richard Borreca, "The New Boss," *Honolulu Star Bulletin*, December 2, 2002, p. A1.

12. Linda Lingle, phone interview with Nichola Gutgold, April 14, 2010.

13. Ken Ige, "This Is Our Time," *Honolulu Star Bulletin*, http://archives.starbulletin.com/1998/10/22/news~tory2.html (accessed February 17, 2010).

14. Linda Lingle, phone interview with Nichola Gutgold, April 14, 2010.

15. Alex Salkever, "Feminine Phenomenon," *Hawaii Business*, Vol. 40, No. 11 (May 1995), Sec. 1. p. 10.

16. Steven A. Holmes, "The 1998 Elections: State by State—West; Hawaii," *New York Times*, November 5, 1998, www.nytimes.com/1998/11/05/us/the-1998-elections-state-by-state-west-hawaii.html?ref=benjamin_cayetano (accessed November 16, 2010).

17. Governor Linda Lingle, Jewish TV, host Phil Blazer, www.youtube.com/watch?v=fGJeRL3baFI YouTube video (accessed March 9, 2010).

18. Linda Lingle, phone interview with Nichola Gutgold, April 14, 2010.

19. Ige, "This Is Our Time."

20. Ibid.

21. Ibid.

22. Ibid.

23. Ibid.

24. Linda Lingle, phone interview with Nichola Gutgold, April 14, 2010.

25. Linda Lingle, Speech transcript accessed from the governor's official website http://hawaii.gov/gov/ (accessed April 19, 2010).

26. Ibid.

27. Linda Lingle, phone interview with Nichola Gutgold April 14, 2010.

28. Ibid.

29. Ibid.

30. Ibid.

31. Ibid.

32. Ibid.

33. Ibid.

34. Ibid.

35. Linda Lingle, speech transcript accessed from the governor's official website, http://hawaii.gov/gov/ (accessed April 19, 2010).

36. Ibid.

37. Linda Lingle, phone interview with Nichola Gutgold, April 14, 2010.

38. Linda Lingle, speech transcript accessed from the governor's official website http://hawaii.gov/gov/ (accessed April 19, 2010).

39. Ibid.

40. Ibid.

41. Ibid.

42. Ibid.

43. Ibid.

44. Melissa Tanji, "Highway Finally Opens to Cheers, Honks, Smoothly Flowing Traffic," *Moui News*, May 28, 2008, p. A1.

45. Linda Lingle, phone interview with Nichola Gutgold, April 14, 2010.

46. Ibid.

47. Michael Keren, "Blogging and Mass Politics," *Biography*, Vol. 33, No. 1 (2010), p. 113.

48. "The Art of the Possible," http://shmooth.blogspot.com/2008/10/whats-wrong-with-linda-lingle.html.

49. Linda Lingle, phone interview with Nichola Gutgold, April 14, 2010.

50. Michael O'Brien, "Hawaii GOP Gov. Lingle Says She'll Look at Senate race in 2012," *The Hill*, October 10, 2010, http://thehill.com/blogs/blog-briefing-room/news/122569-hawaii-gop-gov-lingle-says-shell-look-at-senate-race-in-2012 (accessed December 23, 2010).

51. Borreca, "We Likely Haven't Seen the Last of Linda Lingle."

11

Conclusion: What Must a Presidential Woman Be?

As suggested in this book's preface, generalizing from the stories of nine political women may not pass the tests of empirical research. Nonetheless, doing so can lead to several hypotheses that further investigations can indeed test. The women we chose were from both parties and several regions, and they run the gamut in age from Kassebaum to Lingle. Although not a high enough n, the group of nine are representative.

As one might expect, their political stories differ, suggesting that there is no one route into politics for a woman. The same might be said of men. And the fact that we can say the same of women and men is a positive sign, for in earlier times, the way in for women was appointment upon one's husband's death.

Different stories, different routes, but some commonalities that we can point to that may make the path to "Madam President" more torturous than the path to "Mr. President." These commonalities do not apply to all, but they apply to more than one. They are therefore useful hypotheses.

First, women who are being considered for the presidency must have the appropriate credentials. The same is, of course, true for men, but there seems to be different measuring sticks being used for the two genders. Women are expected to have more experience as elected officials than men. Women not only have to have government experience but successful campaigning experience. And, as the case of Elizabeth Dole suggests, that campaigning experience must be for yourself, not for your spouse. The assumption seems to be that a prospective president must both have the requisite knowledge and the ability to get elected.

More specifically, a future female president should have foreign policy experience. The same is, of course, true of men, but a Barack Obama is permitted to acquire that international expertise by adding Joe Biden to the ticket. A Kathleen Sebelius, on the other hand, would be viewed as weak because she had to add a Joe Biden or a John Kerry or a Hillary Clinton to the ticket. Despite the presence of numerous women in international government such as Margaret Thatcher in the 1980s or Angela Merkel today, the America electorate still tends to see the conduct of foreign affairs as male-defined.

Credentials are, of course, important. What is bothersome then is not the insistence on them but the public's toleration of New Jersey's Chris Christie as a presidential contender after less than one term and its nervousness about Elizabeth Dole's high-level appointments in several administrations or Kathleen Sebelius's after the first term as governor is done and the second well underway.

Second, women who are being considered for the presidency must have the ability to raise the money necessary for a long, expensive campaign. Again, the same is true of men, but women have historically found it difficult to garner the financial support men have. The women, like Elizabeth Dole, might be pointed to as examples for young daughters to emulate by fathers and mothers alike, but appreciating Dole's presence among the candidates is not the same as bank-rolling her. Hillary Clinton in 2008 certainly raised a significant sum as did Michelle Bachmann in 2012. No one doubts Sarah Palin's ability to garner financial support. So, perhaps, this "barrier" is no longer the barrier it once was.

Third, women who are being considered for the presidency must be charismatic or, at least, dynamic. Again, the same is true of men, but, whereas for former Minnesota Governor Tim Pawlenty the lack of spark was just a liability, it seems to be more of a disqualifying trait for Christine Gregoire and Kathleen Sebelius. Part of the problem, of course, is gaining media attention. A restrained style may well be highly effective if one is trying to either court business or work with the opposition, but that style does not attract media beyond state lines and, thus, does not set up a candidate with such a style for higher office. Pawlenty, through persistence, was able to overcome the supposition; through the years, others have done so as well. Our study, however, suggests that overcoming would be more difficult for a woman. The man is noticed and noted as presidential timber; if he lacks dynamism, he may fade in the surfacing or primary phase. The woman, on the other hand, is neither noticed nor noted unless she possesses the requisite panache.

A woman, however, cannot push that requisite dynamism too far, for, fourth, women who are being considered for the presidency must not be overly assertive or aggressive. Should they do so, they run the risk of being dismissed with the b____ word. That has been the fate suffered by Barbara Mikulski and Nancy Pelosi. That was the fate that Hillary Clinton constantly back-pedaled from in her 2008 campaign. Here, we see a marked difference in perspective between how male and female aspirants are viewed: aggressive males are said to be in need of reining in their style when it truly becomes uncivil; aggressive females are said to be inherently nasty should they state their views strongly too often.

Fifth, women who are being considered for the presidency must be attractive and, furthermore, must expect their attractiveness to be front-and-center in the media coverage of a campaign. Dianne Feinstein's expensive attire and "Snow White" hairstyle; Barbara Mikulski's short stature and "roly-poly" physique; Kathleen Sebelius's dress color and toenail polish; Nancy Pelosi's mauve designer suits and cosmetic surgery—all of these will be focused on. Men running for the presidency will not draw comparable attention; furthermore, physical traits will rarely disqualify them. Some might note their height (Jimmy Carter, Michael Dukakis), their weight (Chris Christie), and their suit color (Al Gore), but these traits will not be what media coverage notes first and, then, dwells upon.

Related to this fifth maxim is a sixth: women must look the part. The problem here, of course, is that the part has always been taken by a male. Thus, to look the part—especially when it is thought of as Commander-in-Chief—a woman must look masculine but, of course, not too masculine as to be unattractive. Women are then trapped in a double-bind Kathleen Jamieson fails to discuss—between looking presidential, defined in our culture in masculine terms, and looking attractive, defined in our culture in feminine terms for women. Nancy Kassebaum noted that she did not look the part; undoubtedly, Barbara Mikulski, who is even shorter, felt the same. Others most assuredly did as well. Not all can have the commanding stature of a Dianne Feinstein, even though the "Snow White" tag haunted her. As is noted earlier, it's probably no accident that Geena Davis was chosen for the lead in the short-lived television series *Commander-in-Chief*, for she blended stature and attractiveness—read: masculinity and femininity—in ways few real political women will.

Seventh, women who are aspiring to the presidency must have no "spouse problem." The problem might be a spouse whose business or political dealings are questionable. Dianne Feinstein had questions raised about the former; Olympia Snowe, the latter. The problem might be a spouse who cannot be successfully scripted. Elizabeth Dole experienced this difficulty; and, although not discussed in this book, so did Hillary Clinton. The problem might even be the absence of a spouse as is the case for Barbara Mikulski and Linda Lingle. An aspiring woman's spouse must—it seems—be either well in the background or deceased.

Related to this seventh maxim is an eighth: at least for the present, women who are aspiring to the presidency should be heterosexual. Barbara Mikulski has been rumored to be a lesbian; Linda Lingle has been said by persistent bloggers to look like one. On this point, ironically, there is probably little sexism, for the door is probably as closed to a gay man as a lesbian woman.

Ninth, women who are now aspiring to the presidency must remember that their gendered struggle resonates with only a part of their audience. Although we would argue that there still exist many barriers impeding women's movement in life and in the professions, we recognize that this perspective, very much a "second wave feminism" one, no longer has universal appeal. Women need to find a way to talk this talk to women beyond a certain age while acting fully empowered and talking about what they will do as president to women of a younger age. Elizabeth Dole ran into this problem, so did Hillary Clinton, so might Barbara Mikulski *if* Maryland voters ever got beyond reelecting their favorite daughter, politics, personality, and story notwithstanding. To address two different audiences of women, while also addressing men, requires rhetorical finesse.

So, tenth, women aspiring to the presidency must possess considerable rhetorical finesse. Their words will be scanned for the words that suggest high seriousness in a world with major economic and international problems. Their words will also be scanned for the words that suggest compassion but not softness. None of the women studied in this book erred on the soft side, but some may have erred on the high seriousness side and, thereby, made themselves less compelling. Some may well have sensed the rhetorical minefield and done most of their communication out of the public eye. This somewhat invisible work may indeed have been highly effective, but its invisibility left the women rhetoric-less in the view of the media and, by extension, the media-consuming public.

The tendency to do work behind the scenes may have grown out of a desire shared by these women to do the governmental business they have been elected to do. They seem less purely political than many male politicians—not asking, first and foremost, how to advance themselves and their party, but asking how to get the job of legislator or governor done. In so doing, they quickly learned that the partisan extremes, although the ground of rip-roaring speeches and attention-getting soundbites, were not where the business of government gets done. Thus, many were centrists or compromisers. Even the most partisan in the group of nine—for example, Nancy Pelosi—was noted by many, even by Republicans, for her negotiating skills. Others among the nine were famed for them.

Thus, we offer the eleventh maxim: women who aspire to the presidency must have the "right" politics. And a corollary: the "right" politics are rarely centrist.

Nancy Kassebaum, Dianne Feinstein, and Olympia Snowe served their cities, states, and their nation well. Each, however, took positions that distanced them from the wings of the parties that dominate during the surfacing and primary phases of a presidential campaign. Kassebaum was out of sync with Republican conservatives on the question of reproductive rights; Feinstein was out of sync with Democratic liberals on the matter of capital punishment. And recall how polls showed Snowe more popular in her home state with Democrats and independents than with fellow Republicans. Their dissatisfaction is with a voting record that rejects the party line as often as it supports it. During the general election period, when candidates do indeed usually drift to the center to capture independent voters (as well as, maybe, a few moderates from the other party), a centrist candidate may seem ideal. However, to get to the general election period, one needs to make it through the surfacing and primary phases dominated by more conservative and more liberal activists.

These eleven maxims, again, are extracted from the analysis of just nine women we believed to be of presidential caliber. The maxims, therefore, should not be treated as the firm conclusions of extensive research. Rather, they are hypotheses researchers and critics can test. In the preface to this book, we explained why we went forward without hypotheses. Now, others can go forward with something more than guesses.

Two questions need to be addressed in closing: First, were we surprised; Second, are these hypotheses stable?

The conclusions we came to, at first glance, should surprise no one: the previous work on gender and politics surveyed in the introductory chapter may well have led us to a somewhat similar list of maxims. But we said, "Somewhat." Three differences strike us between the list we might have come up with and the list we did.

First, we might have talked in terms of Jamieson's silence/shame double bind. Instead, we offer what we think is a more nuanced "take" on the question of how a political woman must speak. Silence is certainly not going to help a woman who aspires to the presidency. Neither is what seems to be silence—that is, communicating interpersonally and in group settings largely behind the scenes in attempts to get things done. This communication is certainly not silence, but, based on what the media covers and does not cover, many will overlook this important communication and conclude, falsely, that a woman does not speak much. At the other extreme, overly aggressive speaking—or what might get labeled that—is certainly not going to help either. However, to exhibit the requisite rhetorical finesse and to exhibit a measure of charisma, speaking that gets attention because of its strength, is indeed necessary. So, how does the politically aspiring woman negotiate the tension between speaking strongly and speaking aggressively? Especially in a media and a political environment too ready to stereotype the strong as aggressive? There may then be two double binds in Jamieson's silence/shame one: one between productive behind-the-scenes speaking and public speaking; the other between strong public speaking and aggressive public speaking. The minefield might be just a tad more complex than Jamieson's binary suggests.

Second, we might have noted how women in politics are talked about by the media (and others) in terms of their physical appearance, for there is much extant commentary pointing to this problem. Instead, we note how a politically aspiring woman must appear both feminine and masculine. They must appear feminine because they must be attractive and, in our culture, being attractive for a woman means feminine. However, they must also look presidential, look like someone who could be commander in chief. Thus, a masculine gravitas must be added to the feminine. Precisely how to accomplish this feat, however, is not clear. Androgyny is not the answer, for that trips the lesbian alarm. Rather, a woman has to find a way to be undoubtedly feminine (and heterosexual) while having a sufficient number of strong traits that suggest command. This is a slightly different "take" on the feminine/competence double bind Jamieson discusses. Again, the binary is deceptive, for political women are not expected to choose. Rather, they are expected to combine.

Third, we might not have talked at all about the most basic problem some women face—having politics that are too moderate to survive the very partisan primaries. Admittedly, not all women in politics are centrists, but enough of the really committed and talented ones are that there is frequently a mismatch between a political woman's centrism and the extreme conservatism or liberalism demanded early in a presidential campaign. To some extent, this phenomenon goes back to why people enter politics. Many men enter because they enjoy the partisan battling. Some women might enjoy that too, but many women, with households to run and families to raise, enter because they want to address the problems facing their constituents. Politics is less an ego-satisfying game and more problem-solving service. Addressing them drives them to the middle because oftentimes only from the center can legislative or administrative answers be crafted. Men can, of course, move to the center as well. So, these two tendencies are not inherent in gender. Nonetheless, there does seem to be something of a gender divide. The result is that talented women often end up standing outside the politics that wins at the primary stage.

These maxims are, of course, not carved in stone. As our culture changes, so may many of these maxims. One day, a politically moderate, short, overweight first-term governor with modest funding, an outspoken husband, a strictly-business speaking style, and a tendency to do her best policymaking work behind the scenes in conferences might be a viable presidential candidate. Our culture, however, would have to change dramatically before this scenario could play out. These maxims, then, strike us as fairly stable. As a demonstration of that stability—one we are not going to offer—one might assess both Michelle Bachmann and Sarah Palin with these maxims in mind. Such a demonstration would show—we think—why they have gotten as far as they have as well as what will ultimately keep them from the presidency.

Also instructive would be to assess the Hillary Clinton 2008 campaign with these maxims in mind. We can see why she got as far as she did, but also pinpoint where her candidacy was ultimately shaky.

One last point: the barriers standing in the way of "Madam President" are complex. It is tempting to say that once a Catholic seem barred and, then, after Kennedy, that bar fell. So it was for an African American; so, thanks to the positive response Joe Lieberman received as vice-presidential candidate in 2000, it will be for a Jew. These situations, even that facing an African American, we would suggest, are less complex than that facing a woman. If one extracts from the eleven maxims all of the things a female aspirant for the presidency is expected to be and all of the things she is expected not to be and, then, discerns how many of the "do's" and "don't's" are rooted in how our culture defines the genders, one sees how complex the picture is.

Finally breaking through the proverbial "glass ceiling" is then not simply a matter of biding time as aspirant after aspirant hit it: Hillary cracked it, the next woman who proves a major contender cracks it more, and the next finally breaks it. Rather, breaking requires either a change in our culture or a woman who is in line with these maxims. Or—the most likely scenario: some change in our culture and a woman who is more or less in line with the maxims we have extracted from the nine stories we have told in this study.

Selected Bibliography

American Psychological Association. *Report of the APA Task Force on the Sexualization of Girls*. Washington, DC: American Psychological Association, 2007.

The Barbara Lee Family Foundation. *Keys to the Governor's Office, Unlock the Door: The Guide for Women Running for Governor*. Cambridge, MA: The Barbara Lee Family Foundation, 2001.

_____. *Speaking with Authority: From Economic Security to National Security*. Cambridge, MA: The Barbara Lee Family Foundation, 2002.

_____. *Cracking the Code: Political Intelligence for Women Running for Governor*. Cambridge, MA: The Barbara Lee Family Foundation, 2004.

_____. *Positioning Women to Win: New Strategies For Turning Gender Stereotypes into Competitive Advantages*. Cambridge, MA: The Barbara Lee Family Foundation, 2007.

Bennett, W. Lance. "Storytelling in Criminal Trials: A Model of Social Judgment." *Quarterly Journal of Speech*, Vol. 64, No. 1 (February 1978), pp. 1–22.

Burrell, Barbara. "Political Parties and Women's Organizations: Bringing Women into the Electoral Arena." In Susan J. Carroll and Richard L. Fox (eds.), *Gender and Elections: Shaping the Future of American Politics*, 2nd ed. New York: Cambridge University Press, 2010.

Bystrom, Dianne, "Advertising, Web Sites, and Media Coverage: Gender and Communication Along the Campaign Trail," in Susan J. Carroll and Richard L. Fox (eds.), *Gender and Elections: Shaping the Future of American Politics*, New York: Cambridge University Press, 2006, p. 169–188.

_____. "Advertising, Web Sites, and Media Coverage: Gender and Communication Along the Campaign Trail." In Susan J. Carroll and Richard L. Fox (eds.), *Gender and Elections: Shaping the Future of American Politics*, 2nd ed., New York: Cambridge University Press, 2010, pp. 204–232.

Bzdek, Vincent. *Woman of the House: The Rise of Nancy Pelosi*. New York: Palgrave Macmillan, 2008.

Carroll, Susan J. *Women as Candidates in American Politics.* Bloomington, IN: Indiana University Press, 1985.

____. "Voting Choices: Meet You at the Gender Gap." In Susan J. Carroll and Richard L. Fox (eds.), *Gender and Elections: Shaping the Future of American Politics*, New York: Cambridge University Press, 2006, pp. 74–96.

____. "Voting Choices: The Politics of the Gender Gap," in Susan J. Carroll and Richard L. Fox (eds.), *Gender and Elections: Shaping the Future of American Politics*, 2nd ed. New York: Cambridge University Press, 2010, pp. 117–143.

Carroll, Susan J., Carol Heidman, and Stephanie Olson. "She Brought Only a Skirt: Gender Bias in Newspaper Coverage of Elizabeth Dole's Campaign for the Republican Nomination." Unpublished paper, White House Project Conference, Washington, DC, February 20, 2000.

Carroll, Susan J. and Richard L. Fox, eds. *Gender and Elections: Shaping the Future of American Politics.* New York: Cambridge University Press, 2006.

____. *Gender and Elections: Shaping the Future of American Politics*, 2nd ed. New York: Cambridge University Press, 2010.

Cialdini, Robert B. *Influence: The Psychology of Persuasion.* New York: Harper Collins, 2007.

Cliff, Eleanor and Tom Brazaitis. *Madam President: Women Blazing the Leadership Trail.* New York: Routledge, 2003.

Conover, Pamela Johnston. "Feminists and the Gender Gap." In Karen O'Connor, Sarah E. Brewer, and Michael Philip Fisher (eds.), *Gendering American Politics: Perspectives from the Literature.* New York: Pearson Education, Inc., 2006, pp. 111–20.

Costantini, Edmond. "Political Women and Political Ambition: Closing the Gender Gap." In Karen O'Connor, Sarah E. Brewer, and Michael Philip Fisher (eds.), *Gendering American Politics: Perspectives from the Literature.* New York: Pearson Education, 2006, pp. 79–85.

Crister, Greg. *Fat Land: How Americans Became the Fattest People in the World.* London: Penguin, 2003.

Darcy, R., and Sarah Slavin Schramm. "When Women Run against Men." In Karen O'Connor, Sarah E. Brewer, and Michael Philip Fisher (eds.), *Gendering American Politics: Perspectives from the Literature.* New York: Pearson Education, 2006, pp. 183–88.

Dolan, Julie, Melissa Deckman, and Michele L. Swers. *Women and Politics*, 2nd ed. Glenview, IL; Pearson Education, 2011.

Dole, Robert, Elizabeth Dole, Richard Norton Smith, and Kerry Tymchuk. *Unlimited Partners: Our American Story.* New York: Simon and Schuster, 1996.

Duerst-Lahti, Georgia. "Presidential Elections: Gendered Space in the Case of 2008." In Susan J. Carroll and Richard L. Fox (eds.), *Gender and Elections: Shaping the Future of American Politics*, 2nd ed. New York: Cambridge University Press, 2010, pp. 13–43.

Fikkan, Janna, and Esther Rothblum. "Weight Bias in Employment." In Kelly D. Brownell, et al. (eds.), *Weight Bias: Nature, Consequences, and Remedies.* New York: Guilford Press, 2005.

Fox, Richard Logan. *Gender Dynamics in Congressional Elections.* Thousand Oaks, CA: Sage, 1997.

Fox, Richard L., and Jennifer L. Lawless. "Family Structure, Sex-Role Socialization, and the Decision to Run for Office." In Karen O'Connor, Sarah E. Brewer, and

Michael Philip Fisher (eds.), *Gendering American Politics: Perspectives from the Literature.* New York: Pearson Education, 2006, pp. 87–95.

Frankovic, Kathleen A. "The Ferraro Factor." In Karen O'Connor, Sarah E. Brewer, and Michael Philip Fisher (eds.), *Gendering American Politics: Perspectives from the Literature.* New York: Pearson Education, 2006, pp. 297–306.

Fumento, Michael. *The Fat of the Land: The Obesity Epidemic and How Overweight Americans Can Help Themselves.* New York: Viking Press, 1997.

Gilligan, Carol. *In a Different Voice: Psychological Theory and Women's Development.* Cambridge, MA: Harvard University Press, 1982.

Gregoire, Christine. "Working Together on All Levels of Government." *Vital Speeches of the Day,* Vol. 71, No. 8 (February 2005), pp. 229–230.

Gutgold, Nichola D. *Paving the Way for Madam President.* Lanham, MD: Lexington Books, 2006.

Hall, Jane. "Hillary and Liddy." *Media Studies Journal,* Vol. 14, No. 1 (Winter 2000), pp. 68–69.

Heilemann, John and Mark Halperin. *Game Change.* New York: Harper Collins, 2010.

Helgesen, Sally. *The Female Advantage: Women's Ways of Leadership.* New York: Currency Doubleday, 1995.

Holihan, Thomas A. *Uncivil Wars: Political Campaigns in a Media Age.* Boston: Bedford/St. Martin, 2000.

Horn Sheeler, Kristina. "Marginalizing Metaphors of the Feminine." In Brenda DeVore Marshall and Molly A. Mayhead (eds.), *Navigating the Boundaries: The Rhetoric of Women Governors.* Westport, CT: Praeger, 2000, pp. 15–24.

Horwitz, Linda, and Holly Swyers. "Why Are All the Presidents Men? Televised Presidents and Patriarchy." In Lilly J. Goren (ed.), *You've Come a Long Way Baby: Women, Politics, and Popular Culture,* Lexington: The University Press of Kentucky, pp. 115–34.

Jamieson, Kathleen Hall. *Beyond the Double Bind: Women and Leadership.* New York: Oxford University Press, 1995.

Kassebaum, Nancy Landon. "To Form a More Perfect Union." *Presidential Studies Quarterly* 18 (1988), pp. 241–49.

____. "The Challenge of Change." In Diana Prentice Carlin and Meredith A. Moore (eds.), *The Landon Lecture Series on Public Issues: The First Twenty Years, 1966–1986.* Lanham, MD: University Press of America, Inc., 1990, pp. 847–55.

Katz, Sidney. "The Importance of Being Beautiful." In James M. Henslin (ed.), *Down to Earth Sociology: Introductory Readings.* New York: Prentice-Hall, 1997.

Keith, Sheree. "Women Who Spoke for Themselves, Working Women, Suffrage, and the Construction of Women's Rhetorical Style." In Janis L. Edwards (ed.), *Gender and Political Communication in America,* Lanham, MD: Rowman and Littlefield, 2009, pp. 29–36.

Keren, Michael. "Blogging and Mass Politics." *Biography,* Vol. 33, No. 1 (2010), p. 113.

Kornblut, Anne E. *Notes from the Cracked Ceiling: Hillary Clinton, Sarah Palin, and What it Will Take for a Woman to Win.* New York: Crown, 2009.

Kozar, Richard. *Elizabeth Dole.* Philadelphia: Chelsea House, 2000.

Kunin, Madeleine M. *Pearls, Politics, & Power: How Women Can Win and Lead.* White River Junction, VT: Chelsea Green, 2008.

Lakoff, Robin Tolmach. "The Politics of Nice." *Journal of Politeness Research*, Vol. 1, No. 1 (2005), pp. 168–178.

Landy, David and Harold Sigall. "Beauty is Talent: Task Evaluation as a Function of the Performer's Physical Attractiveness." *Journal of Personality and Social Psychology*, Vol. 19, No. 2 (Spring 1974), pp. 294–301.

Latner, Janet D., Albert J. Strunkard, and G. Terence Wilson. "Stigmatized Students: Age, Sex, and Ethnicity Effects in the Stigmatization of Obesity." *Obesity Research*, Vol. 13, No. 1 (2005), pp. 122–126.

Lawless, Jennifer L., and Richard L. Fox. *It Still Takes a Candidate: Why Women Don't Run for Office*, revised ed. New York: Cambridge University Press, 2010.

Lehman, Kay Schlozman, Nancy Burns, and Sidney Verba. "Gender and the Pathways to Participation: The Role of Resources." In Karen O'Connor, Sarah E. Brewer, and Michael Philip Fisher (eds.), *Gendering American Politics: Perspectives from the Literature*. New York: Pearson Education, 2006, pp. 57–65.

Marshall, Brenda DeVore, and Molly A. Mayhead. "The Changing Face of the Governorship." In Brenda DeVore Marshall and Molly A. Mayhead (eds.), *Navigating Boundaries: The Rhetoric of Women Governors*. Westport, CT: Praeger Publishers, 2000, pp. 1–14.

Marshall-White. Eleanor, *Women, Catalysts for Change: Interpretive Biographies Of Shirley St. Hill Chisholm, Sandra Day O'Connor, and Nancy Landon Kassebaum*. New York, Vantage Press, 1991.

McGlen, Nancy E., Karen O'Connor, Laura van Assendelft, Wendy Gunther-Canada. *Women, Politics, and American Society*, 4th ed. New York: Longman, 2002.

Ng, Assunta. "Women Still Face Many Hurdles on Way to Presidency." *Northwest Asian Weekly*, Vol. 16, No. 10 (May 1997), pp. 6–7.

Norton, Eleanor Holmes. "Elected to Lead: A Challenge to Women in Public Office." In Deborah L. Rhode (ed.), *The Difference "Difference" Makes: Women and Leadership*. Stanford, CA: Stanford University Press, 2003, pp. 109–20.

O'Connor, Karen, Sarah E. Brewer, and Michal Philip Fisher (eds.). *Gendering American Politics: Perspectives from the Literature*. New York: Pearson Education, 2006.

Oliver, J. Eric. *Fat Politics: The Real Story Behind America's Obesity Epidemic*. New York: Oxford University Press, 2006.

Ouerishi, M. Y. and Janet P. Kay. "Physical Attractiveness, Age, and Sex as Determinants of Reactions to Resumes." *Social Behavior and Personality*, Vol. 14, No. 1 (March 1986), pp. 98–105.

Palmer, Barbara and Dennis Simon. "Political Ambition and Women in the U.S. House of Representatives, 1916–2000." In Karen O'Connor, Sarah E. Brewer, and Michael Philip Fisher (eds.), *Gendering American Politics: Perspectives from the Literature*. New York: Pearson Education, 2006, pp. 97–102.

Patzer, Gordon L. *The Physical Attractiveness Phenomenon*. New York: Plenum, 1985.

Paul, David and Jessi L. Smith. "Examining Voter Preferences When Women Run Against Men for the Presidency." *Journal of Women and Politics*, Vol. 29, No. 4 (Winter 2007), pp. 449–453.

Peters, Ronald M., Jr. and Cindy Simon Rosenthal. *Nancy Pelosi and the New American Politics*. New York: Oxford University Press, 2010.

Puhl, Rebecca and Kelly D. Brownwell. "Bias, Discrimination, and Obesity." *Obesity Research*, Vol. 9 (2001), pp. 788–790.

Rhode, Deborah L. *The Beauty Bias: The Injustice of Appearance in Life and Law.* New York: Oxford University Press, 2010.

Ries, Paula and Anne J. Stone, eds. *The American Woman 1992–93: A Status Report.* New York: W.W. Norton & Company, 1992.

Roberts, Jerry. *Dianne Feinstein: Never Let Them See You Cry.* New York: Harper Collins, 1994.

Robson, Deborah. "Stereotypes and the Female Politician: A Case Study of Senator Barbara Mikulski." *Communication Quarterly*, Vol. 48, No. 3 (Summer 2000), pp. 205–222.

Robson, Deborah and Jane Blankenship. "A 'Feminine Style' in Women's Political Discourse: An Exploratory Essay." *Communication Quarterly*, Vol. 43, No. 3 (Summer 2005), pp. 353–366.

Rothblum, Esther D. "The Stigma of Women's Weight: Social and Economic Realities." *Feminism and Psychology*, Vol. 2 (1992), pp. 88–93.

Sandalow, Marc. *Madam Speaker: Nancy Pelosi's Life, Times, and Rise to Power.* New York: Modern Times, 2008.

Schreiber, Ronnee. "Injecting a Woman's Voice: Conservative Women's Organizations, Gender Consciousness, and the Expression of Women's Policy Preferences." In Karen O'Connor, Sarah E. Brewer, and Michael Philip Fisher (eds.), *Gendering American Politics: Perspectives from the Literature*, New York: Pearson Education, 2006, pp. 141–151.

Sheckels, Theodore F. *When Congress Debates: A Bakhtinian Paradigm.* Westport, CT: Praeger, 2000.

Sheckels, Theodore F. *Maryland Politics and Political Communication, 1950–2005.* Lanham, MD: Lexington Books, 2006.

Sheeler, Kristina Horn. "Marginalizing Metaphors of the Feminine." In *Navigating Boundaries: The Rhetoric of Women Governors*, edited by Marshall, Brenda DeVore, and Molly A. Mayhead. Westport, CT: Praeger Publishers, 2000, pp. 15–30.

Soblosky, Kate. "'Probative Weight': Rethinking Evidentiary Standards in Title VII Sex Discrimination Cases." *New York University Review of Law and Social Change*, Vol. 30, No. 1 (2006), pp. 333–335.

Solovay, Sondra. *Tipping the Scales of Justice: Fighting Weight Based Discrimination.* New York: Prometheus Books, 2000.

Sullivan, Daniel B. "Images of a Breakthrough Woman Candidate: Dianne Feinstein's 1990, 1992, and 1994 Campaign Television Advertisements." *Women's Studies in Communication*, Vol. 21, No. 1 (Spring, 1998), pp. 74–83.

Traister, Rebecca. *Big Girls Don't Cry: The Election That Changed Everything for American Women.* New York: Free Press, 2010.

Weatherford, J. McIver. *Tribes on the Hill: The U.S. Congress Rituals and Realities,* revised ed. Westport, CT: Bergin & Garvey, 1985.

Wertheimer, Molly Meijer and Nichola D. Gutgold. *Elizabeth Handford Dole: Speaking from the Heart*/Westport, CT: Praeger, 2004.

Witt, Linda, Karen M. Paget, and Glenna Matthews. *Running as a Woman: Gender and Power in American Politics.* New York: Free Press, 1994.

Index

Pelosi, Nancy D'Alesandro, ix-x, 9, 11, 16, 37, 62, 87–102, 105, 132, 144–145, 170–172, D; barriers, 97–100; biography, 87–89; rhetorical style, 90–97
Perry, Rick, x
Peters, Ronald, 90, 98
Philadelphia Inquirer, 74
Politico, 91
Pollack, Jack, 54
Powell, Colin, 74
Princeton University, 83
public speaking, 71, 72, 74–76, 89–90, 121, 164, 173. *See also* rhetorical style

Quayle, Dan, 30, 144, 147
Quigley, Mike, 97–98

radio addresses, 112, 120, 123
Rather, Dan, 73–74
Reagan, Ronald, 23, 28, 30, 55, 72, 74, 147
Reid, Harry, 144–145
religion, 77, 157; as a barrier, 37, 48, 164, 175
Rell, M. Jodi, 159
reproductive rights, 43, 173. *See also* abortion
Republican National Convention, 10–11, 18, 28, 73, 76, 80, 83, 158, 161–163
rhetoric, viii, ix-x, 7–9, 12, 20–27, 62, 98, 107, 136–137, 155, 164–165
rhetorical finesse, 90, 172–173. *See also* rhetorical style
rhetorical style, ix-x, 21, 27, 40–46, 57–60, 65, 74–82, 89–97, 107–113, 122–127, 136–142, 157–164, 172–173. *See also* public speaking
Rhodes, John J., 28
Rice, Condoleezza, 49, 113, 143
Riehle, Thomas, 122
"right" politics, 11, 48, 172–173
RINO, 114
Roberts, Pat, 135
Robson, Deborah, 9, 60, 65, 98
Rockefeller, Nelson, 18

Roeper, Richard, 28–29
Romney, Mitt, ix-x
Roosevelt, Franklin D., 17
Rosenthal, Cindy, 90, 98
Rossi, Dino, 122, 127
Roy, William "Bill," 19–20

Salter, Susannah Medora, 15
San Francisco, 11, 37–40, 44–45, 47, 55, 61, 65, 88–90, 93, 100
San Francisco Chronicle, 45, 101n1
Schockman, Eric, 45
Schroeder, Pat, 8, 82–83, 105
Schumer, Charles "Chuck," 80
Seattle Times, 122
Sebelius, Edward "Ned," 133
Sebelius, Gary, 133
Sebelius, John, 133
Sebelius, Kathleen Gilligan, ix-x, 9, 10, 11, 16, 111, 113, 131–152, 157, 159, 170–171, G; barriers, 142–148; biography, 131–135; rhetorical style, 136–142
Sebelius, Keith, 10, 133
sexual orientation, 65–66, 125, 164, 171–172, 174
sexism, 40, 55, 71, 172
Shaheen, Jean, 157
Shallenburger, Tim, 134
Smith, Bob, 42
Smith, Chris, 94
Smith, Margaret Chase, 11, 21, 31, 71, 103–104
Snowe, Olympia J., ix, 9, 11–12, 03–118, 143, 171–173, E; barriers, 113–116; biography, 104–107; rhetorical style, 107–113
Snowe, Peter, 11, 104
Sotomayor, Sonia, 121
Souter, David, 121–122
Specter, Arlen, 113
Stanford University, 38
Stanton, Elizabeth Cady, 15, 112
State of the State address, 120, 124, 137, 140, 158, 163–164
State of the Union address, 138, 144; response to, 138, 144

About the Authors

Theodore F. Sheckels is professor of English and communication studies at Randolph-Macon College, Ashland, Virginia. He received his B.S. from Duquesne University and his M.A. and Ph.D. from Penn State University. He is co-editor of *Readings on Political Communication*, editor of *Cracked but Not Shattered: Hillary Rodham Clinton's Unsuccessful Presidential Campaign*, co-author of *Political Communication: A Case Approach*, and author of *When Congress Debates: A Bakhtinian Paradigm* and *Maryland Politics and Political Communication, 1950–2005*. Sheckels has also published book-length studies of South African literature, Australian film, Canadian women writers, and Canadian author Margaret Atwood. He has published essays on these topics as well as on international political discourse in journals such as *Communication Quarterly*, *Southern Journal of Communication*, *Howard Journal of Communications*, and *Rhetoric & Public Affairs*. He chairs the Communication Studies Department at Randolph-Macon and has, since 2007, co-directed the National Communication Association's Institute for Faculty Development.

Nichola D. Gutgold is associate professor of communication arts and sciences at Penn State Lehigh Valley. She received her B.A. from King's College, her M.A. from Bloomsburg University, and her PhD. from Penn State University. She is author of *Almost Madam President: Why Hillary Clinton 'Won' in 2008* (Lexington Books, 2009); *Seen and Heard: The Women of Television News* (Lexington Books, 2008); and *Paving the Way for Madam President* (Lexington Books, 2006). With Molly Wertheimer she co-authored *Elizabeth Hanford Dole: Speaking from the Heart* (Praeger Press, 2004). She has received teaching, research, and service awards from Penn State Lehigh Valley and in 2009 was awarded the Pennsylvania Communication Association Donald Ecroyd Research and Scholarship Award. She leads Penn State students through China communication course field studies. She serves as discipline coordinator for the arts and humanities faculty, a University senator, and was a visiting scholar at California State University–Chico.

Diana B. Carlin, associate vice president for graduate education and professor of communication at Saint Louis University, is a national expert in political debates. She received both her bachelor's and master's degrees in education from the University of Kansas and her Ph.D. from the University of Nebraska–Lincoln. She taught at Washburn University in Topeka and the University of Kansas where she also served in several administrative positions. Her work as an advisor to the Commission on Presidential Debates from 1987–2000 led to research that changed political debate formats and created a national voter education project, DebateWatch. She has worked on a variety of election and civil society projects in new democracies. Her research in political and gendered communication has yielded eight books or monographs and many other publications. Her most recent work includes a study of media coverage of Hillary Clinton and Sarah Palin that appeared in *Communication Studies* and a chapter in the Sheckels volume on Hillary Clinton's campaign. She has taught courses on women in politics, the rhetoric of women's rights, and first ladies.